Astrid Ley, Md Ashiq Ur Rahman, Josefine Fokdal (eds.)
Housing and Human Settlements in a World of Change

Habitat-International: Series on International Urbanism | Volume 25

Editorial

Habitat-International is a publication series of the department of International Urbanism (Städtebau-Institut) at the faculty of architecture and planning at University of Stuttgart. The series is dedicated to the sociocultural and development policy aspects of contemporary urbanisation and architecture. In this context the series presents outstanding doctoral theses and research results.
The series is edited by Astrid Ley, Peter Herrle, Josefine Fokdal und Sonja Nebel.

Astrid Ley is chair of International Urbanism and course director of the international master program MSc Integrated Urbanism and Sustainable Design (IUSD) at the University of Stuttgart. She also works as an urban development consultant to bilateral and international development agencies (oikos human settlement research group). She holds a degree in architecture and urban design from RWTH Aachen and a PhD from TU Berlin. Her expertise and publication record include topics related to urbanization in the Global South, housing processes, the role of local governance, participation, co-production, and civil society.

Md Ashiq Ur Rahman is a professor of Urban and Rural Planning Discipline of Khulna University, Bangladesh. He is highly invested in the field of pro-poor housing initiatives in Bangladesh and other developing countries. He gained his MSc in the Urban Development Planning programme at University College London and was awarded with a PhD in Urban Studies from Heriot Watt University, Edinburgh, United Kingdom. His research interest and career motivation lies in pro-poor urban development initiatives. He believes that individuals have their own capabilities and combining those capabilities towards democratic development is essential.

Josefine Fokdal is interim chair of the department of Local and Regional Planning at the University of Stuttgart. She has been working as a researcher and lecturer at the department of International Urbanism at the University of Stuttgart since 2015. After completing her degree in architecture and international urbanism from TU Berlin, and a master's from Ball State University (USA), Josefine obtained her PhD in 2014 from TU Berlin. Her research and writings span the fields of spatial theory, housing, governance, co-production and rapid urbanization with a geographical focus on Asia.

Astrid Ley, Md Ashiq Ur Rahman, Josefine Fokdal (eds.)
**Housing and Human Settlements
in a World of Change**

With Forewords by Raquel Rolnik and Mohammed El Sioufi

[transcript]

This publication has been enabled by the support of Alexander von Humboldt Foundation through the Georg Forster Research Fellowship

Bibliographic information published by the Deutsche Nationalbibliothek
The Deutsche Nationalbibliothek lists this publication in the Deutsche Nationalbibliografie; detailed bibliographic data are available in the Internet at http://dnb.d-nb.de

© 2020 transcript Verlag, Bielefeld

All rights reserved. No part of this book may be reprinted or reproduced or utilized in any form or by any electronic, mechanical, or other means, now known or hereafter invented, including photocopying and recording, or in any information storage or retrieval system, without permission in writing from the publisher.

Cover layout: Maria Arndt, Bielefeld
Cover illustration: Astrid Ley
Layout: Shaharin Annisa
Proofread by Glenna M. Jenkins
Printed by Majuskel Medienproduktion GmbH, Wetzlar
Print-ISBN 978-3-8376-4942-0
PDF-ISBN 978-3-8394-4942-4
https://doi.org/10.14361/9783839449424

Printed on permanent acid-free text paper.

Content

FOREWORDS

Foreword
Mohamed El Sioufi | 9

Foreword
Raquel Rolnik | 15

Introduction: Housing and Human Settlements in a World of Change
Md Ashiq Ur Rahman, Josefine Fokdal and Astrid Ley | 25

PART I: HOUSING IN THE NEOLIBERAL PARADIGM

Chapter 1: Indonesian Housing Policy in the Era of Globalization
Jo Santoso | 47

Chapter 2: Let's Get Down to Business – Private Influences in The Making of Affordable Housing Policies
Anthony Boanada-Fuchs | 65

Chapter 3: Mutual Aid, Self-Management and Collective Ownership
Marielly Casanova | 89

PART II: HOUSING AND MIGRATION

Chapter 4: Understanding the Housing Needs of Low-Skilled Bangladeshi Migrants in Oman
Shaharin Annisa | 119

Chapter 5: Between Need for Housing and Speculation
Fabio Bayro-Kaiser | 129

Chapter 6: Influence of Migrants' Two-Directional Rural-Urban Linkages on Urban Villages in China
Shiyu Yang | 147

Chapter 7: Urban Environmental Migrants
Syed Mukaddim, Md. Zakir Hossain, Sujit Kumar Sikder | 165

PART III: HOUSING AND CLIMATE CHANGE

Chapter 8: Heat-Stress-Related Climate-Change Adaptation in Informal Urban Communities
Franziska Laue | 189

Chapter 9: From the Hyper-ghetto to State-subsidised Urban Sprawl
Gerhard Kienast | 219

Chapter 10: Learning from Co-Produced Landslide Risk Mitigation Strategies in Low-Income Settlements in Medillín (Colombia) and São Paulo (Brazil)
Harry Smith, Soledad Garcia-Ferrari, Gabriela Medero, Helena Rivera, Françoise Coupé, Humberto Caballero, Wilmar Castro, Alex Abiko, Fernando A. M. Marinho, Karolyne Ferreira | 243

Bio Notes | 267

Forewords

Foreword

Mohamed El Sioufi

This publication is a timely contribution as it addresses the mounting unmet demand for housing that stems from the almost global absence of government interventions since the 1990s. During the last few years, the international community has joined hands to articulate and formulate major goals, agendas and strategies. These 15- to 20-year perspectives set the backdrop against which key actors, including governments, academia, professionals, developers, civil society and the private sector, should further develop them into programmes, interventions and actions on the ground.

Challenges: Access to affordable housing globally is becoming more and more elusive to large numbers of urban populations. As many cities mature and expand, affordable land for housing becomes increasingly scarce and costly and thereby beyond the reach even of the middle class. In most developing countries, housing demand, from the rapidly growing lower and middle-income group, is neither met by the public sector (national and local authorities) nor by the private sector (the forces of the market). Planning the development of affordable serviced land and housing as well as providing financial and mortgage schemes are either absent, undeveloped or, if they exist at all, they do not target the informally employed lower-income groups.

Government responses: Over the last 60 to 70 years, housing policies have shifted the roles of the public sector from direct delivery by the central government to a laissez-faire role that is limited to enabling the market. Only in rare situations has the market worked and, even then, there has had to be some support to vulnerable groups through social and financial programmes. The private sector, in the majority of cases, favoured earning rapid high profits by focussing on housing for higher income groups that could buy housing units thus enabling the developers to recoup their investments in the shortest possible time. In many cases, housing plans are sold before construction commences. In most countries, long-term investment in rental housing and other tenure modalities has nearly vanished, depriving the younger generations from accessing decent affordable housing. For the most part 'enablement of the market and the withdrawal of the public sector from the housing scene has proved ineffective as it has resulted in disastrous urban and human consequences.

In cases where governments have addressed housing through delivery they have, unfortunately, failed to reach the target populations. Often, housing policies and strategies aimed at building a certain number of housing units per year; for example, "building 100,000 housing units", etc. These output-based, quantitative policies only provide photo opportunities for officials who stand in front of usually towering housing projects. In reality, however, these schemes result in vacant abandoned settlements in a phenomenon referred to as "Ghost Towns". These are now abundant globally.

These expensive urban failures are the result of strict zoning regulations that segregate residential areas from other urban uses. The myth of low-cost public-owned land situated far away from urban areas is another culprit. It is only cheap for ministries of housing that are looking to reduce the costs of these housing units. However, this type of urban development shifts the real costs of infrastructure to other ministries (infrastructure, transportation, etc.). The real costs, however, are shouldered by the targeted low-income groups who have to commute to jobs, or to seek employment and social and economic amenities. Commuting costs are usually prohibitive for lower-income groups as they reduce their net incomes by 30% to 50%, thereby resulting in their moving back to well-located informal areas. Such cases are documented in a variety of developing countries.

Finally, many of these housing programmes have incurred very high costs that resulted from centralised delivery, inefficiencies and, in many cases, corruption. The failed laissez-faire policies and attitudes of the public sector towards producing affordable land and housing have left one third of urban dwellers living in informal settlements.

People's responses: In response to the absence of affordable options for land and housing, about 1 billion lower-income urban dwellers have taken it upon themselves to find alternatives through the development of informal settlements and housing. In extreme cases, they have resorted to illegally squatting on land which they then developed into their own settlements. In other cases, they have acquired land that was unsuitable for development, usually in climatically vulnerable areas, including in cyclone paths, and flood- and mudslide-prone areas.

In other cases, they have settled in hazardous zone where they have been exposed to high-tension power lines, or situated along railway lines or in toxic areas etc. Consequently, the most vulnerable urban residents are exposed to life-threatening and health hazards and end up living under inhumane conditions.

Global Responses: In recognition of past policy failures and in order to address the increasing housing demand, social segregation and urban divides; there has been a recognition for the need for new approaches to both urban development and housing delivery. The international community has developed some high-level frameworks for addressing these challenges:

The Sustainable Development Goal (SDG) 11 "Sustainable Cities and Communities" surpasses the ambitions of its predecessor Millennium Development Goals'. It's first target aims to "By 2030, ensure access for all to adequate, safe and affordable housing and basic services and upgrade slums".

The New Urban Agenda (NUA) further unpacks SDG 11 by developing appropriate concepts and strategies. Paragraph 109, for example, calls to "… consider increased allocation of … resources for: upgrading and … prevention of slums … with strategies that go beyond physical and environmental improvements, to ensure that slums are integrated into the social; economic; cultural; and, political dimensions of cities. These strategies should include … access to sustainable, adequate, safe, and affordable housing; basic and social services; and safe, inclusive, accessible, green, and quality public spaces; and they should promote security of tenure and its regularisation, as well as measures for conflict prevention and mediation."

UN-Habitat developed The Global Housing Strategy (GHS) as a collaborative global movement towards further supporting the concept of adequate housing for all and improving the housing and living conditions of slum dwellers. It was developed to explore ideas to be included in the NUA. Its main objective is to assist member states in working towards the realisation of the right to adequate housing.

Paradigm shift in thinking and practice: The above frameworks aim to go beyond the classic 'in the box' thinking that confines the housing debate to its limiting components: land, infrastructure, design, building materials and labour. Housing is to be situated "at the centre" of urban thinking and of cities as an integral part of urban development, thus avoiding many of the previous drawbacks.

The NUA treats housing as an integral part of an urban development approach within a larger cluster of thematic areas. The aim is to achieve sustainable urbanization that is based on the urban planning principles of high density and mixed land uses and integrating social groups with efficient street networks while reducing the urban environmental footprint. Through urban land management, fiscal instruments are combined with a focus on available affordable serviced land for urban uses that are intermixed with housing. Legal and regulatory frameworks would aim to enable and encourage investments in housing at all levels, thereby contributing to local economic development and income-generating opportunities for lower-income groups. Revitalised urban economic development would target growth in sustainable affordable jobs and the development of income-generating opportunities that would render housing and other services affordable. Policies are to include cross-subsidies between various land-use categories and, when necessary, subsidies and incentives are to be utilized to stimulate the supply and demand sides of housing. Slum upgrading and prevention are central to ensuring human rights are respected and are a corner stone to leaving no one behind.

Further effectiveness would be achieved through ensuring that a variety of housing tenure types provide a diversity of options that address different social, economic and cultural needs. Governance and maintenance of housing and neighbourhoods should ensure that the housing rights and needs of women, youth, and special groups are addressed through inclusive, affordable and culturally adequate solutions. Post-disaster reconstruction and the development of resilient solutions for housing in disaster-prone and climate change areas are also growing in importance.

Systemic reforms should promote an active role for the public sector beyond enablement so as to ensure universal access to adequate affordable housing. Linking housing with other parts of the economy should be strengthened to ensure economic development, employment generation and poverty reduction. Decentralized housing production and empowering different actors and modalities of housing development are to be encouraged within these frameworks. Sustainable building and neighbourhood designs and technologies are to be pursued with an aim towards more cost-effective, flexible and energy-efficient solutions. Most importantly, all efforts should result in significant and measurable improvements in housing and living conditions for all, while facilitating the role of housing as an important support for poverty reduction.

Forward looking – working together: While these recommendations might seem overwhelming, they rather provide a variety of avenues to better address housing needs. These frameworks are designed to support key stakeholders in focussing on targeted conceptualisation and innovations and the research needed to operationalise them. Concerted integrated collaborative partnerships between key actors are vital to mobilising the added values they can each contribute, including central and local government leaders' political will; academia's creativity and innovation; the private sector's efficiency; civil society and the media's advocacy; the professional community's knowhow; and local communities' and individuals' deep understanding of their needs and their ability to harness their energies, resourcefulness and commitment.

Foreword

Raquel Rolnik

My input[1] might seem rather provocative as it is very difficult to talk about the Right to the City and the Right to Adequate Housing these days. I think it is crucial for us, who are related to questions of housing and cities, urbanism and urban planning, to understand that a new colonial empire that is faceless and flag-less – is seizing territories and reshaping cities. The name of this new colonial empire is global finance. It is a global process, which means that it is a process that is de-territorialized, abstract, fictitious and speculative. This is the very nature of finance. In this process, built space has more and more a key role in the promotion and expansion of finance. It is a global process, it is general, it is everywhere, but it is also particular in each place (states, and even regions and cities), path-dependent on political economies of land, housing and built space.

We will talk more specifically about how central the role of built space is as a fundamental part of the circuits of appreciation and valorisation of finance and how much it affects and shapes cities and urban policies. We could then talk about those rent-seeking landscapes that are made of shopping malls, corporate towers, international chain hotels, cultural centres, all built by brand architects, which look exactly the same everywhere. They look spectacular in their uniqueness but nevertheless repeat themselves everywhere, as abstract and disconnected from real territories as is finance itself.

When I received my mandate as Special Rapporteur on the Right to Adequate Housing, I had to travel long hours and sometimes arrived in some city half dead, half sleepy. From my taxi or car, I then saw those towers and shopping malls, and I found myself asking: Am I in Chicago? Or am I in Dubai? Am I in Astana? …the same rent-seeking landscapes were everywhere. This kind of

---

1 This Keynote was delivered at the 19thN-AERUS conference on "Housing and Human Settlements in a World of Change", held in Stuttgart 8-10th of November 2018.

built space is precisely the type of architectural and urban products that are perfectly suitable for international investors.

However, let us talk about these rent-seeking landscapes through the lenses of housing and urban policies, which actively create the material, symbolic and normative conditions for the capture of lived territories by finance. I have not mentioned the word "neo-liberalism" so far, but now it is time to name it: Yes, I am talking about neo-liberalism, which among its discourses includes a big lie: "State get out of the business and let the market do what is needed!" Yet in truth states, through their public policies, have actively created and reproduced all of the conditions for financial capital to seize cities and the built space. So, we are not talking about having the state in or out but about the specific new role of the state, from a distributive role, where it captures part of surplus capital so as to deliver goods and services to citizens, to one where it is dedicated to open territories being captured by surplus capital. We are not even talking about having state money or not, because most of the state money is directed towards promoting development that is made for providing interest to the capital invested in real estate.

When I had arrived in Dubai during one of my trips as Rapporteur, I realised that some of the fantastic buildings that were created were empty. By that time I was so idiotic and thought: "Poor investor, they must have lost a lot of money with these investments". But no! One of the crucial things about financial capital and its relation to the built space is that the built space is an asset, a sort of parking place in a wide financial circuit. As such, it can be "on the books" and by that alone it provides interest and rating for those investors and investment funds, even if it's not used. We can see this around the world, a lot of empty spaces, which eventually become wonderful opportunities for future funds to take over. Yet, we are not only talking about the opening of the ground for these international fluxes of financial capital to come and take over the space but also a global process of dispossession.

Accumulation by dispossession – there is nothing new about that, but it is a new version with a new scale and a new speed. We need to ask ourselves and inquire: who is dispossessed, where are the displaced, and, even more importantly, what are the forms and tactics of the displaced, of the dispossessed, to emplace themselves and to create, what I call in opposition to the rent-seeking landscapes, generating their landscapes for life?

During my mandate as Special Rapporteur for the Right to Adequate Housing from 2008 to 2014, I could witness the effects of the financial crisis of 2008, which was the first crisis of this new form of financial capital in its relation to real estate and built space, especially with its new relation to housing. By that time, in 2008, what I could witness was a housing crisis. A housing crisis in countries like the US, like the UK, countries that used to have residual problems of housing, I would say, compared with other countries in Latin America, Asia or Africa. Of course, we cannot say that everybody in the US, UK, Netherlands or Sweden was living in wonderful and adequate housing before 2008, but I would say that most of the people had access to adequate housing. Which was a result of years of promoting housing as an essential part of the welfare state, a result of a particular political pact which was generated in those countries, from the late 19th/ early 20th century (depending on the particular history of the country), between capital, labour and the state to direct some surplus of the wealth produced towards social housing and social housing products. But in 2008 we saw foreclosures and homelessness worldwide, in the US, in Spain, in Ireland. I could witness a hunger strike in Kazakhstan, where the government and the new president – the former head of the communist party – convinced everybody to take out loans, to take credit, to buy homes that were built by Turkish construction companies with basically German and other European investment capital. By the time the crisis of 2008 started, the invested capital just went away from the construction companies, which went bankrupt, leaving buildings unfinished and people, whose savings were in the buildings, homeless. In Spain or the US, thousands and millions of houses were foreclosed, forcing people who had bought apartments or houses built by private entrepreneurs to give them back to the banks as they could not pay their debt any more. Worse even, in the case of Spain, these people still have a debt as the value of their houses after the crisis was much lower and insufficient to cover all the value of their mortgages. I also witnessed demonstrations in Tel Aviv, demonstrations of young Israelis without homes and without any possibility of getting one, because Israel also embarked on a neo-liberal policy of taking housing out of the welfare state; instead, transforming it – and this is the common thread between all those countries – from being a part of the welfare state, from a social policy with different versions, into a commodity or financial asset through policies of promoting home ownership as the one and only solution for housing.

So, we are talking about the financialisation of housing, in many terms. One is the possibility of opening a new frontier for this mass of surplus capital which is floating around the planet. Built space is especially relevant for finance for three reasons. First, because one spends a lot of money with built space, this space can absorb much investment capital surplus at once. Just to give you some figure: the investment fund of Apple, the corporation, is bigger than that of the national bank of Germany. And we are talking about national banks, sovereign funds, workers' pension funds, because one part of the dismantling of the welfare system was the dismantling of the public welfare system and pushing all the workers to pension funds. Including us trying to figure out how to maintain some savings to assure retirement and old age in countries where public pension funds do not exist anymore. Secondly, for its durability. It is common, probably in Europe as well, certainly in Latin America, that one's mother or father or aunt advises to put one's money in built space, because it will not disappear over time. The materiality of the house, the fact that the built space can stay for 30, 40, 50 years and more, makes it especially useful for the medium- and long-term investments that need to have returns over time, like pension funds. Finally, built space and (urban) land in general is very important collateral in the financial world. If one has land, if one has built space, then one has an asset that allows one to raise more, ask for more at the bank or on the financial circuit. And this is also something that everybody has experienced: we go to a bank and ask for a loan, and the first question the bank manager asks is whether one has a property or an apartment as a collateral. Built space is collateral. For these three reasons, the building of spaces is tightly integrated with the process and circuits of appreciation of financial capital. Finally, new innovative products that link built space with financial circuits – like real-estate investment funds – made the entry and exit of financial capital into built space much easier, without transaction costs, just with a digital bit.

I have another wonderful story to tell you about the housing crisis in the UK. At the end of the 1960s, 40% of the whole housing stock in the UK was social housing, built either by councils or other non-profits, like churches or unions. Under Margaret Thatcher (and also Reagan in the US) the whole stock was practically privatised, to the sitting tenants. Which, of course, was great for Margaret Thatcher and the way she could enter and destroy Labour-based constituencies, as all the workers practically gained a home: they could buy the home they lived in with a great discount and could become owners of these apartments and homes. We had different versions of this dismantling everywhere: in Eastern Europe, all the social housing stock was privatised, in Britain it was privatised to the sitting tenants. Even in places where there is still social housing, like Germany, some social housing companies were completely privatised, some privatised parts of their housing stock. So, we are talking about the dismantling of housing as a social policy, as part of the dismantling of the welfare state, as a human right, transformed into a commodity and financial asset, through strategies of privatisation (in the UK, Eastern Europe) and financialisation (in the Netherlands, Germany).

But then the question is: What about countries in Latin America and Africa that never had housing policies as a part of a welfare state? While the welfare state was dismantled in Europe, that was not the reality in countries like Brazil or South Africa. Instead, we had a "Southern" version of the commodification and financialisation of housing: the massive production of housing in the peripheries in Chile, Mexico, Brazil, South Africa, adopting a version of the same model of promoting ownership of homes produced by private developers, with, in the case of Latin America, a heavy subsidy from the state. These homes are provided in the outskirts not because of planning problems but because land is cheaper there and thus provides for higher profits for developers. Cheap land, in Latin America for instance, means non-urbanized land, land without a city, which means living in jobless amenities-less environments.

Financial capital was invested directly in construction companies and the owners of these companies became shareholders through IPOs[2] or investment funds, hedge funds and equity funds, through the securitization of mortgages, which allows mortgages to circulate as one type of financial product, from one bank to the other bank, and then to an investment fund, and so on. I found one case in New York, right after the crisis, in which the mortgage of buildings passed through the hands of 80 different investment funds and groups within ten years. So, nobody really knew who the owner was. This is nothing new, this is surplus capital promoting geographical restructuring, the expansion of borders. This is also nothing new in the history of urban planning, the history of the rebuilding of Paris under Haussmann is part of this story. David Harvey talks about the spatial fix, a fix in terms of a situation that needs to be restored but a fix also in terms of fixing something, grounding something. Yet what is new about the process is its scale, its speed: Capital arrives and leaves in a bit. Moreover, now there is instrumental titularization, which is essential to understanding this process as transforming fixed objects into paper, into assets. The new financial instruments, such as real-estate investment trusts, are completely different, because one does not buy or sell a piece of a shopping mall, for instance, but holds a piece of paper, not even a piece of paper, a piece of an electronic gesture, which represents the right and expectation to receive interest payments over time. These new instruments promote a possibility that the space can circulate without changing hands or without being precisely tied to anyone. Yet when it comes to housing, at the end of the day someone took out a mortgage in the first place. This is the one that will be dispossessed at the end, and that is exactly what happened with the foreclosures. Whereas investment banks received their returns from passing these papers from one to the other, to the other, each time

---

2 Initial Public Offerings

receiving some per centage, it was the people that had mortgaged their lives who lost their homes and became homeless when the whole system collapsed.

All of this would have been impossible without the active role of the state, which since the late 1970s removed all barriers for the free circulation of capital, dismantled social housing policies, pushed everybody towards buying their homes, and created home ownership as the one and only model for everybody, everywhere, heavily subsidised by the state. We are not talking about the state not spending money, we are talking about redirecting state money towards home ownership. Another way was to make rental housing less protected, for instance, through the Ley de Arrendamientos Urbanos in Spain or the reform of rent control in New York and Berlin. 'Affordable' in inverted commas, because as a matter of fact, it is not meant for those who do not have any money, and it is seizing and taking out big tranches of land. Chile in the 1970s was the big laboratory for countries where social policies were residual. The housing policy of the Pinochet dictatorship was the destruction of all of the campamentos, the self-built informal settlements, and the displacement of their residents into home ownership on the peripheries. This 'opened' the valuable land in the cities for use that provides more earned interest for the capital that was invested in the place. And the dispossession machinery did not act only in the Global South by evicting informal settlers. In the US and Spain, for example, expanding suburbs were produced during the housing boom years, emptying the centres of the cities and making them more and more playgrounds for rent-seeking capital. That is exactly what happened when renters were pushed out of their well-located apartments, or social housing was demolished to open ground to "affordable" and "mixed" housing, which basically raised the rent of the places and pushed out former inhabitants.

One of the books that are fundamental to understand housing policies and urban policies under neo-liberalism is entitled "Housing: Enabling markets to work" (Mayo *et al.* 1993), which describes the recipe to reforming housing policies in order to promote home ownership through credit and unlocking land value. The latter is the idea that very well-located land cannot be occupied by poor people. This 'unlock land value' is the idea that one can build thousands of houses in the middle of nowhere with the money gained by reallocating very valued land.

In cities were most of the homes are self-built in squatter or non-developed land, there is a specificity. We don't have proper names for these "informal", "illegal", "irregular", "self-built" spaces because our rational utopia is the orderly market of home owners of modernist architecture on private property. But what happens with these other spaces that have no name? They exist in our cities in multiple dimensions of this 'other', often being the majority of the built space, especially in the so-called Global South. What is the role of this space, what is the role of this 'other' and what is the role of housing and urban policies in relation to this 'other'.

The essential condition for space to circulate freely in global markets is that space has one and only one permitted form of relationship between individuals with the territories they occupy: private property. Private property is the very base, the very condition, for titularization and financialisation. It is not necessarily the safer kind of tenure relationship, and we saw this with the housing crisis. But private property is the freest to circulate, is the freest to be part of a market of commodities and a market of finance. To that end it is very important to deny the existence of the hundreds of other types of tenure, especially during the colonial period. Colonialism was based on the denial of these ties, and this permitted massive land grabbing in America, in Africa, in Asia, and in Europe as well, with for instance the denial of the relationship the Roma have with territories. We are talking about 200 years, since the enlightenment, when property is now connected to freedom and citizenship and is becoming a very foundation of the modern state. Utopia is a democracy of freeholders, meaning property holders. And the rest is the rest.

In colonized territories, planning was essential to setting the borders between what is in and what is out: the orderly planned space based on the idea of private property was a way of affirming the cultural hegemony of the elites and also to draw the border between the 'others' and the racialized bodies and the racialized space, which are basically the landscapes for life, the self-built neighbourhoods that were produced under scarce resources without any material support of the state. Today, this precarity has nothing to do with tenure relations or with cultural characteristics. The precarity has to do only with the fact that the wealth of society is not directed towards there. There are no resources and no money directed toward the favelas, bastilles, slums. But if we take the word "slum", we see that "slum" means criminal, scum in English. We are not only talking about a spatiality but also about a territorial stigma, we are talking about discriminatory gestalt. In Brazil, the official statistics institute, IBGE, nominates self-built urban settlements as "aglomerados subnormais", subnormal agglomerates, clearly relating a certain form of spatial arrangement with outlawed criminality and irregularity.

However, it is very interesting to see that those spaces are not completely destroyed. They are maintained, they are tolerated, they are reproduced, including with the action of the state. Rarely are they displaced to the peripheries or destroyed. The most common situation is the ambiguity of everyday life, the permanent transitoriness, a state of exception that is over those settlements. Planning provides the language that sets the perimeter and the borders in order to see who has all of the rights and it is not ambiguous, and who has to live under the "perhaps" – "perhaps you can stay", "perhaps you will be urbanized", "perhaps displaced", "perhaps regularised". And even more perverse, being under the state of exception is the condition which permits, for instance, that the police can enter there, shooting in the streets and houses, killing randomly without any judicial mandate.

The expansion and reproduction of those settlements were, according to the classic analysis of Brazilian sociologist Francisco de Oliveira in the 1970s, an essential condition to maintain wages that were too low to bear the housing cost. And what about today? Today, the ambiguity is essential to maintaining certain parts of the cities as a "reserved" target for financial capital, spaces to be captured by financial capital. Because slum evictions are, first of all, politically justified; because slums are marginal, outcast, outlaw, irregular. And at the same time, slum evictions are very practical because no expropriation has to be paid, basically, so they are cheap, cheaper at least than expropriating land in middle-class neighbourhoods or private property. We have thousands of examples of this, such as evictions that take place during preparations for mega events, for which new urban developments are often located exactly where those settlements existed before.

All of that expresses the tight relationship between urban policies and housing policies, as the massive production of homes in the outskirts of cities are connected to the real state of complex financial expansions into central locations, with their shopping malls, corporate towers and cultural centres.

After the 2008 financial crisis ended, the financialisation of housing persisted and advanced. The new wave, the new version of financialisation of housing, was not home ownership any more, but rental housing, which is corporate landlordism. The same hedge funds and equity funds that were behind the construction companies during the massive production of home ownership have been cheaply buying foreclosed apartments and houses so they could rent them out. Blackstone alone presently owns 85,000 housing units in 17 different cities in the US, and this is only one international investment fund. Some of these funds have even bought public housing in Madrid or Berlin and put them up for rent, of course pushing out 'bad' renters, that is, the ones who have been either unable to pay the higher rents or are considered racialized bodies. Those evicted in New York or Atlanta have been mainly African-Americans, the ones evicted in some German cities are basically immigrants and the ones having difficulties paying rent in Spain are mostly Latin American immigrants. This machinery of dispossession has now been reproduced through rental housing.

Let me finish my input on a brighter note, outlining some responses. What can we do with this powerful electronic cloud that made all states, even states under the rule of socialist parties or coalitions, adhere to adopting the same instruments, removing the same barriers, and developing and upholding the same policies? I think we have to reverse this story. Saying that the only constraint, the only barrier to financial capital taking over of all territory and all cities are the very places that are occupied by the poor, by the people with not-so-clear tenure relations. These people are the real constraint for this massive wave to go on. Here, we are not only talking about resistance to evictions. More than about resistance, I want to talk about existence. I want to talk about emplacements, which means the construction of the city by the people, and the fact that these people are there and that these cities are built under the logic of people's lives and prosperity.

We are talking about an urban warfare (Rolnik 2019), a contemporary rebellion in which space is more than the scenery where the battles take place, but are the object of the battles themselves, battles around appropriation. We are seeing battles around the occupation of public space, thus creating a symbolic geography, which means a political confrontation between territories that are either understood as landscapes for life or as playgrounds for financial capital. Longtime occupations can exercise forms of organisation, decision-making and self-government, and can rehearse possible futures. Today, they are, of course, confronted by a militarized control of space, which also corresponds to private control, or the so-called new forms of governance, which are embedded in public-private partnerships, public-private transformations and urban transformations, with their use of repressive technologies in the absence of the necessary political mediation of space.

I finish by interrogating the Right to the City in this context. The Right to the City is not a set of words written in a by-law, in a resolution, or in conference proceedings. The Right to the City is the recognition and valorisation of the material and cultural landscapes that emerge from urban struggles everywhere: in movements against evictions, in the platform for people affected by mortgages in Spain, in the rebuilding of tenant unions in Spain, the UK and the US, in the demonstrations against gentrification in the Global North and Global South. The Right to the City is alive and on the streets.

REFERENCES

Mayo, S. K., S. Angel, and A. Imhoff. (1993) "Housing: Enabling Markets to Work (with Technical Supplements)." World Bank policy paper. World Bank.

Rolnik, R. (2019) *Urban Warfare. Housing Under the Empire of Finance.* London:Verso.

Introduction: Housing and Human Settlements in a World of Change

Md Ashiq Ur Rahman, Josefine Fokdal and Astrid Ley

The housing challenge is becoming increasingly recognised in international policy discussions[1]; however, its broader links to the processes of migration, climate change, and economic globalisation are not yet fully understood. Despite the fact that, in principle, housing is recognised as a basic human right and is essential for human development, in practice, securing safe and adequate housing for everyone remains a major global development challenge of the 21st century – as pointed out in the two forewords by respectively El Sioufi and Rolnik. Issues associated with housing, such as its scarcity (including the lack of accessible land), affordability and quality, are persistent but changing in magnitude, over time. This book aims to situate housing in relation to the processes of global transformation. In this sense, it highlights the processes of economic globalisation, migration, and climate change as three major dynamics in relation to the global housing crisis. Obviously, there are also further global transformations in place but they are either not yet as widely discussed in terms of their effects on housing (such as information and communication technology) or they include very particular local forms and effects (such as demographic changes). This book is an attempt to identify the influencing dynamics of the three key transformation processes. As such, it does not discuss housing in isolation but rather

---

1 International agreements address housing and its role in urban development and call for systematic approaches to the housing challenge (Agenda 2030 for Sustainable Development, with goals to reduce extreme poverty, the Sendai Framework for Disaster Risk Reduction 2015; the Addis Ababa Action Agenda on Financing for Development 2015; the Paris Agreement under the United Nations Framework Convention on Climate Change 2015; and the New Urban Agenda 2016).

takes a holistic perspective toward housing in a world that is changing on both local and global scales.

Over the last twenty years, the process of economic globalisation has resulted in significant changes that have not only affected livelihoods in human settlements and reshaped the institutional settings of a housing delivery that is often framed under neo-liberal policies and so-called enablement approaches but has also turned housing into a product that is traded under a system of globally operated finance. Thus, the commodification of housing largely affects the overall housing process (see Rolniks' contribution in the foreword for an elaboration). Apart from this financialisation process of housing, rural-urban migration as well as the upsurge in forced migration across international borders (due to crises, or economic or environmental reasons) are also emerging issues which have implications for cities and human settlements (UN-Habitat 2016).

Independent of these diverse push factors, the process of migration is directly resulting in rapid urbanisation, globally. This process is also causing the spatial expansion of urban settlements through the annexation and reclassification of rural areas to make more space for housing provision for a growing urban population. However, the question is whether these changes are addressing the housing needs of migrants and how these processes are taking place in different contexts. Apart from the two dynamics of migration and economic globalisation, this book also highlights the influence of climate change. The question, here, is whether climate change and its direct link with housing and human settlements is a persistent or emerging issue. This book seeks to highlight how a changing climate is affecting the housing process and how human settlements are responding through everyday practice and policies. The three global trends discussed here (economic globalisation, migration and climate change) apply to developing, transitional and developed countries alike but are most strongly discussed in relation to developing countries, which are severely affected but have addressed these issues only to a limited degree in spite of their relevance. This is reflected in this book in the number of chapters that contextualise the three global dynamics of economic globalisation, migration and climate change in relation to housing in developing and transitional countries across diverse regions worldwide.

This chapter raises three different but interlinked questions related to the aforementioned dynamics. These questions are: (i) What outcomes have economic globalisation and related neo-liberal policies and "enabling" ideas brought to the ground to address the issue of housing over the last two decades? (ii) How are the dynamics of migration reshaping the urban housing provision? And (iii) How are human settlements able to respond with different housing approaches to extreme climate events? To frame the above questions, this chapter draws on various sources to understand the housing processes in relation to the impacts of the three global dynamics addressed in this book. Later, this chapter contextualises the theoretical discourses by reflecting on the case studies outlined in the following chapters of this book.[2]

HOUSING AND ECONOMIC GLOBALISATION

The evolution of pro-poor housing policies is not an isolated event; rather, these policies have been enacted with the various macro-economic changes that took place in developing countries, starting since the post-WWII period. This evolutionary process is related to the development discourse that associates urban poverty within the political, economic, social and cultural context (Jenkins *et al.* 2007). The particular link between the destruction of local economies and livelihoods through extending production chains to low-income countries is a case in point for economic globalisation as it is affecting livelihoods and thereby housing finance. Moreover, over the last three decades, neo-liberal policies have been particularly influential in reshaping housing systems and housing opportunities globally. Neo-liberal housing approaches have involved the privatisation of state housing assets, the promotion of individual home ownership, and increased rents, reduced subsidies, the deregulation of private housing and mortgage lending, the weakening of planning controls for new and existing housing, reduced state intervention in social and economic affairs and the firmly established assertion of the superiority of market processes (Rolnik 2013; Forrest and Hirayama 2009; Mukhija 2004).The consequence has been a deliberate attempt by policy-makers to make housing policies more market friendly and to encourage the private sector to be further involved in housing delivery (Sengupta 2009; Berner 2001). However, the type of neo-liberalism implemented and its particular outcomes in relation to housing differ across political, economic, social and cultural contexts.

Although, conceptually, the neo-liberal approach refers to the market and the withdrawal of the state, in practice, there is a duality. As Peck and Tickell (2006) have observed, "Only rhetorically does neo-liberalism mean less state" (p. 33). Brenner and Theodre (2005) explain this understanding of neo-liberalism as

---

2   This publication and its contributions are based on selected papers that were presented at the 19th N-AERUS conference on "Housing and Human settlements in a World of Change", held in Stuttgart 8-10th of November 2018 and financed by the German Research Foundation (DFG).

being a "neo-liberalism [that] is not a fixed end-state or condition; rather, it represents a process of [a] market-driven social and spatial transformation" (p. 102). Thus, this approach is always intensely contested by diverse social forces concerned with preserving non-market forms of actions (ibid). This proposition provides the scope for understanding different forms of neo-liberalism. In an effort to clarify how neo-liberal policy has developed, Peck and Tickell (2002) identify two interrelated phases or processes: "roll-back neo-liberalism" and "roll-out neo-liberalism" (p. 36). Roll-back neo-liberalism refers to "the active destruction or discreditation of Keynesian-welfarist and social-collectivist institutions" (Ibid, p. 37). This process is often termed privatisation and involves a retreat from state regulations and the governmental control of resources, including public services, nationalised industries, and labour and social rights (Aguirre et al. 2006). The second neo-liberal process, roll-out neo-liberalism, refers to "the purposeful construction and consolidation of neo-liberalised state forms, modes of governance, and regulatory relations" (Peck and Tickell 2002, p. 37). The concept of roll-back neo-liberalism has always been contested by the fact that the local context depends on both the political regime and the impact of the market on urban social structures (Brenner and Theodre 2005). In the context where roll-back neo-liberalism fails to cater to the urban poor, roll-out neo-liberalism acts as an alternative form of urban governance by involving different actors (ibid). This approach to roll-out neo-liberalism is evident, in developed countries, in different urban upgrading and housing programmes (e.g., social housing programmes in the United Kingdom). However, roll-out neo-liberalism as a modality of urban governance is still limited and Brenner and Theodre (2005) mention it as being a problem of political will as opposed to criticising the idea of neo-liberalism. Therefore, it is of significance to contextualise how the globalised economy has made an impact on livelihoods and housing. Against this notion it becomes relevant to ask how neo-liberal "enabling" ideas have been modified in different countries in order to address the issue of housing, particularly housing for the urban poor.

HOUSING AND MIGRATION

Worldwide more than 65 million people are on the move due to conflict or natural disasters (UNHCR 2015). In addition, rural-to-urban migration continues to increase pressure on urban infrastructure and housing demand. While this issue has persisted in the developing countries and countries in transition for decades, the recent influx of refugees in Europe has put affordable and safe housing back on the agenda in the Global North. Here, high pressure on urban areas and the failure of local governments to provide access to affordable housing has led to a condition where more than one billion urban dwellers are living in informal and underserviced settlements worldwide (UN-Habitat 2016). This situation calls for addressing inefficient housing policies, stringent regulations and inaccessible housing finance as well as to acknowledging the informal solutions and efforts undertaken by the urban poor, themselves, in order to achieve an inclusive and empowering approach. The role of migrants in this process has always been conceptualised as a cheap source of labour (Schiller and Caglar 2009). However, the role of migration can be conceptualised at different scales as migrants are creating and reproducing different social institutions in the absence of states' responses to their basic needs, including housing and employment.

Therefore, the link between migration and housing can be explained through a process of symbiotic relationship-building. As Saunders (2011) explains, the arrival of migrants or the development of transitory neighbourhoods that often lie at the fringes of established cities provide hope for migrants in making use of their socio-cultural resources and economic capital for a better future. However, this hope is always contested through physical segregation and the policy measures of different actors who want to make their cities competitive in a neo-liberal way (Sassen 2016; Saunders 2011; Schiller and Caglar 2009). In response to these segregation policies and in order to explore the opportunities available in their arrival cities, migrants often resort to their own informal and adaptive solutions to make use of a spectrum of available housing options. Therefore, informality is a common feature when we discuss the provision of housing for migrants. This notion of informality has two interrelated outcomes. One is related to migrants' housing prospects and the other is related to a speculative future. In terms of prospects, informal housing support and housing solutions are often self-arranged. More often, these housing solutions are the determinants of migrants' identity and self-actualisation; they strengthen confidence among migrants who act collectively for their survival in their arrival cities, from both the social and economic perspective (Moser and Stein 2011; Tipple 2005; Rakodi 2002; Mitlin 2001). The speculative future is associated with the temporary status of such housing provision and citizen rights. Migrants' autonomous adaptation to secure housing is often constrained by a lack of secure tenure and household capacity, with most migrants having neither the physical nor the financial capacity to afford large-scale market-driven housing projects (Banks 2012; Schiller and Caglar 2009). Therefore, it is of great importance to understand whether and how the dynamics of migration reshape the provision of urban housing.

HOUSING AND CLIMATE CHANGE

The continuing extension of the built environment has severe effects on climate change and is a key factor that needs to be addressed in climate-change mitigation measures. The third part of this book, however, sets its focus on the vulnerability of human settlements due to climate change. In particular, cities in developing countries and countries in transition are at risk due to the impacts of climate change for a number of reasons: high population density, where sometimes the majority of people are living in slums or informal settlements; a high concentration of solid and liquid wastes in these settlements; informal urban growth that disrupts natural drainage systems and urban expansion on particularly risky sites (Tanner *et al.* 2009; Pelling 2003), to mention just a few.

Climate change is having an increasingly important influence in that it is exacerbating the already vulnerable livelihoods of the urban poor (Banks 2012; Roy *et al.* 2012). The effects of climate change are adding an additional layer of shocks the urban poor must face in the context of limited services and infrastructure, densely populated and environmentally vulnerable habitats, and their limited adaptive capacity to cope with climate-change impacts (Roy *et al.* 2012; Banks 2012; Banks *et al.* 2011; Roy *et al.* 2011; Jabeen *et al.* 2010). Despite these challenges, present climate-change-adaptation strategies have largely ignored the issues of housing (Hossain and Rahman 2018; Tanner and Mitchell 2008; Mitlin 2005). A large proportion of informal urban dwellers reside in risky locations that are prone to natural disasters; for instance, on river banks that are prone to flooding or in areas that face the potential danger of landslides. With climate change, the frequency of natural disasters and issues such as urban heat islands often intensify, in many instances leading to disastrous consequences for the most vulnerable groups (UNISDR 2012). Thus, access to safe and adequate housing also means access to land that is situated in safe locations (Boonyabancha 2009). The assessment and perception of risk, however, is not without contestation. Poor urban communities that are situated in high-risk sites are also exposed to the threat of eviction and relocation, which causes further vulnerability. This contested situation calls for upscaling all of the levels on which housing is being discussed and, thus, for city-wide approaches to move toward a strategy of safe and affordable housing. Housing can provide a pathway and has been identified, in the literature, as being the major component of the physical capital that contributes to urban resilience (Rakodi 2002). Here, resilience can be understood as "the capacity of a system, community, or society potentially exposed to hazards to adapt, by resisting or changing in order to reach and maintain an acceptable level of functioning and structure," and this implies learning from past experiences to improve future protection by implementing "risk reduction measures" (UNISDR, 2012). Thus, a capacity-based understanding of resilience contemplates the poverty issue that is at the heart of the disaster-risk reduction and climate-change-adaptation nexus. In this context, the development of capacity within a social system that includes poor communities and different organisations is built on a system that links climate-change adaptation and disaster-risk reduction as an important step because it creates an enabling environment for poverty reduction in a changing climate (Béné et al. 2014). Therefore, integrating (community-based) risk-mapping into urban development and a discussion of land and infrastructure development tools that are associated with housing can be a first step in identifying safe, well-connected locations city-wide. In this context, to understand the dynamics of urban resilience, it is important to identify how human settlements are able to respond with different housing approaches to extreme climate events.

OVERVIEW OF THE BOOK

The book is divided into three parts, each covering one thematic area. Part I deals with the issue of housing in a globalising economy as it relates to market-oriented policies. In this section, three chapters illustrate the evolution of housing policies and the emergence of alternative modes of housing provision under the process of the financialisation of housing. These three chapters cover case studies on approaches to social housing in Indonesia, Argentina, Uruguay and Brazil. Part II of the book contains four chapters that highlight the issue of migration and its relation to housing and human settlements in the context of Oman, Bolivia, China and Bangladesh. These chapters also use the case-study method to highlight the exclusion of migrants from policy initiatives on housing and the everyday routines and habits of migrants in relation to tenure, housing and the collective spaces they use to develop intervention strategies for housing and employment in the face of government neglect. The final section - Part III of the book presents three chapters that cover the issues of housing and climate change. Here, the authors showcase case studies from Egypt, South Africa, Columbia and Brazil to portray different strategies of adaptation to extreme climatic events in order to reduce the physical vulnerability of different urban neighbourhoods. In the following, we will reflect on the major arguments of each of the chapters under the thematic areas.

Part I consists of contributions related to the link between "Housing and Economic Globalisation". The first chapter in this section is entitled "Indonesian

Housing Policy in the Era of Globalisation". Here, Jo Santoso discusses two new housing initiatives of the national government of Indonesia; namely, the "City Without Slums" and "The National Affordable Housing Program". Drawing on the case-study context, he argues that the successful implementation of these housing programmes depends not only on their ability to effectively overcome the conditions of the existing stock of housing but it also has to deal with the negative impacts of the transnational-global orientation of Indonesian economic development, which continuously deepens social gaps and produces urban poverty. Finally, he argues that Indonesia's housing problems cannot be overcome only by successful governments programmes but, in the long run, this highly depends on the success of the community-based programme "City for All" in empowering urban communities to develop their own capacities to be part of the solution. This does not mean withdrawing the state's responsibility but rather sharing the responsibility between the state and the communities.

The second chapter of Part I is entitled "Let's get down to business – Private Influences in the Making of Affordable Housing Policies: The case of Minha Casa Minha Vida in Brazil." Anthony Boanada-Fuchs focuses on the involvement of market actors in the housing sector and the impact of the global financial crisis on Brazil. The findings of this chapter underline the high level of policy influence developers and construction companies have had on the affordable housing programme, from introducing the idea of a large-scale national housing program to the constant policy and regulatory adjustments to the Minha Casa Minha Vida housing programme, over the years. He argues that formal communication channels have enabled these actors to influence housing policy, but they have also benefitted from informal or, at best, institutionalized practices that have developed in the absence of any official regulation. Finally, this chapter argues that the lack of democratic participation and accountability in the housing process has led to a biased institutionalization that guarantees profit margins and preferential development conditions for developers at the expense of Brazilian cities and society at large.

The final chapter of Part I, by Marielly Casanova, is entitled "Mutual Aid, Self-Management and Collective Ownership: Social Capital as a Housing Finance Counter-Mechanism to Neo-liberal Policies". This chapter draws on different sources of international literature. Casanova argues that the economic system has been putting intense pressure on the housing market as it has been following a logic of accumulation and speculation, which has driven up prices and excluded a great majority of the urban population. Referring to the case-study context of Argentina and Uruguay, the author claims that, in response to these challenges, transformative initiatives from social groups or organised communities are fostering mutual aid, self-management and the development of collective property assets from social organisations and these have become the tools the urban poor use to counteract their unfulfilled citizen rights. As evidence, Casanova presents the case of the tenant movement in Argentina called MOI (Movimiento de Ocupantes e Inquilinos) to secure housing rights against the threat of forced evictions, by developing tenant cooperatives and taking over and occupying abandoned properties. She further draws on the case of a housing cooperative called FUCVAM (Federación Uruguaya de Cooperativas de Viviendapor Ayuda Mutua–the Uruguayan Federation of Mutual-aid Housing Cooperatives), which developed its activities by learning from Argentina's MOI movement. Casanova identifies that, in both case-study contexts, self-management, mutual aid and collective ownership played important roles in developing social capital as an alternative mechanism to financing low-income housing.

Part II of this book contains the contributions of different authors on the issue of "Housing and Migration". In the chapter entitled "Influence of Migrants' Two-Direction Linkage on Urban Villages in China: The case of Shigezhuang village in Beijing", Shiyu Yang notes that, in China, urban villages grow informally and with their prime location and low living costs they have become ideal destinations for China's internal migrant population. Highlighting the case-study context, she argues that migrant workers' constant linkage to their rural origins and social networks are based on place bonds which may contribute to more working opportunities, a better sense of belongingness and strong neighbourhood attachments. At the same time, however, this deepens their vulnerable and inferior status in their urban destinations. Drawing on the everyday lives of migrants in urban villages, Shiyu explains that temporary migrants as circulators consider the city as a place for work instead of a place for living; thus, they are reluctant to invest money in their city living and only demand substandard housing. Therefore, strong community leadership is a missing element in urban villages in China in terms of negotiating with other stakeholders regarding migrants' right to the city.

The second chapter of Part II by Fabio Bayro Kaiser, entitled "Need for Housing or Speculation? Urban Expansion of the City of Tarija-Bolivia", raises the question of land speculation in the City of Tarija in Bolivia and reflects on the severe consequences of neglecting this issue in the context of the recent influx of migrants and the increasing levels of population density due to rural-urban migration. In this chapter, Bayro Kaiser identifies that urban expansion in the case-study context is the outcome of centralism in housing policies and programmes that make the operationalisation of development agenda(s) quite difficult as existing programmes are not designed to respond to site-specific circumstances. Referring to the case-study context, he explains that land speculation has deprived the city of valuable natural land and has also destroyed important water bodies in an illegitimate way. He also argues that informal urbanisation is an opportunity to develop cities, but inadequate municipal controls and/or regulations mean that speculation has led to over-priced plots of land. Moreover, through an analysis of the urban expansion that has taken place in the areas studied, he argues that the new (planned) neighbourhoods as an outcome of urban expansion are larger in terms of surface than the older neighbourhoods; however, they house significantly fewer people.

In her chapter entitled "Understanding the Housing Needs of Low-Skilled Bangladeshi Migrants in Oman", Shaharin Elham Annisa identifies that cities across the Gulf region are increasingly shifting the location of migrant workers' housing away from city centres and closer to the work sites of low-skilled migrants. This chapter seeks to reveal these migrants' housing needs by studying a labour camp and shared housing developed in Al-Hamriya, Muscat. Annisa notes that the temporary alteration of indoor and outdoor spaces, in the case-study settlements, can be considered an indication of city management's failure to cater to the basic social and spatial needs of these low-skilled migrants. In this chapter, she argues that such alterations to housing units and the built environment are linked to the livelihood strategies of low-skilled migrants, ranging from finding income-generating opportunities to building strong social cohesion. Finally, she identifies that housing for low-skilled migrants in the Gulf region does not comply with these migrants' livelihood opportunities, and the manner in which migrants alter their housing and the built environment, in an informal way, brings about more opportunities in terms of enhancing their capital so as to pursue different livelihoods.

The fourth and last chapter of Part II is entitled "Urban Environmental Migrants: Demands for a Unique Category of Human Refugees to Ensure Their Right to Land and Resettlements", by Syed Mukaddim and his co-authors. Using the case-study context of Khulna city, Bangladesh, the authors call for the basic recognition of people who are forced to migrate due to environmental events. They argue that environmental factors are not the sole influence but they certainly put heavy pressure on to the other drivers of migration. This chapter identifies that even though the link between environmental factors and migration has been realised in the different policies and programmes of governmental and non-governmental organisations, the people who face forced resettlement either due to conflict or to climate-related disasters are yet to be categorised separately so as to receive appropriate assistance. Finally, the authors argue that environmental migrants are largely acknowledged as either a usual "migrant" or a "refugee", both terms that undermine the significance and gravity of the conditions in which they live.

Part III covers the issue of "Housing and Climate Change" and opens with the contribution by Franziska Laue, on "Heat Stress Related Climate Change Adaptation in the MENA Region - Reflections on Socially Inclusive Approaches". In this chapter, the author explains the theoretical interconnected aspects of housing and climate change and claims that climate-change-related vulnerabilities differ across neighbourhoods, based on the physical conditions of the housing structures, the built environment and the demographic compositions. Laue uses the case-study method to highlight this issue and identifies that all neighbourhoods in the Greater Cairo Region (GCR) are exposed to heat stress, but climate-change-related vulnerabilities are an increasingly relevant topic particularly for low-income neighbourhoods and neglected and contested historic areas and informal settlements. She argues that, in the context of the above-mentioned vulnerable neighbourhoods, adaptation can crucially rely on the local community's awareness, interactions, and mechanisms for adaptation. To highlight the importance of community involvement, Laue presents the findings of a project in a neighbourhood called Ezzbet El-Nasr, which is located in the GCR and had received aid from an international organisation. Her findings are that community-based climate-change adaptation requires a particular balance of individual and collective awareness and community interaction and support, whereas these communities (potentially) face continuous neglect in terms of both the services they need and formal governance.

The following chapter, "From the Hyper-Ghetto to State-Subsidised Urban Sprawl: Old and New Vulnerabilities in Buffalo City, South Africa", by Gerhard Kienast, highlights the local practice of emergency resettlement and the redevelopment initiatives that are triggered by shack fires and severe floods in Duncan Village, Buffalo City, South Africa. Kienast uses the case-study method and argues that a non-participatory relocation has created new vulnerabilities in the area studied. He notes that the new settlements, in the case-study area, were only serviced with the most basic infrastructure, lacked integration in the local economy and were also problematic for inhabitants because transport costs were prohibitive. In addition, he points out that the spaces that opened up due to the relocation of shack owners were soon filled by migrants who set up new informal housing. Therefore, he argues that the reoccupation points to the simple fact that there is a high demand for a place in the city, that the state-subsidised housing programme is nowhere close to filling this gap and that the formal, bureaucratic, long-term planning system has failed to reduce the risk of disasters. Finally, he argues that when the formal long-term planning process fails to implement climate-change adaptations, a poverty-ridden area like Buffalo City must be balanced with interim services and disaster-management plans.

The final chapter of Part III and of the book is on "Learning from Co-Produced Landslide Risk Mitigation Strategies in Low-Income Settlements in Medellín (Colombia) and São Paulo (Brazil)". In this chapter, Harry Smith *et al.* use the case-study method to investigate two projects that involve community-based efforts that range from developing financial mechanisms to the co-production of arrangements set up to deal with disaster-prone areas in Medellín (Colombia) and São Paulo (Brazil). The authors argue that current risk governance and management practices focus on post-disaster and recovery scenarios rather than prevention and mitigation, with the latter manifesting mostly in interventions that run counter to establishing relationships of co-production. This chapter shows that different levels and ways of understanding disaster risk can be found within different communities and are linked to the history of each particular settlement; this, in turn, affects how such communities engage with external agencies (e.g., local government, utilities companies) in relation to dealing with disaster risk. In addition, the authors argue that risk governance and management involve different approaches in different cities but are linked to a general approach that is used in informal settlements in each city and also to state capacity. The projects described in this chapter showcase alternative ways of engaging vulnerable communities and the local government in each city in co-producing landslide-risk-management strategies. Drawing on the lessons learned from the participatory action research projects in the case-study contexts, the authors argue that developing ways of co-producing landslide-risk mitigation that optimise the use of community and state capacities to provide safe homes depends on the shared objectives of the stakeholders involved.

CONCLUSION

Reflecting on the contents of this book, we investigated three different but interlinked questions related to the thematic issues it addresses: (i) What outcomes have the globalising economy and the aligned neo-liberal "enabling" ideas brought to the ground to address the issue of housing over the last two decades? (ii) How are the dynamics of migration reshaping the provision of urban housing? And (iii) How are human settlements able to develop different housing approaches that will enable them to respond to extreme climate events? The three chapters on "Housing and Economic Globalisation", in part I of this book, give evidence to how market-based enabling mechanisms under neo-liberal development approaches have failed to address the housing needs of the urban poor and how in contrast a participatory enabling approach has the potential to adopt the informal networked actions of the urban poor in order to scale up community-led projects and programmes. However, the lack of public policies that affect the function and creation of organisational arrangements for social housing is detrimental to such participatory approaches. Thus, it is time to bring back the state, in a collaborative form, for restructuring housing policy around the condition and provision of housing for the urban poor. Moreover, this implies that political will is essential for such a re-engagement in the era of financialisation.

Reflecting on the chapter by Jo Santoso, we conclude that the transformation of housing policy in Indonesia follows the enabling approach advocated by the World Bank, which essentially replicates the roll-back form of neo-liberalism. Although the case studies in the chapter present community-led initiatives, it is obvious that these have not been mainstreamed through public policy for housing on a city or country-wide scale. Similar cases have been observed in the case of Brazil, as pointed out by Anthony Boanada-Fuchs. In these two chapters, we can observe that the common feature of the roll-back form of neo-liberalism follows the World Bank approach that asks for the restructuring of organisational arrangements and legislation to ensure market friendly environments (Waeyenberge 2018). However, in the case-study context of Brazil, Boanada-Fuchs asserts that the state's market-enabling approach to a housing solution did not necessarily include legislative restructuring but rather a profit-seeking commodification process of housing development. Therefore, reflecting on two papers that present the roll-back form of neo-liberalism, we want to refer to Raquel Rolnik (2013) as she describes the whole process of "the commodification of housing and the increased use of housing as an investment asset [that has] profoundly affected the prevailing idea across the world that adequate housing was a human right" (Rolnik 2013, p. 1059). Also, Marielly Casanova highlights the importance of community-led approaches under an enabling paradigm; however, the case study presented in her chapter follows the idea of a "participatory enabling approach" under the roll-out form of neo-liberalism. In these cases, the government becomes the facilitator of the actions of all of the participants involved in the production and improvement of shelter (Sarfoh 2010). However, in reviewing different international practices, we have observed that these initiatives failed to reach the necessary scale and in multiple cases the urban poor still face challenges where formal governance has not blended with informal governance in an institutionalized way (Rahman *et al.* 2016; Fokdal *et al.* 2015; Mitlin 2008). Therefore, we would like to draw attention to our claim that political will is the essential component for reaching the appropriate scale for community-led housing initiatives and tackling the commodification of housing in an era of economic globalisation under the neo-liberal paradigm.

The chapters of Part II on "Housing and Migration" point to inefficient housing policies, stringent regulations and inaccessible housing finance and how this is creating an informal bubble of housing solutions for migrants. It seems that housing policies and programmes are not at all inclusive in relation to migrants and often migrants are treated as a non-existent population. Further, their efforts to undertake an empowering approach to achieve inclusion have been very fragile. Highlighting the chapters of Shiyu Yang and Fabio Bayro Kaiser, it is evident that the physical segregation of migrants is a factor globally, and this is mainly due to the policy measures of different actors and the competitive nature of cities. In both cases, housing for migrants is provided informally and developed outside the city not because of planning problems but because land is cheaper there. In the case of China, this land has officially remained non-urbanised land; and in the case of Bolivia, these areas were declared urban without the provision of urban amenities. These cases show a clear policy of the segregation and marginalisation of migrants in relation to their housing provision. Similar issues have also been identified by Syed Mukaddim et al. in the case presented on Bangladesh, where environmental migrants do not receive any special attention from policy-makers but are left alone in the city, like the rest of the urban poor, and this makes their lives more vulnerable. In response to these segregation policies, we have often observed, globally, an autonomous response from migrants wherein they have developed incremental housing or altered the built environment (Moser and Stein 2011; Tipple 2005). The chapter by Shaharin Elham Annisa showcases similar responses from migrants in Oman, where they are altering the built environment and going beyond formal rule to appropriate spaces for generating different opportunities to pursue livelihoods. However, these solutions are very fragile and always under threat of demolition (Banks 2012). Therefore, as we highlighted in the last section, the issue of migrants must be treated as a political priority in local development plans. The motivating factor for such a transformation in the political process could be triggered by the idea of Schiller and Caglar (2009, p. 189), where they noted that "migrants may also participate in rescaling a city by contributing to a re-evaluation of a city's global image".

Reflecting on the issues of housing and climate change, in Part III, it can be assumed that the changing nature of climate, together with the housing condition, increases vulnerability in low-income urban neighbourhoods. In this section, the authors have identified that housing can present a pathway for increasing urban resilience. They point toward acknowledging the nature of the changing climate and the associated risk of climate-induced disaster and argue that it is now essential to explore alternative ways of engaging vulnerable communities and the local government at the city scale in co-producing risk-management strategies. In the chapter on climate-change adaptation in the MENA region, Franziska Laue reflects on those living in environmentally vulnerable settings and substandard housing and notes that poor urban households and communities are also attempting to find strategies of adaptation in order to reduce their physical vulnerability to extreme weather events. These strategies can be considered as "physical impact minimising strategies" (Hossain and Rahman 2018). Therefore, institutionalizing these efforts resonates with the capacity-based understanding of resilience (Béné et al. 2014). Such institutionalized processes and their forms can be applied through the frameworks of co-production/co-management in which citizen and state relations are amended to take account of communities' potential to self-organise (Mitlin 2008). On one hand, the case study presented by Harry Smith et al., in Part III, showcases a perfect example of such co-production in dealing with issues of climate change on a neighbourhood scale. On the other hand, state negligence and the lack of community leadership in the case of Duncan Village in Buffalo City, South Africa, presented by Gerhard Kienast, shows a neighbourhood's vulnerability to different climatic events. In summary, the findings indicate that where the representative community-based organisations can build partnerships with local or national governments, the possibilities for building resilience to climate change are much greater.

Finally, this book unpacks the dynamics of housing under three key thematic areas of a world in change. Although the cases presented in this book are very much local and reflect on current statuses, they are still connected to global transformations and show that the changing nature of economic globalisation under neo-liberalism, migration and climate change is producing varied outcomes in relation to housing. Therefore, a global consensus and an understanding of local issues will be significant to dealing with the challenges of housing in the near future. The cases presented in this book are a testimony of the informalisation of the housing process, the increased diversity of actors involved and the lack of efficient and responsive housing policies to adequately adapt to the respective contexts. The New Urban Agenda and Sustainable Development Goals could provide a background of such a consensus. Nevertheless, how to contextualise both agendas in order to deal with the issue of housing needs to be addressed in both academia and in practice. The contributions of this book provide some examples and indications of such a contextualisation. In doing so, this volume wants to encourage policy-makers, planners, researchers and social activists to take an integrated perspective on housing and human settlement in a world of change.

REFERENCES

Aguirre, A., Eick, V., & Reese, E. (2006) Neoliberal Globalization, Urban Privatization, and Resistance. *Social Justice,* 33(3), pp. 1–3.

Banks, N. (2012) *Urban poverty in Bangladesh: Causes, consequences and coping strategies.* BWPI Working Paper 172, Manchester: Brooks World Poverty Institute.

Banks, N., Manoj, R. & and David H. (2011) Neglecting the Urban Poor in Bangladesh: Research, Policy and Action in the Context of Climate Change. *Environment and Urbanization,* 23 (2), pp 487–502.

Béné, C., Newsham, A., Davies, M., Ulrichs, M., and Wood, R. G. (2014) Review article: Resilience, poverty and development. *Journal of International Development,* 26(5), pp. 598–623.

Berner, E. (2001) Learning from informal markets: innovative approaches to land and housing provision. *Development in Practice,* 11 (2), pp. 292–307.

Brenner, N. & Theodore, N. (2005) Neoliberalism and the urban condition. City, 9(1), pp 101–107.

Boonyabancha, S. (2009) Land for housing the poor by the poor. *Environment and Urbanization,* 21(2), pp. 309–329.

Fokdal, J., Ley, A., & Herrle, P. (2015) 'From Grassroots Shacks to the Towers of Power: Relationship Building of Transnational Urban Poor Networks. Experiences from Africa and Asia' in Peter Herrle, Astrid Ley and Josefine Fokdal (eds), *From Local Action to Global Networks: Housing the Urban Poor,* Ashgate Publishing Limited, United Kingdom.

Forrest, R. & Hirayama, Y. (2009) The uneven impact of neo-liberalism on housing opportunities. *International Journal of Urban and Regional Research,* 33(4), pp. 998-1013.

Forrest, R. and Hirayama, Y. (2009) The uneven impact of neo-liberalism on housing opportunities, *International Journal of Urban and Regional Research,* 33(4), pp 998-1013.

Hossain, M. Z. and Rahman, M. A. U. (2018) Adaptation to climate change as resilience for urban extreme poor: lessons learned from targeted asset transfers programmes in Dhaka city of Bangladesh. *Environment, Development and Sustainability,* 20(1), pp. 407–432.

Jabeen, H., Johnson, C. and Allen, A. (2010) Built in resilience: learning from grassroots coping strategies for climate variability. *Environment and Urbanization*, 22(2), pp. 415–431.

Jenkins, P., Smith, H., & Wang, P. Y. (2007) *Planning and housing in the rapidly urbanising world.* London; New York: Routledge Publishers.

Mitlin, D. (2008) With and beyond the state co-production as a route to political influence, power and transformation for grassroots organizations. *Environment and Urbanization*, 20(2), pp. 339–360.

Mitlin, D. (2005) Editorial: Chronic poverty in urban areas. *Environment and Urbanization*, 17(2), pp. 3-10.

Mitlin, D. (2001) Civil Society and Urban Poverty – Examining Complexity. *Environment and Urbanization*, 13 (2), pp 151–173.

Moser, C. and Stein, A. (2011) *The importance of assets in current development debates: Millennium Development Goals, social protection and climate change,* Global Urban Research Centre Working Paper 7, Manchester: Global Urban Research Centre.

Mukhija, V. (2004) The contradictions in enabling private developers of affordable housing: A cautionary case from Ahmedabad, India. *Urban Studies*, 41, pp. 2231–2244.

Peck, J., & Tickell, A. (2002) Chapter 2: Neoliberalizing Space, pp 33-57, Neil Brenner and Nik Theodore (eds.), Spaces of Neoliberalism: *Urban Restructuring in North America and Western Europe,* Malden, MA: Oxford's Blackwell Press.

Peck, J. & Tickell, A. (2006) Concepualizing Neoliberalism: Thinking Thatcherism' in Helga Leitner, Jamie Peck and Eric S Sheppard (eds) *Contesting Neoliberalism: Urban Frontiers.* New York: Guildford Press.

Pelling, M. (2003) *The vulnerability of cities: Natural disasters and social resilience.* London: Earthscan.

Rahman, M. A. U., Hossain, M. Z., and Kabir, M. E. (2016) Operationalizing community-led housing in practice: Lessons from Bangkok, Thailand and Mumbai, India. *International Journal of Sustainable Built Environment*, 5(2), pp. 564–578.

Rakodi, C. (2002) 'A livelihood approach – conceptual issues and definition', in C. Rakodi and T. Llyod- Jones (eds.), *Urban Livelihoods: A People Centred Approach to Reducing Poverty* (pp. 3-22). London: Earthscan.

Rolnik, R. (2013) Late Neoliberalism: The Financialization of Homeownership and Housing Rights. *International Journal of Urban and Regional Research*, 37(3), pp. 1058–1066.

Roy, M., Jahan, F. and Hulme, D. (2012) *Community and institutional responses to the challenges facing poor urban people in Khulna, Bangladesh in an era of climate change,* BWPI Working Paper 163, Manchester: Brooks World Poverty Institute.

Roy, M., Guy, S., Hulme, D. and Jahan, F. (2011) *Poverty and climate change in urban Bangladesh (ClimUrb): an analytical framework,* BWPI Working Paper 148, Manchester: Brooks World Poverty Institute.

Sarfoh, K. O. (2010) Lost in Translation – *The Nexus of Multi-Layered Housing Policy Gaps:* The Case of Ghana. University of St Andrews, United Kingdom.

Sengupta, U. (2009) Government intervention and public–private partnerships in housing delivery in Kolkata. *Habitat International*, 30, pp. 448-461.

Sassen, S. (2016) A Massive Loss of Habitat: New Drivers for Migration. *Sociology of Development*, 2(2), pp. 204–233.

Saunders, D. (2011) Arrival city: *How the largest migration in history is reshaping our world.* Vintage.

Schiller, N. G. & Çaglar, A. (2009) Towards a comparative theory of locality in migration studies: migrant incorporation and city scale. *Journal of Ethnic and Migration Studies*, 35, pp. 177–202.

Tanner, T., Mitchell, T., Polack, E. and Guenther, B. (2009) *Urban governance for adaptation: Assessing climate change resilience in ten Asian cities.* IDS Working Paper 315, Brighton: Institute of Development Studies.

Tanner, T. and Mitchell, T. (2008) Entrenchment or enhancement: Could climate change adaptation help to reduce poverty? *IDS Bulletin*, 39(4), pp. 6-13.

Tipple, G. (2005) The place of home-based enterprises in the informal sector: evidence from Cochabamba, New Delhi, Surabaya and Pretoria. *Urban Studies*, 42(4), pp 611–632.

United Nations Office for International Strategy for Disaster Risk Reduction (UNISDR) (2012) How to Make Cities More Resilient: A Handbook for Local Government Leaders. A Contribution to the Global Campaign 2010 – 2015: "Making Cities Resilient – My City is Getting Ready!" UNISDR, Geneva.

United Nations Human Settlements Programme (UN-HABITAT) (2016) World Cities Report 2016, Urbanization and Development: Emerging Futures. UN-Habitat, Nairobi.

United Nations High Commissioner for Refugees (UNHCR) (2015) Every life matters, UNHCR global report. UNHCR, Geneva.

Waeyenberge, E. V. (2018) Crisis? What crisis? A critical appraisal of World Bank housing policy in the wake of the global financial crisis. Environment and Planning A: Economy and Space, 50(2), pp. 288–309.

Part I: Housing in the Neoliberal Paradigm

Chapter 1: Indonesian Housing Policy in the Era of Globalization

Jo Santoso

INTRODUCTION

In the early1970s, the Government of Indonesia introduced a liberal market-oriented housing policy that focused on growth-oriented urban development. This new housing policy was based on the privatization of the housing sector and prioritized home ownership, factors that initiated the establishment of Indonesia's real estate sector. This new liberal policy also produced a number of negative impacts on housing, particularly in the cities, where the capability to anticipate and prepare for the urbanization process was significantly reduced. In the three decades that followed, the Indonesian government attempted to overcome the negative impacts of these policies by introducing two strategic programmes: one aimed to upgrade housing and settlement and the other subsidized housing.

Between 1980 and 2000 as urbanization in Indonesia reached its peak, its cities failed to address the problems inherent in urbanization, including the availability of adequate, affordable housing. Despite efforts to overcome the issues of poverty and housing for the poor in urban areas, the social discrepancy within the cities grew, resulting in an even bigger problem in new construction of substandard housing and an increase in the incidence of squatters in cities. In 2001, which marked the middle of the region's recovery from the Asian Monetary Crisis, the Indonesian government initiated a study called Enabling the Housing market to work in Indonesia(HOMI), which was supported by the World Bank (World Bank 2001). In its final report, in 2002, the HOMI study accepted that for a certain period of time affordable housing could only be delivered through subsidies. At the same time, however, the study maintained the basic concept, that housing can only become more affordable if market distortions could be addressed. In short, housing market needed to work more efficiently. At the same time, if the housing were to become more affordable, then the housing subsidy could be reduced (Hoek-Smit 2005). The HOMI study's recommendation to reform the housing delivery system was never implemented. So, once again, the need to reform housing policy became the objective of under President Joko Widodo's government (2014-2019). This government integrated the various housing programmes into two "main strategic programmes": City without Slum (Indonesia: Kota TanpaKumuh – Kotaku) and the National Affordable Housing Programme (NAHP), both of which had long-term financing in loans from the World Bank. The main question of this chapter is how effective were these two strategic programmes in solving the housing problem in Indonesian cities and what main hurdles did they need to overcome? Further the chapter discusses approaches to affordable housing in the Indonesian context under neo-liberal conditions; it also provides an overview of the related challenges to the implementation of affordable housing on both national and local levels.

Urbanization in the Era of Globalization – The Case of Indonesia

Before continuing with a discussion on housing policy and programmes, it is important to understand that in a newly developing country such as Indonesia the housing problem has a strong relation with the capacity of cities to deal with the impacts of rapid urbanization. The poor condition of housing in a particular city is only one of many problems' cities encounter when they are dealing with rapid urbanization. External factors also influence a particular city's ability to deal with the housing problem, although these factors are not the main reasons for the housing problem. One external factor is global financial restructuring, which has direct impacts on internal factors that are related to all levels of urban structures (Marcuse and van Kempen 2002; Agyeman 2003). This paper points to three transformation processes of globalization and their impacts on urbanization as it relates to affordable housing.

The first transformation is in the relationship between cities within the same country. It should be noted that due to globalization the function of the "national system of cities" has lost its relevance as a tool for states to balance welfare across regions (Young 1990; Harvey 1992). Previously, the "national system of cities" was the instrument national states implemented the most to provide social equity (Kusno 2012). Through state-sponsored interventions, the discrepancies between economic regions could be reduced by improving infrastructure and public services in under developed regions, so as to create "equity in opportunities". Under the neo-liberal economy of the past two decades, the state withdrew from its role as the caretaker of social equity. The national system of cities was displaced by individual competition between cities. Now, each city works in isolation on a platform of global competition where it must concentrate its energy on upgrading its international position through the commoditization of its local assets (including its natural environment and urban land) and human resources (Logan and Harvey 2002; Friedman 2005). The second transformation is the changing relationship between the city and its hinterland. Almost all urbanists maintain the same position regarding the overall dominant position of urban culture (Marcelloni 2007). In general, the city today is no longer the economic and social-cultural centre of its hinterland. The role of the city as a market place for products from the hinterland has been substituted by its position as a globalized city that provides a market for all kinds of consumer products, including the same goods that were previously produced locally, such as vegetables or fruits. In short, the formation of the city and its hinterland as a spatial-ecological entity no longer exists (Marcelloni 2007). Balanced development in the greater metropolitan region cannot be achieved because the conversion of the land use cannot be controlled and the private sector now drives a development that is heedless to a city's spatial-ecological aspect. The third transformation process is in the restructuring of the city itself, which began in Jakarta during the Soeharto regime in the late 1970s. After a short pause due to the 1997-1998 monetary crisis, the spatial restructuring of the inner city accelerated. The original domestic land use in the inner city has continuously been converted into large-scale commercial buildings, sometimes combined with apartment blocks. The subsequent reduction in the housing stock led to a decrease in the inner-city population. Between 1980 and 2004 the urban districts of Gambir and Tanah Abang, which are located in the centre of Jakarta, lost more than 40% of their registered population or from 1.4 to only 0.9 million population over the twenty-five year period (Santoso and Al-Hadar 2004). Lot by lot, land speculators acquired inner city areas with development potential and reassembled these areas into bigger lots that were later developed as commercial superblocks. The first and second transformation produced push factors on the process of urbanization. The impacts of the third transformation are a reduction in the housing stock in the city centre, followed by the city's expansion to the outskirts. Jakarta's city centre is occupied by what Marcuse and van Kempen (2002) call "the new citadels" or "exclusionary enclaves" of the rich and extremely mobile upper class. The hundreds of towers that dot the skyline have shaped Jakarta into an image of a citadel that stands out from the rest of the city (Marcuse and van Kempen 2002). New elites, professionals, and highly paid managers now occupy some areas behind the city centre, and these are all surrounded by historic urban settlements. This mixed characteristic is typical of the central business districts of many large Asian cities. On the outskirts of the city, the full privatization of urban development has caused the disappearance of an integrated "social-mixed new town". With literally hundreds of private housing estates, each designed according to its target market, there has been a pattern of uncontrolled growth along with its inherent unpredictable social and irreparable environmental impacts (Harvey 1992).

Urbanization and the Problem of Housing

In a very large country like Indonesia, the characteristics of urbanization such as speed, dimension, gender and the spatial distribution of migrants differ from region to region. Those cities with lower population growth may benefit from incoming migrants, while the majority of the cities with higher population growth may not. This section presents the negative impacts of rapid urbanization on existing urban environments (Santoso 2018a).

Between 1961 and 1971, Indonesia's population increased from 97.1 to 119.2 million or by more than 20% during the 10-year period. At the end of the 1970s, as the country's total population growth rate began to decrease its urban population increased at a faster rate than the average overall population. According to the Indonesian Bureau of Statistics, the population of Indonesia between 2000 and 2010 increased by around 1.5% yearly, with the urban population increasing from between 42% and 50.6%. It is expected that the country's urban population will reach its highest growth rate over the period between 2025 and 2050, from around 182.1 million to approximately 227.7 million. After the year 2050, population growth is expected to gradually decline. But this slower growth in urbanization will not reduce the housing problem. Rather, the cities will face two new issues: the first is the decreasing number of persons living in one household and the second is the need for more urban land coverage. These two factors will have negative impacts on the availability of residential land. The decreasing average household size (i.e., the average number of persons per household) will automatically mean the same population size will create a higher demand for housing units. The need for housing will be determined by the growth in the number of household units. From 2000 to 2010 the number of housing units grew from 21.4 million to 30.0 million units, while the average number of persons per household decreased from 4.1 down to 3.9. The forecast from 2025 to 2050 is for the average number of persons per household to continue to decrease from 3.75 to 3.6 persons per household and, thus, an increase in the number of households from 44.1 to 63.9 million (see Table A). At the same time, a higher income per capita will increase the average size of the housing unit. Table A shows that as the population is expected to grow by around 90% from 2010 to 2050; the urban land coverage is expected to grow by 115% from 30.600 to 65.280 square kilometre; and, accordingly, the average density will decrease from 39.22 to 34.88 persons per hectare. All of these factors will create additional pressures on housing affordability.

Table A above shows that between 2000 and 2050 the population density of Indonesian cities is predicted to trend downward from an average of 51.59 p/ha in 2000 to 34.88 p/ha in 2050.

Table A: Urban Population of Indonesia.

Year	2000	2010	2025	2050
Population total (Million)	208.8	237.6		
Urban population (Million)	87.7	120.0	170.0	227.7
Percentage (%)	42.0 %	50.6%		
Households (person/unit)	21.4 (4.1)	30.8 (3.9)	44.1 (3.75)	63.9 (3.6)
Urban land coverage (sqkm)	17.000	30.600	45.850	65.280
Density person/Sqkm	5,159	3,922	3,708	3,488

Source: Urban Laboratory Taumanagara (compiled from different sources). The increasing growth of the urban land coverage is calculated following the methods proposed by Angel (Angel 2012).

This reduced density is expected to occur because newly developed urban areas will have a much higher percentage of non-domestic land use, such as land for commercial use and other uses dedicated to urban services. The population density in inner-city areas will decline because of the conversion of existing domestic areas to non-domestic land use (Santoso 2016). Other data show that there will be a big difference between the average urban density nation-wide and the actual densities of large metropolitan cities in Indonesia. Large metropolitan cities, like Jakarta, Bandung, and Surabaya with their high economic growth, have densities of between 70 to 150 persons per hectare. Table B shows that, currently, the average density of six large metropolitan Indonesia cities is 114.86 p/ha, which is more than two to three times higher than the density of average-size cities, which is 34.88 p/ha. The problem of housing in Indonesian cities cannot be generalized only on the basis of the average city density. Every housing programme must develop appropriate implementation strategies on how to accommodate the different characteristics of these cities.

Table B: Population Density in Large Metropolitan Cities in Indonesia (2015).

City	Area (hector)	Population	Density
Jakarta	65.600	10,075,310	153
Bandung	16.700	2,470,802	147
Surabaya	35.000	2,853,661	81
Medan	26.500	2,191,140	83
Bandar Lampung	12.900	960,000	73
Denpasar	12.398	863,000	70
Total 6 cities	*169.098*	*19.412.914*	*114.86 p/ha*
Average Density (from Table A)			*34.88*

Source: Urban Laboratory Tarumanagara (unpublished data).

THE INDONESIAN HOUSING POLICY

The Indonesian government's neo-liberal market-oriented housing policy has given absolute priority to the privatization of the housing supply while at the same time supporting the demand for home ownership. This policy has negative impacts on the housing situation in the cities and the capability of these cities to adjust to the urbanization process. Two strategic housing programmes have been introduced to address the negative impact of this neo-liberal urban policy: the first is The Housing &Settlement Upgrading Programme and the National Affordable Housing Programme (NAHAP). The following discusses the implementation of these two housing programmes, with special attention paid to the period 1999 to 2016.

The Housing & Settlement Upgrading Programme (1999 – 2016)

From 1999 to 2016 the Indonesian government implemented a number of different housing and settlement upgrading programmes. Indonesia's current housing upgrading programme – City Without Slums can be understand as a new variant of housing and settlement upgrading with a similar conception. The following is a summary of the differences between the programmes that were introduced during this period.

In 1999, in the midst of the Asian financial crisis, the Indonesian government implemented a project called Urban Poverty Alleviation (P2KP) (Bahasa: *P2KP: Proyek Penanggulangan Kemiskinan di Perkotaan*). The programme operated until 2006 and consisted of two phases: the rescue phase and the consolidation phase. The basic concept of P2KP was to empower the urban poor to increase their ability to improve their social condition and rise out of poverty. In 2007, P2KP was replaced by a new programme called Empowerment Program for the Urban Population (*PNPM – Program Nasional Pemberdayaan Masyarakat Perkotaan*). The target of this new programme was not limited to the urban poor but it also included the low-income urban community in general. The remarkable characteristics of these two programmes (P2KP and PNPM) was that they focused on empowerment than to investing in the physical aspects of development. In this regard, poverty was understood to be the result of a helplessness that should be overcome through community-based social transformation. Of course, this focus on empowerment was strongly correlated to the fact that the Indonesian state at the time was close to bankrupt.

However, turning to the concept of community-based social transformation is not due to the state's lack of funds but on the positive experiences of similar previous programmes that show that even the poorest members of the urban population have significant potential to help themselves rise out of their poor socio-economic and environmental conditions. But there are other reasons behind the government's decision to substitute the PNPM in 2015 with the programme City Without Slums (*Kotaku*). The first is to accommodate the consequences of Decentralization Law No.22/1999, which is later modified several times until its last version, Law No.23/2014, obligates the government to decentralize its administrative structure (Government of the Republic Indonesia 2014). Following the promulgation of this new law, the housing sector becomes the full responsibility of the local governments. The decentralization of the housing sector is also supported through the new Housing and Settlement Area Law (Undang-Undang Tentang Perumahan Dan Kawasan Permukiman, UU no.1/2011) (Government of the Republic Indonesia 2011). Following the spirit of the new housing law, the main activities of the national housing agencies moved toward capacity building and institutional development. The first initiative of the housing programme City Without Slums is to accommodate the new decentralized structure by giving local governments more authority in the coordination and execution of the housing upgrading programme. The second initiative is to support the first through the mobilization of local financial resources. In line with the concept of empowerment, the national agencies are encouraged to allocate their financial resources more toward capacity building as the aim is to shift the cost of the physical aspects of housing more to local stakeholders, such as local government agencies, CSR (Corporate Social Responsibility), community-based organizations, and NGOs, among others (Management Programme NSUP – *Kotaku*, 2019). The third new innovation in the City Without Slums programme is an establishment of so-called operations and maintenance committee on the neighbourhood/district level; this committee is responsible for managing the housing settlements. One of the explicit tasks of these committees is to prevent the construction of poorly built houses in district areas, under a programme called Transformation Community-based Development Programme, which is introduced in 2019.

These additional innovative components are integrated into the City Without Slums programme. However, the implementation of the additional components is not without problems. First, because of its high grade of complexity, City Without Slums can only be successful if executed by highly experienced specialists. Know-how, such as defining the appropriate size of the upgrading area, understanding the importance of community awareness, understanding the timing for these types of projects and whether and how local governmental institutions should be involved and other prerequisites, can only be delivered by qualified and fully experienced field managers. It is not easy to find persons with the requisite training and experience even though Indonesia already has more than fifty years of experience in carrying out similar programmes. The main weakness of all upgrading programmes is this type of programme cannot significantly influence an increase in the production of affordable housing nor can it prevent the replication of new substandard units outside of these projects' locations (Santoso 2018b).

The Subsidized Housing Programme

The Indonesian government began its first subsidized housing programme in 1976 in the form of reductions in mortgage interest for members of low-income groups. To support the programme the government established Bank Tabungan

Negara (BTN) as a special mortgage bank. Further, the government established the National Urban Development Agency, which is a state-owned developer known as Perumnas. Perumnas develops large-scale housing projects, the units of which can be bought with subsidized mortgage loans from the BTN. During the 1970s and 1980s Perumnas developed several large-scale housing projects, some in the outskirts of Jakarta and other big cities, others as smaller-scale housing projects in the inner city (The Government of the republic of Indonesia 1974). On the whole, Perumnas built approximately 500,000 low incomes housing and apartment units in more than 300 locations spread throughout Indonesia (http://www.perumnas.id/perum-perumnas). At the end of the 1980s, when the oil bonanza was over, Perumnas moved away from its original purpose to act as the National Urban Development Corporation. Further, after the monetary crisis of 1997-1998, Perumnas is no longer continued to carry out its particular mission in the housing sector. Its status as a "special enterprise for developing social housing projects" disappeared as it became an ordinary state enterprise with a limited social mission of providing low-interest (subsidized) mortgages (Silas 2005). In recent years there is a plan to revitalize the role of Perumnas as champion in production of low-income housing in particular in relation to provision of land for low income housing, but the plan is never actualized.

The mortgage subsidy programme consists of an allowance that reduces the interest on housing loans for eligible members of a defined target group; here, the government pays the difference between the market interest rate and the actual interest the borrower pays. In implementing this programme, the government works together with private developers. The private developer manages the construction and the new houses are sold at a maximum price only to those who are eligible for the subsidized mortgages. Since the programme began in 1976, it has undergone many revisions, especially since 1999 when housing prices were repeatedly adjusted for inflation. The other problem is in providing financial resources. According to the new version of Decentralization Law No.32/2004, the authority and responsibility of housing affairs should be decentralized to the local government. But years after the first Decentralization law was promulgated in 1999, only a few local administration was able to initiate a low-income housing program (Kusno 2012).

Experiences from implementing and operating different housing-subsidy programs between 2005 and 2013 offer the following conclusions: In general, the implementation of the different "top-down" housing programs has been ineffective. The main reason is that on one hand the national institutions could not effectively control what happened on the ground and the local governments cannot carry out their important role as mediator between the stakeholders at the local level and the government institution at the national level. On the other hand, the national government's financial support was misused as it was seen as an opportunity to earn short-term benefits and not as an opportunity for the decentralization of programme delivery. Local governments and other local players also failed to adjust the programme to the specific conditions of local areas. An indicator for this, among others, is the need to adjust programmes to local conditions such as using local building materials, adjusting housing prices to the local minimum salaries or the UMR (minimal monthly salary), and other considerations. In Jakarta or Surabaya, for example, the actual UMR is around Rp 3.6 million (around U$ 250), but in some areas in Eastern Indonesia the UMR is valued at only 45-50% of this amount (Santoso 2018a). Further, there was insufficient effort to enable local players to participate in these projects. There was no significant improvement in the awareness of the involved stakeholders about the importance of housing programmes for low-income people living in their communities. The end result of all this is that the goal of transferring housing affairs from the national to the local level utterly failed.

Another important finding is that, in general, the quality of subsidized housing is far from acceptable. Poor coordination between the responsible institutions and the attitudes of profit-oriented contractors and housing developers created situations where the involved players are accusing each other and nobody was doing their homework. The Ministry of Home Affair has the opinion that in order to decentralize the housing affair, the Ministry of the Public Works and Housing is responsible to empower the local housing stakeholders, but the Ministry of Public Works and Housing has the view that the Ministry of Home Affair is responsible to do the capacity building of government institutions on local level. The mortgage Bank of BTN has primary interest to distribute the subsidized mortgage to so many clients as possible. In the end, the quality of the products becomes uncontrolled and no involved is willing to take the responsibility that a high percentage of the houses is not full fill the minimal standard. Under the bottom line, the home buyers assumed all of the risks and have to make an extra effort to repair and maintain the condition of their houses. The biggest risk is that if the buyer cannot cover the high cost of depreciation in the early years then they will have to move to another house and will stop paying the mortgage instalments on the original one. The results are a large number of abandoned houses and the rapid increase of non-performing loans by the mortgage bank.

The Concept of Affordable Housing

The notion of housing affordability became widespread in Europe and North America during the 1980s. In the words of Alain Bertaud, former principal planner at the World Bank and now of New York University, "It is time for planners to abandon general objectives and to focus their efforts on two measurable outcomes that have always mattered: workers' spatial mobility and housing affordability" (Bertaud 2014). Most of the literature on affordable housing applies to mortgage programmes and many other programmes that exist along the same continuum – from emergency shelters to transitional housing to non-market rentals (also known as "social housing") to formal and informal rentals, indigenous housing, and ending with affordable home ownership. In many countries, there are affordable housing committees that consist of social-housing experts and government representatives. The Australian National Affordable Housing Summit Group developed their definition of affordable housing as housing that is adequate in standard and location for lower or middle-income households and does not cost so much that a household is unlikely to be able to meet other basic needs on a sustainable basis (ACTU 2012).

In the United Kingdom, affordable housing includes social rental and intermediate housing provided to specified eligible households whose needs are not met by the market. Here, affordability is calculated based on the capacity of those in a specific income group to use a percentage of their disposable income to pay their "total housing cost". This seems a simple solution but the actual calculation is rather complicated while at the same time it must include a number of factors in the demand and supply side of the housing market, such as the willingness to save and spend money for housing, the number of persons in a particular household, the actual cost of operating/managing a house, the construction cost of the house, the inflation rate, the cost of capital, the cost of utilities, the cost of the depreciation of the building and the quality of the infrastructure, etc. (Gabriel *et al.* 2005).

One of the greatest strengths of following the housing affordability concept is to develop what is called the housing affordability index (HAI). Following a housing affordability index developed by a team at MIT, housing affordability is the ability of a household group to capture the "total cost of occupying the individuals' housing", which consists of the cost of rent or mortgage payments along with all of the everyday housing expenditures (MIT Centre for Real Estate, 2019). With regards to affordability, this total housing cost is more relevant than the market price of housing. This statement means that the housing price is indeed a "relative cost" in relation to affordability. Therefore, understanding the challenges of affordable housing requires understanding trends and disparities in income and wealth. The conventional approach to affordable housing is to measure the relationship between income and the market price of housing. However, a better method of measuring housing affordability has been to consider the percentage household income spent on (total) housing expenditures.

Further, if the market-oriented way of thinking is to understand buying housing as an act of property investment, then its quality should be measured in the relation to the amount of the investment and the actual value of the property. The core idea of this approach is to define affordability in relation to the local-specific conditions. In Indonesia, both the minimum wage (Indonesia: UMR) and living costs are very strong local-specific conditions where the high percentage of people whose incomes are less than 60% of the median income is very city specific (Rodda 1994).

The other strong influencing factor is the dynamic of the world economy. Since 2000 the world has experienced an unprecedented boom in house prices not only in magnitude and duration but also in the synchronization of these factors across countries. Never before have house prices risen so fast, for so long, in so many countries. Prices have doubled in many countries. In Ireland housing prices nearly tripled as the country became a target of foreign investors. When the biggest financial bubble in history burst in 2008, this wreaked havoc on the housing market globally.

By 2011 home prices in Ireland had plunged by 45% from their peak in 2007. In the United States prices fell by 34% while foreclosures increased exponentially. In Spain and Denmark home prices dropped by 15%. However, in spite of the bust, home prices continue to be overvalued by about 25% or more in Australia, Belgium, Canada, France, New Zealand, Britain, the Netherlands, Spain, and Sweden (Cox and Pavletich 2012). Many researchers argue that income inequality is partly to blame for the shortage of affordable housing. This same condition can be found in globalized cities in Europe, Australia, and Asia: In many of these globalized metropolitan cities a new form of "illegal rental condition" is sprouting up and in a situation city administration have failed to control. Typically, only legal, permitted, and separate housing is considered when calculating the cost of housing. The low rental costs for a room in a family home or an illegal garage conversion or a college dormitory are generally excluded from the calculation, no matter how many people in an area live in such situations. In cities like Singapore or Hongkong, we find that home owners have subdivided their apartments in order to make it more affordable. In many cases the home owner are renting all the bed rooms and they only keep the living room for them.

Faced with few affordable options, many people attempt to find less-expensive housing by buying or renting farther from the city centre. But long commutes often result in higher transportation costs which erase any savings on shelter. Some call this the "drive until you qualify" approach, which causes far-flung development and forces people to drive long distances to get to work, to buy groceries, to take their children to school, or to engage in other activities. A well-located dwelling might save significant household travel costs and therefore improve not only family economics but also the overall quality of family life. The trend is going more toward sacrificing domestic life for a "better" house; but this is not the case of a minimum-wage worker in an industrial factory on the outskirts of Jakarta. These workers normally share a rental accommodation with friends so as to reduce theirs dwelling cost as much as possible. This is because migrant workers want to save money for their family who are still living in their home villages, so they spend as little as possible on their own housing.

The conclusion is that the housing affordability index follows the dynamics of the market. In many countries, housing is becoming less affordable because the market economy is causing social inequality to deepen. This is causing home seekers to lower their expectations as much as possible; it is also the real reason we are seeing increasing incidences of poor squatters in high-density urban areas across large metropolitan areas world-wide. All of this is the consequence of integrating the housing sector within the market economy.

THE DIFFICULTIES TO IMPLEMENT NAHP IN INDONESIA

The idea of housing affordability is to move away from housing programmes as part of a "social-corrective" programme and toward integrating a housing delivery system into the market mechanism. There is no housing policy that addresses the problem of the production of substandard houses; as long as there is a demand, these types of housing will continue to be produced. Following the concept of the neo-liberal housing concept, housing has become more unaffordable through a so called "market distortion". The HOMI study (2001) had the goal of dealing with this distortion by enabling the Indonesian housing market to work properly. Here, the assumption was that the market distortion should be addressed before the housing market can work more efficiently and be able to supply more affordable housing at a reasonable standard of quality. The HOMI study accepted the importance of the relationship between housing and social disparity and also recognizes the importance of subsidized housing programmes. But as housing becomes more affordable, the subsidy should be reduced simultaneously. Marja Hoek-Smit, the leader of the HOMI study, repeatedly underlined the importance of gradually reducing subsidy programmes following an increase in market efficiency (Hoek-Smit 2005). Alain Bartaud also noted that the core of the housing problem is in how to integrate the housing delivery system into the market mechanism. The weakness of the HOMI study is that the study does not recognize the importance of the local characteristics of the housing problem.

From the different concepts of affordable housing mentioned above, it can be concluded that housing expenditure, income and local economic conditions are the most critical indicators of the housing affordability index. By consequence, the factors that influence the HAI at the local level should be observed. That is, each local area or region should have its own specific HAI; otherwise, this measure would not give us the real picture of the housing problem. All of the three above-mentioned indicators are strong, depending on the local economic situation. Housing is, in general, a local matter. The quality of the housing in a particular city is strongly determined by the willingness and ability of the local stakeholders involved in the housing delivery system and not by the extent of the financial subsidy. If the willingness to provide a housing delivery system at a reasonable standard does not exist at the local level, then no national government can change that. Even if the City Without Slums are to be successful in establishing a housing management committee, if social equitability cannot be achieved then nobody will be able to avoid the incidence of new miserable squatters springing up somewhere else in the city.

Indeed, the Indonesian national government must play several essential roles to support the decentralization of the housing sector. With regards to the limited availability of financial resources for housing, many experts in Indonesia are of the opinion that this should be the core of housing policy on the national level. In particular, the necessary long-term financial resources cannot be transferred to institutions that operate at the local level (LPPPPI 2015). Although the nature of housing development is a long-term enterprise, with people building houses to last for 40 to 75 years or longer, it is not easy to mobilize funding. The availability of a long-term housing fund can protect housing production from the ups and downs of national and global economic cycles. Further, government policy should protect investments in the housing sector from short-term speculative manoeuvres.

The concept of affordable housing is seen as an individual act of buying a house as an investment (in property), which is a domestic affair. A person's housing stock is an individual asset that can be used as a collateral guarantee to borrow money from a bank. Also owning a house enables a person to become involved in the process of capital accumulation. Affordable housing needs can be addressed through public policy instruments that focus on the demand side of the market and programmes that help households reach the necessary financial benchmarks that make housing affordable. National policies define banking and mortgage lending practices, and taxation and regulatory measures that affect the cost of building materials and professional practices (i.e., real estate transactions). The purchasing power of individual households can be enhanced to a certain degree through tax and fiscal policies that result in reducing the cost of mortgages and the cost of borrowing. Public policy may include the implementation of subsidy programmes and incentives for average households. The national government must also develop a platform for a housing information system, and this should be installed in every city that wants to deal with housing problems. The information provided should also include the socio-economic conditions of people who are working and living outside the market system.

Furthermore, in relation to enabling housing stakeholders, the national government should help cities form housing affordability committees. Other issues where there still needs to be national-agency interventions regarding local stakeholders are: the management skills needed to ensure the quality of the design and construction of social housing. The trend today is to sacrifice quality for lower cost. This has an impact on reducing the lifetime of the product. The development of technology is also relevant as it can increase quality and avoid higher costs. Making use of local-specific building materials and traditional building cultures are possibilities that move in this direction.

But what national government cannot do is protect the housing market and the quality of new construction from the negative impacts of the rise and fall of the global economy. In all globalized cities, the appearance of foreign workers with much higher incomes that sometimes allow for investments in housing has had an impact on the over-proportional increases in rental costs and housing prices, especially where city governments allow foreigners to buy these properties.

FINAL REMARKS

In the mid-1970's the Indonesian government began to establish liberal housing policies that privatized the national housing delivery system and prioritized housing ownership. In the same time, the government introduced two strategic programmes whose goals were to upgrade substandard housing and provide mortgage subsidies to members of low-income groups. Three decades later,

Indonesians must accept the reality that the condition of low-cost housing has become worse than ever. Although the Indonesian economy was continuing to grow, during that time, this did not automatically make housing more affordable. After the end of Soeharto regime, in 1998, the Indonesian government increased its efforts to eliminate substandard housing, especially in urban areas. At the same time, it also attempted to increase the efficiency of housing production and the number of subsidized housing programmes. But 15 years later, the Indonesian government should realize that the problem of housing in the cities cannot be solved by permanently increasing housing subsidies and upgrading substandard homes. Indonesia has to learn that the problem of housing can be solved only if the production of new substandard housing can be stopped; this calls for a big effort to make housing more affordable. To achieve those goals, the Indonesian government introduced two new housing programmes: City Without Slums and The National Affordable Housing Programme, both of which have long-term financial backing from the World Bank. This chapter shows that these two programmes can be successfully implemented only if two main problems can be overcome: the first is to enable stakeholders in local housing to assume leadership positions in a decentralized housing delivery system; the second is to find a way to control the main factor, which is to make housing more affordable in the present market-oriented economic system where there is a gap between housing expenditure and the disposal incomes of people who need housing. This latter objective can only be achieved if social inequality can be overcome.

REFERENCES

Australian Council of Trade Unions (ACTU) (2012) Affordable Housing: Issues, Principles and Policy Options, Australian Council of Trade Unions.

Asian Development Bank (ADB) (2019), Cities and Economic Dynamism in Indonesia, Key Indicators for Asia and the Pacific (Cities and Economic Dynamism: Challenges and Opportunities), ADB Manila.

Angel, S. (2012) Planet of Cities, Lincoln Institute of Land Policy: Cambridge, Mass.

Agyeman, J., Bullard, R.D., Evans, B. (2003) Just Sustainabilities: Development in an Unequal World, Earthscan: London.

Bertaud, A. (2014) Housing Affordability and Freedom to Build [online], available:http://legacy.urbanizationproject.org/uploads/blog/Bertaud_Housing_Affordability_Freedom_to_Build_10.30.14_copy.pdf [accessed 23 Feb 2019].

Cox, W., Pavletich, H. (2012) 8th Annual Demographia International Housing Affordability Survey: 2012 Ratings for Metropolitan Markets, available: http://www.iut.nu/wp-content/uploads/2017/07/InternationalHousingAfforda bility-Survey.pdf [accessed 23 Feb 2019].

Friedman, A. (2005) Homes within Reach: A Guide to the Planning, Design, and Construction of Affordable Homes and Communities., J. Wiley: Hoboken, N.J.

Gabriel, M., Jacob, K., Arthurson, K., Burke, T and Yates, J. (2005) Conceptualising and Measuring the Housing Affordability Problem, National Research Venture 3: Housing Affordability for Lower Income Australians, Australian Housing and Urban Research Institute, Melbourne, available: https://core.ac.uk/download/pdf/43326790.pdf [accessed 23 Feb 2019].

Government of the Republic of Indonesia (2014) Local Government and Decentralization, UU No. 23/2014.

Government of the Republic Indonesia (1974) Establishment of PerumPerumnas, PP No. 29/1974.

Government of the Republic Indonesia (2011) Housing Law.

Harvey, D. (1992) 'Social Justice, Postmodernism and the City', International Journal of Urban and Regional Research, 16(4), 588–601.

Hoek-Smit, M.C. (2005) 'The Housing Finance Sector in Indonesia', available: http://siteresources.worldbank.org/INTEAPREGTOPFINFINSECDEV/Reso urces/5897481144293317827/EAFinance_bkgrnd_Housing_Finance_Indone sia.pdf [accessed 23 Feb 2019].

Kusno, A. (2012) PolitikEkonomiPerumahan Rakyat Dan Utopia, Ombak: Yogyakarta. (English: Economic Policy of Public Housing and Utopia Jakarta)

Logan, J.R. and Harvet, L.M. (2002) 'The City as a Growth Machine', in Fanstein, S. and Campbell, S., eds., Readings in Urban Theory, Blackwell: Malden, Mass, 199–238.

LPPPPI (2015) 'BTN, LokomotifPembiayaan Program SejutaRumah', in HUDMagz, Lembaga PengkajianPengembanganPerumahan dan Perkotaan Indonesia, 22-23. (English: 'BTN, the locomotive of a funding programme for a million houses', in HUDMagz,The Housing and Urban Development Institute).

Marcelloni, M. (2007) 'The Challenge of Governing the New Scale of the Contemporary City', in Rosemann, J., ed., Perma City, Technical University Delft: Delft, 223–227.

Marcuse, P. and van Kempen, R. (Eds.) (2002) Globalizing Cities: A New Spatial Order, Wiley-Blackwell: Oxford.

MIT Center for Real Estate [online] (2019) available: https://mitcre.mit.edu/ [accessed 23 Feb 2019].

Pengendalian Program NSUP – KotakuTahun 2019 (English: Management Programme NSUP-Kotaku Year 2019)' (2019).

'Perjalanan Program Pembangunan BerbasisKomunitas (English: Transformation community-based Development Programme)' (2019).

Rodda, D. (1994) Rich Man, Poor Renter: A Study of the Relationship Between the Income Distribution and Low-Cost Rental Housing, Ph.D.

Santoso, J. (2016) 'The Pro Global-oriented Urban Policy and The Impacts on The Local-specific Character of Asian Urbanity', Presented at the Great Asian Streets Symposium, National University of Singapore: Singapore.

Santoso, J. (2018a) StudiDesentralisasiSistemPenyediaanPerumahan Di Daerah, Urban Laboratory Tarumanagara University, Jakarta. (English: Study on Decentralized Housing Delivery System.)

Santoso, J. (2018b) StudiEvaluasi Program PerumahanUntuk Masyarakat BerpenghasilanRendah, Urban Laboratory Tarumanagara University, Jakarta. (English: Evaluation of Housing Programme for Low Income Group.)

Santoso, J., Al-Hadar, I. (Eds.) (2004) 'CatatanMengenai Dasar-Dasar PengembanganSistemPerumahanSosial', in SistemPerumahanSosial, Centropolis UNTAR: Jakarta, 127–134. (English: Notes on basic principles for the development of social housing.)

Silas, J. (2005) 'Perjalanan Panjang Perumahan Indonesia Dalam dan Sekitar Abad XX', in Colombijn, F., Barwegen, M., Basundoro, P. and Khusyairi, J., eds., KOTA LAMA, KOTA BARU: Sejarah Kota-Kota Di Indonesia Sebelum Dan Setelah Kemerdekaan, Ombak: Yogyakarta. (English: The Long Journey of Indonesian Housing Within and Around the 20thCentury.)

World Bank (2001) HOMI Study, Enabling the Housing Market in Indonesia to Work, World Bank, Jakarta.

Young, I. (1990) Justice and the Politics of Difference [online], Princeton University Press, available at: https://press.princeton.edu/titles/9562.html [accessed 23 Feb 2019].

Chapter 2: Let's Get Down to Business – Private Influences in the Making of Affordable Housing Policies

The Case of Minha Casa Minha Vida

Anthony Boanada-Fuchs

INTRODUCTION

When thinking of housing in Brazil, the favelas no doubt first come to mind. This paradigmatic slum typology has become a large part of Brazil's visual dictionary because it is seen as a lasting manifestation of the country's dysfunctional urban planning and housing markets. Similar to other countries in the Global South, informal housing solutions emerged during the course of the early 20th century but these approaches only proliferated during the 1980s and 1990s (in Brazil, the 'lost decade') when national governments passed neo-liberal reforms that were in line with the Washington consensus.[1] With decreasing government spending on housing, infrastructure and basic services, urban growth largely took place in an unplanned manner and informal settlements quickly turned into slums. The number of people living in households situated in slums increased worldwide, throughout the 1980s and 1990s, to reach 921 million in 2001 (UNCHS 2003).

In the specific case of Brazil, the housing supply in the early 2000s showed signs of severe dysfunctionality: the formal market catered to only the top 20%

---

1   This consensus between three Washington D.C. based lending institutions (the International Monetary Fund, the World Bank and the United States Department of the Treasury) aligned their respective demands of institutional reforms targeted at developing countries requesting financial assistance.

of total demand. The remainder of the population needed government support or relied on informal mechanisms (Maricato 2009). This housing situation was the result not only of roll-backs in state expenditures but also of the institutional legacy a former military regime left behind (1964-1986). Brazil's transition toward democracy created major institutional disruptions (In chapter 9, Kienast describes similar mechanisms that existed in the South African context after apartheid). The dissolution of The National Housing Bank of Brazil (BNH), in 1986, in combination with a stabilization plan that was brought in to respond to an unfolding economic crisis, in the 1990s, led to reduced credit for housing and reduced government spending on urban development. As local governments were unable to fill the shoes of an absent national government, the question of housing and urban planning remained largely unsolved, at the institutional level, until the beginning of the 2000s when the growth of cities largely took place in an irregular manner. While reliable data are largely missing for that time period, Brazilian scholars agree that the 1980s and 1990s are marked by a decline in the housing situation on a national level (Cardoso and Aragão 2013).

In early 2000s, the governments of President Luiz Inácio Lula da Silva and, subsequently, President Dilma Rousseff launched several initiatives that recognised the importance of cities and reaffirmed the role of government in providing infrastructure and basic social and economic programs. In a neo-Keynesian rolling out of the state, major investment projects were launched (such as the Growth Acceleration Program). This culminated in Minha Casa, Minha Vida (MCMV), a public housing program that was launched in early 2009 in order to address the country's housing backlog. The MCMV has been presented as pursuing a dual goal of improving the housing situation (by reducing the existing backlog of 7 million units (FJP 2008)) and, at the same time, countering the global financial crisis by generating jobs and stimulating investment (D'Amico 2011; Cardoso et al. 2013b). While such a dual view was reflected in the media, in official government communications and in academic discourse, a closer look at the program's conditions, the nature of the changes it brought, and the underlying mechanisms of these views clearly shows the overemphasis on involving market actors at the expense of civil society, participation, and ultimately the liveability of cities.

This chapter aims to show the close interconnections between market actors and public decision-making by looking at the policy-formulation process that led to the MCMV and the interactions between the government and large-scale developers. By doing so, it provides more academic evidence for the broadly stated criticism that the housing program was and continues to be too market friendly. A deeper analysis of the private influences on public policy-making is needed to advance an understanding of the political economy of urban development and also to uncover the underlying forces that are shaping our built environment.

This chapter is structured as follows. First, an explanation of the characteristics of the national housing programme and an outline of the research design are presented. Next, the Brazilian housing sector and the main institutional changes that led up to the MCMV are discussed. Then we take a step back and retrace the precise genealogy of the policy ideas and their institutionalization. The analytical part of this chapter discusses not only the role of the private companies that have been involved in shaping the idea of a national housing programme but also the underlying premise behind the programme's institutionalization and the regulatory changes that were passed between 2009 and 2015. The conclusion stresses the need for further research on the role of developers in the planning and implementation of urban policies.

THE BRAZILIAN AFFORDABLE HOUSING PROGRAM

Minha Casa, Minha Vida is an ambiguous program. On one hand, it represents a paradigmatic shift in Brazilian affordable housing strategy while at the same time featuring many elements that are direct continuations of the initiatives of former governments. Particularly influential have been the aforementioned Growth Acceleration Program (Programa de Aceleração do Crescimento, PAC), the Solidarity Credit Programme (Programa Crédito Solidário), and the Residential Leasing Programme (Programa de Arrendamento Residencial, PAR). The MCMV incorporated the Growth Acceleration Program's monitoring and decision-making processes and branding effects, the institutionalization of autoconstruction under the Solidarity Credit Program, and the PAR's insurance purchase and supply incentives as well as its unified social-housing fund. From an institutional lens, and even to a certain extent from a programmatic angle, the MCMV builds upon former housing-related government programs. The major novelty is in its unprecedented scale of investment; in its first phase, between 2009 and 2011 alone, R$34 billion (USD 19.5 billion)[2] were allocated to finance a broad range of subsidies and incentives, as well as a reduction in registration and legal fees on both the demand and supply sides of the program.

In order to understand how market actors influenced the way the programme was set up and how it changed in the course of its operations, it is necessary to take a closer look at the nature of its initial programme. The MCMV is a national

---

2   All values in Real are converted to US dollars, based on the 2009 exchange rate.

housing program that attempted to address a national housing backlog of 7 million units (as of 2009) by offering differentiated demand targets and several sub-programmes and by using a combination of subsidies aimed at both supply and demand. The programme targets households that are living under different socio-economic realities that span from poor and low-income families up to the lower middle class. The programme additionally differentiates in space by acknowledging housing differences between rural and urban areas.[3] In urban areas, official minimum salaries (MS) are used to determine the housing needs and demand benefits. The demand benefits, output targets, and supply modalities all differ by income track. Track 1 is targeted at families earning up to 3 minimum salaries; track 2, up to 6 MS; and track 3, up to 10 MS (see Table 1).

Two different sub-programmes were established to address Brazil's urban housing deficit:[4] The National Programme for Urban Housing (Programa Nacional de Habitação Urbana; PNHU) deals with market-oriented supply and Entidades is based on self-organisation. The PNHU is at the heart of the MCMV. At the outset, the government's aim was to deliver 1 million housing units (14 percent of the deficit) by allocating 14 billion Reias (8 billion USD) within the programme's first phase (2009-2010). The demand benefits, which may include a direct subsidy, beneficial loans and repayment conditions, as well as reductions in registration charges are adjusted to the different tracks. The programme entails the construction of new housing units in urban areas, the redevelopment of existing properties in consolidated areas, and the purchase of urban allotments (the latter two were only regulated later, see Rolnik et al. 2010). The government fixes the ceilings for the unit prices of the houses provided for recipients in all income tracks, the minimum floor plan areas (only for track 1), and the limits on the unit costs that are applied to the reduced unified tax rate and the registration charges. As can be seen in Table 1, these different limits are partially disconnected from each other.

---

3 In rural areas, demand is categorized based on the official average yearly wage for an agricultural worker. Families in track 1 can earn salaries up to R$ 10,000/year; in track 2, up to R$ 22,000/year; and in track 3, up to R$ 55,800/year (USD 5,741; 12,631; 32,036; respectively).

4 Presently, there are three sub-programs and a special development modality for municipalities with fewer than 50,000 inhabitants under which projects are developed based on a public offering. This segment has only been included in the program since 2010.

Table 1: Demand and supply benefits of MCMV per track.

Benefits MCMV	Track 1: MS 0-3	Track 2: MS 3-6	Track 3: MS 6-10
Income level	USD 801	USD 1,602	USD 2,670
Max. unit cost	USD 29,280	USD 74,635	USD 74,635
Max. unit size: house / apartment	32 / 37 sqm	-	-
Subsidy	USD 13,205	USD 1,148	USD 0
Interest rate	0%	5%	6%
Interest differential	Fully	Fully until 1,335 USD	None
Repayment	10% (min R$ 50)	-	-
Notary reduction	100%	90%	80%
Mortgage security	Government	Guarantor Fund, 36 months	Guarantor Fund, 24 months
RET (unified tax regime supply)	1%	1% to 34,447 USD; above 6%	
Notary reduction (supply side)	90%	90% to USD 34,447, 80% to USD 45,929; 75% to USD 74,635	

Source: Table produced by the author, based on legal documentation of the different programs.

Entidades is a housing modality that is based on self-organisation for the urban housing demand of those in track 1 and is carried out by non-profit organisations. The work can be entirely given to a main contractor or it can be done through self-built/assisted construction. For the first phase, the government allocated R$ 500 million (USD 287 million) to the Entidades programme.

While the MCMV is clearly social in nature as its aim is to build housing units for low- and middle-income families and to reduce the national backlog, it can hardly be seen as the driving force behind the institutionalization of Brazil's housing programme. Its priority is to create volume in the number of houses but not quality, in other words its intention is to use the country's building industries to realise floor space and not homes that are adapted to the needs of the population (this is further discussed below).

Figure 1: Minha Casa, Minha Vida in practice.

Source: http://www.brasil.gov.br/noticias/infraestrutura/2015/04/mucuri-ba-recebe-casas-populares-do-minha-casa-minha-vida/minha-casa-minha-vida.jpg/image_view_fullscreen.

Brazil's affordable housing programme was clearly formulated as a counter-cyclical measure in the context of the unfolding global financial crisis. Similar to other governments around the world, the Brazilian government reaffirmed its role in the housing sector. The financial shock of 2007/08 and the consequent global recession had considerable impacts on global consumption, investment flows, affordability levels, and inadequately housed populations (homelessness, slum populations, etc.). Large-scale housing initiatives were seen as adequate socio-economic policy responses as they were viewed as stimulating both national production and consumption simultaneously. From 2007 to 2013, national governments in Mexico, Malaysia, India, and several other countries of the Global South launched housing programs aimed at assisting low-income people; however, these programmas almost exclusively relied on real-estate-market actors to construct up to 500,000 housing units yearly (Buckley *et al.* 2016; see also contributions in this book; for the example of Indonesia (Santos 2020, chapter 1), for Argentina and Uruguay (Casanova 2020, chapter 3)). The market for low-income housing in countries in the Global South amounted to almost 200 million units with an investment requirement of USD 9-11trillion (GIZ 2014). These projects were rendered financially viable through lower profit margins and savings in economies of scales. In view of the billions of dollars in investment opportunities this presented, the question arises as to whether governments actually managed to balance both the country's social and economic needs.

The role of developers and the financialisation of housing

Real-estate developers are central agents of change as they construct a large majority of the built environment. Despite the centrality of these stakeholders in steering urbanisation processes and their spatial manifestation, the existing body of literature on this topic remains thin (Adams and Tiesdell 2010; Coiacetto 2009). One of the first books on development and developers was edited by Guy and Henneberry (2002); this publication shows that in the early 2000s and prior there was a broad range of approaches to improving our institutional understanding of real-estate markets (see also Fainstein 1994). Currently, the theoretical and practical insights on developers remain fragmented, with little dialogue among their many parts. While interest is slowly developing in terms of investigating this issue as it relates to the Global South (Fauveaud 2014; Rouanet and Halbert 2016; Sanfelici and Halbert 2015; Searle 2014), knowledge remains very limited on the role of real-estate developers in urban development (see Rolnik in the foreword of this book for an elaboration). This imbalance between the relevance of this issue and currently deployed research efforts is particularly worrisome in a period of the increasing globalisation of financial flows and the financialization of the real-estate sector (Aalbers 2016).

RESEARCH DESIGN

An analysis of the policy-formation process in Brazil is often carried out by relying on the Advocacy Coalition Framework (ACF), which ideally requires unrestricted access to the actual meetings that underlie policy negotiations or at least the associated documentation on these meetings (Crow 2001; Sabatier and Weible 2007; Hersperger *et al.* 2013). In the case of the MCMV, this access could not be established because discussions on programme elements relied on several informal communication channels. Furthermore, the same communication channels may support corrupt practices as is suggested by the central role of construction companies in the corruption scandal of 2014 onwards (Cardoso and Jaenisch 2017). The Governance Analytical Framework (GAF) provides the advantage of being flexible enough to enable an indirect research workflow (Hufty 2007, 2011; Kübler 2012). Instead of analysing actual interactions between competing actors, the existing research is limited to the detection of communication channels. However, the GAF is based on four main concepts: agents, nodal points, values, and norms, of which the first two are essential for this study as it conceptualises the policy-formation process as a series of nodal points where different agents convene. In the absence of academic alternatives, an analysis of secondary sources and newspaper clippings is used to retrace the chain of nodal points. These are placed in relation to the actual policy outcomes. This workflow does not allow for the detection of causalities in terms of influencing decision-making but it at least helps illustrate the range of communication channels available to market actors who exert pressure on government decisions. These insights can help create a first step toward understanding the policy influences within the MCMV and the different ways developers managed to shape the regulatory framework that ultimately defines the possibilities and restrictions of their own business activities.

THE HOUSING SECTOR IN BRAZIL AND ITS INSTITUTIONAL CHANGES UP TO THE MCMV

Traditionally, housing in Brazil was built by private individuals and, later, companies that offered housing units for their own workers so they could live close to their factories. In the second half of the 20th century, the country's housing sector was institutionalized and relied on a pension and welfare system in which funds were used to finance government-produced houses (such in the Casa Popular program of 1946). The idea of tapping into these financial possibilities continued throughout very different political systems, including under Brazil's military regime (1964-86) and after it became a democracy (1986 onwards). The military government recognised the economic importance of housing and created the first country-wide housing policy (Loureiro, Macário, and Guerra 2013, pp. 1886-8), a national housing bank (BNH), the Workers Severance Fund (Fundo de Garantia de Tempo de Serviço; FGTS), which is a mandatory program that is still central today, and the optional Brazilian Savings and Loans System (Sistema Brasileiro de Poupança e Empréstimo; SBPE). Access to both funds boosted the availability of housing finance and enabled the development of a large-scale housing supply in the country (Cardoso et al. 2013b). The system of a national housing bank, the SBPE and the FGTS stimulated economic growth and the establishment of a real-estate sector that consists of the same main actors and institutions as today (Cardoso and Aragão 2013).

Brazil's peaceful transition to democracy was less smooth in economic and institutional terms. The new democratic government had to find ways to respond to the economic crises that brought down the military regime; it also had to develop a national stabilization plan. Political instability and hyperinflation coupled with very limited public spending resulted in a power vacuum, where the absence of state actions (the extinction of the BNH created an institutional hole in relation to housing) translated to the spread of slums[5] and increasing signs of urban malfunction. The private real-estate market contented itself with catering to the housing demands of the country's top 20 percent income earners (Maricato 2009) and the scarce available funds mainly benefitted those who earned higher incomes.[6] Housing policy at the federal level showed institutional fragility and administrative discontinuity, with isolated programmes and planning that failed to take into account larger urban considerations (Cardoso *et al*. 2011). Government programmes that targeted those earning lower incomes (Habitar-Brasil, Projeto Pro-Moradia) were characterised by discontinuity, low efficiency and decreasing output (Cardoso *et al.* 2013b). Also, the government structure was highly fragmented in relation to programmes for housing and urban development. Only toward the end of the 1990s were some reforms passed to address urban development and the housing sector.

The Cardoso government remodelled housing finance according to international best practices, which included the provision of certificates of real-estate receivables (CRI) and mortgage-backed securities, both of which were informed by the American model. The idea of unifying governmental structures that were in charge of urban and housing issues had already emerged during this period, but this was only realised when the labour party came to power (Romagnoli 2012). In 2003, the Lula government created the Ministry of Cities.[7] While this institutionalization represented a huge step toward streamlined planning for urban and housing development, it fell short of uniting financial flows with its housing-development model. The FGTS remained under the decision-making of Caixa (short for Caixa Econômica Federal which reported directly to the Ministry of Finance); this considerably eroded the ministry's financial emancipation (see Bonduki 2008). Caixa had been operating de facto as the state bank since the dissolution of the BNH, in 1986, in a function it was neither initially conceived for nor had the legal status to carry out (Dias 2009).

---

5   In the 1990s, the slum population outgrew the country's normal overall demographic growth by close to a factor of three (Maricato 2009).

6   Between 1995 and 2003, fully 79 % of all financial resources went to households with incomes in excess of 5 MS (USD 390) and only 8.5 % for families that earned less than 3 MS (USD 234). The indicated dollar values are based on the official MS limit and the dollar exchange of 2003 (Bonduki 2008, p. 80).

7   The issue of housing was assigned to its own secretariat (Secretaria Nacional de Habitação, SNH), which consisted of three departments, one for housing, another for technical and institutional development, and another for slum rehabilitation.

An important preoccupation of the Lula government was to remove major institutional bottlenecks from private-market activities. In 2004, three major reforms were introduced in important changes to the aforementioned CRI to further decrease investment risk, the introduction of a special tax regime, and access to the stock market; these profoundly restructured the functioning of Brazil's real-estate sector. In combination with more favourable macro-economic conditions, these new policies triggered a major economic boom in the country that should have lasted throughout the 2000s. The Lula government's wage policies also increased the percentage population in the middle and upper-income brackets, thereby ensuring they had the financial means to access formal market-based housing options. Construction companies that had traditionally catered to the demands of high-income earners now created subsidiaries in order to move down the income ladder (Bonduki 2009). But the favourable developments experienced by the Brazilian economy and the housing sector were suddenly threatened by the unfolding global financial crisis. It is in this context that the government developed and launched the MCMV as a social-housing program with clear economic aims.

The global financial crisis affected various sectors, including real estate where demand for housing (measured in sales) dropped by 90 percent at the individual firm level (Arantes and Fix 2009). In order to avoid entering into the major recession that was unfolding throughout the world, the government initiated immediate countermeasures to support national industries and consumption, such as expanding the credit limits of major banks and lowering tax rates for industrial products (D'Amico 2011). A more comprehensive stimulation package was launched through the MCMV in the beginning of 2009. Conceptualised as a neo-Keynesian initiative, this social-housing program received a budget of 34 billion Reais (USD 19.5 billion) in order to build one million housing units within 2 years. It was expected that the program would stimulate employment creation and consumption as well as alleviate the national housing deficit by 14%; thus, combining social and economic targets.

Institutionalization of the MCMV

The idea of Minha Casa, MinhaVida was directly connected to the global financial crisis. The government's official discourse, and also that of large parts of academia, was that the program had been formulated as a direct response to changes in the global macro-economic climate.

While from an overall view the MCMV might appear to be a novel national approach to housing, an investigation of the programme's institutional framework shows a complex imbroglio of old and new ideas. The housing programme incorporated several institutional precedents while ignoring others. For the following discussion, it is essential to carefully dissect the programme's innovative characteristics from its more path-dependent developments.

The selective institutional influence of former housing programs

The MCMV is an unprecedented initiative in Brazil in terms of budget and scale. However, this housing programme stands at the end of a broader and rather continuous learning curve, particularly when considering its institutional configuration. The MCMV directly benefitted from the successes and failures of the previous Solidarity Credit Programme, the Residential Leasing Program, and Growth Acceleration Programme.

The Solidarity Credit Programme can be seen as the direct ancestor of both Entidades and the MCMV. This program was created to include families that lacked adequate savings capacities to access the formal housing market. Families with incomes under MS 3 were organised into associations, cooperatives, or other civil-society organisations (Fernandes and de Silveira 2010). More specifically, the program assisted the construction of low-income housing and could be seen as a direct outcome of social movements that gained access to federal funds after putting pressure on the government (Cardoso and Aragão 2013).

The Programa de Arrendamento Residencial was created by the Cardoso government in order to stimulate housing supply. It aimed to increase the supply of rental housing and represented the government's main programme for housing between 1999 and 2009. In contrast to the neo-liberal agenda that pervaded the Brazilian economy, this housing programme reaffirmed the role of the state and linked public subsidies to the private housing supply (Arantes 2010). Still, PAR can be seen as having been another step toward the greater commercialization of social housing in a system that put the production of social housing in the hands of private enterprise and became seduced to the logic of capital accumulation.

Construction companies were attracted by land donations and additional development rights (Cardoso and Aragão 2013). The main housing bank's mortgage-loan assurance considerably decreased investment risks. Caixa was in charge of project control but was limited to merely conducting techical/financial viability studies and was not concerned with overseeng housing's architectural or locational features. The bank also filtered the demand established by the local government, based on risk assessments. With the help of PAR funds, rent repayment was subsidised over a period of 15 years. At the end of their contracts, beneficiaries were given the option to buy their rental unit through a system whereby they received credit for the rent they had already paid (which is quite considerable) or by requesting a new unit and/or contract (Arantes 2010).

The proclaimed target group included those who earned from 3 to 6 MS. In practice, the 200,000 realised units within the first five years went to families with incomes ranging between 4 to 8 MS). PAR was remodelled under the Lula government to better target lower-income families (MS < 4). As government funding was not increased, the construction of these new units was largely achieved by government-stipulated reductions in project and building standards (in particular, unit sizes), while the market reduced construction costs by choosing peripheral land on which to build new housing units (Arantes 2010).

The Growth Acceleration Program was launched at the beginning of 2007 (January) and used the newly available financial resources that were the indirect result of the positive economic growth the country had been experiencing up to that year. This programme further promoted economic growth through an ambitious initiative in infrastructure investment (Cardoso et al. 2011) and had a major impact on the infrastructure coverage throughout the country. In housing, investment went primarily into upgrading slums to alleviate poor living conditions and into improving access to civic services. Slum upgrading was also very visible and marketable as a political success.

While the proportional share of available funds within the overall program budget was rather negligible, overall it led to a 20-fold increase in the budget allotted to slum upgrading for the period between 2002 and 2008 (Bonduki 2009). The funds used for this initiative came directly from the Casa Civil ministry and were not restricted to the same social-control mechanisms other funds were (Cardoso et al. 2013a). Two institutional innovations of the Growth Acceleration Programme are relevant for a discussion of the MCMV. Under this programme, the Brazilian government discovered the importance of discourse and the symbolic advantage of uniting various programmes under a single label (Cardoso et al. 2013a). As a consequence of these multi-ministerial undertakings, the programme required refined institutional configurations to answer the challenges of project planning, approval, implementation, and control. Special steering committees were established to streamline decision-making processes and compliance. Situation rooms enabled the collection of sector-specific data, and monitoring of the physical and financial schedules and, thus, ensured that deadlines and targets were met. These institutional innovations managed to reduce the procedural friction and ministerial fragmentation of former housing programmes (Loureiro et al. 2013).

The MCMV was ultimately built on the large shoulders of former progamsme. The Growth Acceleration Program has shown that a large-scale public programme that relies on the construction sector to create jobs and stimulate economic growth can be a success. This programme's steering and monitoring committees were developed to address the major challenges of national programmes that are attached to quick feedback loops and were directly translated into the MCMV.

The Solidarity Credit Program fine-tuned the traditional model of auto-construction and set up an institutional structure that was based on unified social funds that should have been the role model for Entidades. The learning experience from PAR has been highly influential due to its own less-controlled (and publicly accountable) fund for social housing as this created a gatekeeper position for Caixa as the central control agent positioned between the government and the construction companies.

The discontinued branches of housing programs

The MCMV has partly or completely ignored several institutional innovations. The inclusion of insights from PAR was highly selective. Despite including large parts of the programme almost one for one, the idea of rental units was completely discarded despite their obvious advantage in offering geographic flexibility to the beneficiaries of these units. Programming also incurred greater discontinuity and followed a similar logic in the almost complete dismissal of the new housing policy.

In the second half of the 2000s, PlanHab was developed and introduced. As a direct result, social movements engaged in the reform of a decision-making process in Brazilian cities that had become institutionalized under the National Council of Cities (October 2002). In August 2007, the National Housing Secretariat initiated discussions on PlanHab in order to consolidate efforts on a national housing policy. For the next two years, housing policy was jointly developed through initiatives between representatives of civil society, states, municipalities, and academics (Loureiro et al. 2013). The policy document that was launched in January 2009 aimed to establish a long-term strategy to address the country's current and future housing needs, based on the idea of decent housing (moradia digna, Bonduki 2009). In the end, however, PlanHab remained a pipe dream. While some political staff decisions undermined government support for the national housing plan, the unfolding of the economic crisis of 2007/08 pushed forward quick-fix solutions that combined the desire for immediate results with the economic stimulus of a sector that is one of the country's major employers. At the same time, the MCMV largely ignored the preparatory work of PlanHab8 and only used its financial insights (budget allocation, tax relief, the guarantee fund), while adopting the most optimistic scenario proposed by the plan (Bonduki 2009).

Given the level of detail and the elaboration process inherent in PlanHab, the MCMV can only be seen as a rather clumsy and rudimentary approach to the challenge of affordable housing in a framework that largely favours construction companies at the expense of society as a whole. In the next section, I attempt to provide some explanations of the instrumental influence of private-sector actors that may cast some light on the political economy of institutional change in Brazil. Indeed, real-estate developers were behind the idea of the MCMV, its institutionalization, and adjustments to the programme throughout its years of operations.

HOW TO CREATE YOUR OWN REGULATORY FRAMEWORK: THE ROLE OF REAL-ESTATE DEVELOPERS IN THE MCMV

Planting the idea: The policy-formation process of the MCMV

The introduction of the MCMV was announced in March 2009 as a counter-cyclical measure to the global financial crisis of 2007/08; but the idea of a large-scale national housing programme had been planted much earlier.

In the mid-2000s, SindusCon-SP, the country's most influential real-estate umbrella organisation, began to collaborate with FGV Projetos, an important university-led thinktank, to publish a magazine on the construction sector (Conjuntura da Construção). By the end of 2006, a special issue discussed the merits of strong government involvement in the housing sector (based on historical analyses). In 2007 and 2008, two out of four annual issues were dedicated to the idea of a national public housing programme (including a special issue that featured Mexico). These nodal points represent direct communication channels to influencing public opinion and using the legitimacy of (quasi) scientific research. Specific stories and special issues of these magazines were commonly featured in the country's most important newspapers, in combination with expert interviews.

---

8 The planning and land mechanism tools have largely taken over, such as prioritizing municipalities that make use of increased property taxes for underutilized lands or donated land. In practice, however, these tools were largely non-operational.

In parallel to these efforts, the Rio branch of SindusCon attempted to influence public decision-makers even more directly. In 2007, the association organised a government delegation to visit Mexico. Delegates from the construction sector found both the Mexican and Chilean housing policy experiences to be the most appropriate model for housing production in Brazil (Cardoso et al. 2011). In both countries, the stimulus of the supply structure led to the construction of monotonous, large-scale, poor-quality housing projects that were situated in urban peripheries (see Rolnik 2012). Nevertheless, from the impressions collected abroad, a pilot project called sustainable housing was initiated under the Cardoso government and later presented to Dilma Rousseff at the beginning of 2008 (De Andrade 2011; Cardoso and Aragão 2013). These attempts by the real-estate lobby to create a positive momentum for large state-led housing programmes quickly yielded concrete results.

At the end of 2008, informal meetings took place between the minister of the Casa Civil Dilma Rousseff (Chief of Staff Office) and several major construction companies. Rousseff had invited six large construction companies (Cyrela, Rossi, MRV, WTorre, Rodobens, and Gafisa) to discuss the feasibility of such an undertaking (Loureiro et al. 2013). According to the CEO of Wtorre, the private-sector actors in this conversation proposed several measures to President Lula da Silva, such as the creation of a guarantee fund and reduced notary costs for land records, of which almost all were directly included in the government's proposal which formed the basis for the later law (MP 459 2009; Blanco 2009).

The importance of the real-estate sector received a symbolic dimension when the programme was introduced to the broader public. In a television broadcast that took place on March 25, 2008, President da Silva left the main presentation to the minister of the Casa Civil. Dilma Rousseff's speech was followed by a discourse between the president of the Brazilian Chamber of Construction Industries and a comment by the developer Gafisa (by then the country's largest developer). This public event can be seen as a nodal point that visually enshrined the different levels of importance attributed to each sector: the government and the private sector took centre stage, while representatives of social movements were present but visually marginalised (De Andrade 2011).

Influencing the institutional frame of the MCMV

The MCMV was institutionalized by Law No 11.977 (June 7, 2009). The first phase initially ran to the end of 2010, with the overall target of delivering one million new housing units. Phase 2 was envisioned to last from 2011 to 2014 and to have a total budget of R$125 (USD 67) billion9 allocated to building a further two million houses (later increased by 600,000 and to take an additional year to complete). In both phases, those in track 1 should have received around 40% of all contracted units. Phase 3 began in 2016 with the allocation of R$211 (USD 64.9) billion10 for constructing 3 million housing units (see Table 2). At this time, however, the program was caught up in the national government's budget crises and new construction contracts basically came to a halt.

Besides monitoring progress, the government set up regular meetings in Brasília that brought together representatives from the private market, civil society, and academia. These round-table discussions were used on a regular basis to collect feedback and decide on any required changes. Due to frustrating experiences that took place in other sectors,11 these discussions became de facto industry-government feedback moments. This alignment of interests in specific nodal points was also reflected in the changes that were made. While various problems emerged throughout the MCMV's years of operations (discussed in a separate forthcoming paper),12 for the most part the regulatory changes followed the logic of improving market benefits (Loureiro et al. 2013; Dias 2015).

Various federal government measures for the financial viability of projects also took place under the MCMV. For example, setting maximum permissible unit prices was one of the primary measures used to influence market response: increasing housing prices without changing other requirements (such as unit size and housing standards) was seen as broadening the geography in which MCMV

---

9   Based on the 2011 exchange rate.
10 Based on the 2016 exchange rate.
11 Representatives of academia and social movements expressed their concerns as soon as the program was announced. The government largely ignored their criticisms; thus, generating feelings of being unheard (Loureiro *et al.* 2013, 1886:8). This is confirmed by a comparative study by Pires and Gomide (2014, p. 20), which shows that the MCMV relied on the "active engagement of construction firms, [but] housing movements and urban planning professionals never had much opportunity to influence the implementation of the program."
12 The problems that occured during the MCMV's different phases ranged from specific reported shortcomings (delays, intransparent selection processes, resales, abandoned units, invasion by criminal groups), more systemic problems (default rates, units that were too small, projects that were too distant, lack of infrastructure, land speculation, too costly, insufficient quality, too market friendly) to institutional limitations (rushed process, absence of certain concerns, non-participatory, not aligned with urban planning frameworks, no consideration for rental and vacant housing, corruption).

projects were possible (while increasing profitability in areas where such projects were already possible). The result was a more active supply of housing units.

For the urban-supply modality, the unit sizes, standards, and maximum unit prices were fixed. Between April 2009 and October 2015, unit prices saw particular adjustments: The maximum allowed price increased, over the years, from R$ 51,000 to R$ 63,000 (USD 21,817 to 30,428), or by 128%. For the track 2 and 3 limits, the revisions were even more vivid and represented an increase of 173%, which was much higher than the national-construction-cost inflation rate of 147%.

Table 2: Overview of MCMV phases and their targets.

MCMV 1 (2009-10)	Track 1	Track 2	Track 3	Total
Goal	400,000	400,000	200,000	1,000,000
Contracted	482,700	375,800	146,600	1,005,100
MCMV 2 (2011-14/15)	**Track 1**	**Track 2**	**Track 3**	**Total**
Goal (original)	1,200,000	600,000	200,000	2,000,000
Goal (extension)	2,000,000	1,350,000	400,000	3,750,000
MCMV 3 (2016-2021)	**Faixa 1**	**Faixa 2**	**Faixa 3**	**Total**
Goal	1,600,000	1,000,000	400,000	3,000,000

Source: Table by the author based on program documentation.

A second domain of regulatory changes was in the level of supply incentives. The largest incentives were in considerable reductions in notary fees and a unified taxation regime (so-called Regime Especial de Tributação, RET) being applicable to project budgets. RET applicability was also regulated by maximum unit prices, albeit these were disconnected from the aforementioned track-1 ceilings (see Table 1). This carved out a regulatory loophole where builders could scoop up the main benefits of highly subsidised units but sell their projects at higher prices to track-2 families. As this track was less tightly controlled than track 1, it also opened up the possibility of imposing further payments off-the-book so as to increase the final unit price (see Cardoso et al. 2013c, p. 146).

A third area of policy reform concerned compliance to a minimum standard of building quality. The Ministry of Cities and Caixa imposed qualification standards for construction companies (supply procurement, administration, human resources, etc.) in order for them to participate in the subsidised housing programs. In practice, these qualification standards linked project size to company size and ultimately benefitted large developers.

In contrast to the supply-related changes, other problems that were linked to the MCMV did not receive the same level of attention. The inadequacy of the unit model applicable to an entire country, which was in disregard to the overall cultural, environmental and geographic differences, had been raised from the very beginning (Arantes and Fix 2009). The lack of solutions to account for the heterogeneity of demand (Cardoso and do Lago 2013) was particularly puzzling as the national housing policy of 2008 offered a broad range of options that were based on different family sizes and regional differences (Eloy and Cagnin 2012). Similar stagnation in the programme adjustment can be traced to the issue of land location (Nascimento and Tostes 2011; Maricato 2011), the location of projects (market-dictated peripheral developments) (Arantes and Fix 2009; Nascimento and Tostes 2011), and delayed delivery (Rodrigues 2013; Globo 2013).

CONCLUSION

Programme Minha Casa, Minha Vida has added more evidence for an international critical review of a large-scale national governmental housing programme that has over-relied on market supply and ultimately led to urban sprawl, mass housing of relatively poor quality and a supply that runs aside actual demand. In Brazil, the private sector was instrumental in planting and shaping the idea of this housing programme, defining its actual institutionalization, and influencing the way it changed over time. This was made possible by not only the sector's pro-active engagement and deployment of its own resources but also the ease at which it was able to align its interests with those of the government. A programme that incorporated both of private and public interests came at the expense of Brazilian society and cities.

These private-sector lobby efforts took place largely undetected from public scrutiny as the purpose of this lobbying remained hidden behind a vail of legitimacy in the print media, in its own umbrella associations and in official round-table debates in Brasília. Retracing the involvement of the real-estate sector in shaping public opinion and influencing changes in policy provides evidence on the political economy of urban development and points to important yet largely ignored forces that underlay current urban development trajectories. The direct link between the MCMV and political change (the impeachment of Rousseff; the imprisoning of Lula), economic scandals (construction-related bribery mechanisms) and ultimately re-emerging socio-spatial tensions in the country, underline the necessity of further research on the role of real-estate developers in urban development.

REFERENCES

Aalbers, M. B. (2016) The Financialization of Housing: A Political Economy Approach, Routledge Studies in the Modern World Economy. New York: Routledge, p. 168.

Adams, D. and Tiesdell, S. (2010) "Planners as Market Actors: Rethinking State-Market Relations in Land and Property." *Planning Theory & Practice* 11 (2): 187–207. https://doi.org/10.1080/14649351003759631.

Arantes, P.F. (2010) "Pesquisa Sobre o PAR Apresenta Antecedentes Do Minha Casa, Minha Vida." *Revista Pós* 17 (28): 275–80.

Arantes, P.F. and Fix, M. (2009) "Como o Governo Lula Pretende Resolver o Problema Da Habitação. Alguns Comentários Sobre o Pacote Habitacional Minha Casa, Minha Vida." *Correio Da Cidadania* 30.

Blanco, M. (2009) "Conheça Detalhes Da Aprovação de Empreendimentos No 'Minha Casa, Minha Vida'. E Veja as Plantas." *Construção Mercado 95*.

Bonduki, N. (2008) "Política Habitacional e Inclusão Social No Brasil: Revisão Histórica e Novas Perspectivas No Governo Lula." *Revista Eletrônica de Arquitetura e Urbanismo* 1: 70–104.

———. (2009) "Do Projeto Moradia Ao Programa Minha Casa Minha Vida." *Teoria e Debate* 82: 8–14.

Buckley, R.M., Kallergis, A. and Wainer, L. (2016) "The Emergence of Large-Scale Housing Programs: Beyond a Public Finance Perspective." *Habitat International* 54: 199–209. https://doi.org/10.1016/j.habitatint.2015.11.022.

Cardoso, A.L. and Jaenisch, S.T. (2017) "Mercado Imobiliário e Política Habitacional Nos Governos de Lula e Dilma: Entre o Mercado Financeiro e a Produção Habitacional Subsidiada." In, São Paulo: 17th ENANPUR Conference, 22–26 May.

Cardoso, A.L. and Aragão, T.A. (2013) "Do Fim Do BNH Ao Programa Minha Casa Minha Vida: 25 Anos Da Política Habitacional No Brasil." Rio de Janeiro: Letra Capital.

Cardoso, A.L. and Corrêa do Lago, L. (2013) "O Programa Minha Casa Minha Vida e Seus Efeitos Territoriais." In: O Programa Minha Casa Minha Vida e Seus Efeitos Territoriais, edited by A.L. Cardoso and Observatório das Metrópoles, 7–16. Rio de Janeiro: Letra Capital.

Cardoso, A.L., de Souza Araújo, F. and Jaenisch, S.T. (2013a) "Morando No Limite: Sobre Padrões de Localização e Acessibilidade Do Programa Minha Casa Minha Vida Na Região Metropolitana Do Rio de Janeiro." Anais: *Encontros Nacionais da ANPUR* XV: 1–16.

Cardoso, A.L., Rodrigues Nunes Junior, D., de Souza Araújo, F., Ferreira da Silva, N. and S.T. Jaenisch. (2013b) "Quando Um Direito Vira Produto: Impactos Do Programa Minha Casa Minha Vida Na Cidade Do Rio de Janeiro." *Simpósio Nacional de Geografia Urbana*, XIII. Rio de Janeiro.

Cardoso, A.L. and Rodrigues Nunes Junior, D., de Sousa Araújo, F., Ferreira da Silva, N., Aragão T.A., and Amorim, T.P. (2013c) "Minha Casa Minha Sina: implicações da recente produção habitacional pelo setor privado na Zona Oeste da cidade do Rio de Janeiro." In: O Programa Minha Casa Minha Vida e Seus Efeitos Territoriais, edited by A.L. Cardoso and Observatório das Metrópoles, 143–160. Rio de Janeiro: Letra Capital.

Cardoso, A. L., Aragão, T.A. and de Souza Araújo, F. (2011) "Habitação De Interesse Social: Política Ou Mercado? Reflexos Sobre a Construção Do Espaço Metropolitano." *Encontro National da ANPUR* XIV: 1–21.

Coiacetto, E. (2009) "Industry Structure in Real Estate Development: Is City Building Competitive?" *Urban Policy and Research* 27 (2): 117–35.

Crow, B. (2001) Markets, class and social change: trading networks and poverty in rural South Asia. Springer. https://doi.org/10.1057/9781403900845.

D'Amico, F. (2011) "O Programa Minha Casa,Minha Vida e a Caixa Econômica Federal." O Desenvolvimento Econômico Brasileiro e a Caixa: *Trabalhos Premiados*, Rio de Janeiro: Centro Internacional Celso Furtado de Políticas para o Desenvolvimento, 33–54.

De Andrade, E.S.J. (2011) "Política Habitacional No Brasil (1964 a 2011): 'Do Sonho Da Casa Própria à Minha Casa, Minha Vida'." Master thesis, *Arquitetura e Urbanismo Da Escola de Arquitetura e Urbanismo*. Niterói: Universidade Federal Fluminense.

Dias, E.C. (2009) "Minha Casa, Minha Vida, Minha Política Pública." *Conjuntura Da Construção* 7 (2): 4–5.

———. (2015) "Lucros e Votos: Os Empresários e o Governo Na Política Habitacional Brasileira." *Revista de Economia Política* 35 (4): 763–79.

Eloy, C.M. and Cagnin, R.F. (2012) "Mudanças No Minha Casa, Minha Vida: Em Que Direção?" Valor Econômico, São Paulo, October 31, available at: www.valor.com.br/opiniao/2887278/mudancas-no-minha-casa-minhavidaem-que-direcao, [accessed May 5, 2019].

Fainstein, S.S. (1994) The City Builders: Property, Politics, and Planning in London and New York. Oxford, Malden: Blackwell.

Fauveaud, G. (2014) "Mutations of Real Estate Actors' Strategies and Modes of Capital Appropriation in Contemporary Phnom Penh." *Urban Studies* 51 (16): 3479–94. https://doi.org/10.1177/0042098014552767.

Fernandes, C., do Carmo Pires, and de Fátima Ramos da Silveira, S. (2010) "Ações e ContextoDaPolítica Nacional de Habitação: Da Fundação Casa Popular Ao Programa 'Minha Casa, Minha Vida." II Encontro Mineiro de Administração Pública, *Economia Solidária e Gestão Pública*.

GIZ. (2014) "My Home, Your Business: A Guide to Affordable Housing Solutions for Low-Income Communities." Deutsche Gesellschaft für Internationale Zusammenarbeit GmbH on behalf of German Federal Ministry for Economic Cooperation and Development, Bonn.

Globo. (2013) "Moradores Do 'Minha Casa, Minha Vida' Estão Sem EnergiaEm Imperatriz."Globo G1, available at: http://g1.globo.com/ma/maranhao/noticia/2013/09/moradores-do-minha-casa-minha-vida-estao-sem-energia-emimperatriz.html, [accessed May 5, 2019].

Guy, S. and Henneberry, J. (2002) Development and Developers: Perspectives on Property. Oxford: Blackwell Publishing and RICS Foundation.

Hersperger, A.M., Gennaio Franscini, M. P. and D. Kübler. (2013) "Actors, Decisions and Policy Changes in Local Urbanization." *European Planning Studies* 4313 (July 2015): 1–19. https://doi.org/10.1080/09654313.2013.783557.

Hufty, M. (2007) "The Governance Analytical Framework." WP1, The Graduate Institute, Geneva, 1–19, available at http://graduateinstitute.ch/webdav/site/developpement/shared/developpement/mdev/soutienauxcours0809/hufty_Gouvernance/2.1b.Hufty-Eng.pdf, [accessed January 5, 2015].

———. (2011) "Investigating Policy Processes: The Governance Analytical Framework (GAF)." *Research for Sustainable Development: Foundations, Experiences, and Perspectives*, 403–24.

Kübler, D. (2012) "Introduction: Metropolitanisation and Metropolitan Governance." *European Political Science* 11 (3): 402–8. https://doi.org/10.1057/eps.2011.41.

Loureiro, M.R., Macário, V. and Guerra, P. (2013) "Democracia, Arenas Decisórias e Políticas Públicas: O Programa Minha Casa Minha Vida." Texto Para Discussão. Vol. 1886. Rio de Janeiro: Instituto de Pesquisa Econômica Aplicada (IPEA).

Maricato, E. (2009) "O" Minha Casa" é Um Avanço, Mas Segregação Urbana FicaIntocada." *Carta-Maior, May 27*, available at: https://www.cartamaior.c om.br/?/Editoria/Politica/O-Minha-Casa-e-um-avanco-mas-segregacaourban a-fica-intocada/4/15160, [accessed May 5, 2019].

———. (2011) O Impasse Da Política Urbana No Brasil. Petrópolis: Vozes.

MP 459 (2009) Dispõe sobre o Programa Minha Casa, Minha Vida - PMCMV, a regularização fundiária de assentamentos localizados em áreas urbanas, e dá outras providências, Medida Provisoria No. 459, Presidência da República, Brasília: Casa Civil, March 25.

Nascimento, D. and Tostes. S.P. (2011) "Programa Minha Casa Minha Vida: A (Mesma) Política Habitacional No Brasil." Arquitextos, June, Year 12, 133(3). Vitruvius: São Paulo.

Pires, R.R.C. and de Avila Gomide, A. (2014) "A 'New Democratic-Developmental State' in Brazil? A Comparative Analysis of Governance Arrangements, State Capacities and Policy Results." In 23rd International Political Science Association World Congress, Jul 19-24.

Rodrigues, E. (2013) "Famílias Sofrem Com Atraso Do Minha Casa, Minha Vida." Diario Gaucho, September 23, available at: http://diariogaucho.clicrbs .com.br/rs/dia-a-dia/noticia/2013/09/familias-sofrem-com-atraso-do-minha-c asa-minha-vida-4278371.html, [accessed May 5, 2019].

Rolnik, R. (2012) "Eu Sou Você Amanhã: A Experiência Chilena e o 'Minha Casa, Minha Vida." Blog Raquel Rolnik. May 10, São Paulo, available at: https://raquelrolnik.wordpress.com/2012/05/10/eu-sou-voce-amanha-a-exper iencia-chilena-e-o-minha-casa-minha-vida/ [accessed May 5, 2019].

Rolnik, R., Reis, J., Bischof, R. and Klintowitz. D.C., (2010) "Como Produzir Moradia Bem Localizada Com Os Recursos Programa Minha Casa, Minha Vida? Implementando Os Instrumentos Do Estatuto Da Cidade." Brasília: Ministério Das Cidades, 132.

Romagnoli, A.J. (2012) "O Programa 'Minha Casa, Minha Vida' Na Política Habitacional Brasileira: Continuidades, Inovações e Retrocessos." Master thesis, Universidade Federal de São Carlos: São Carlos.

Rouanet, H. and Halbert, L. (2016) "Leveraging Finance Capital: Urban Change and Self-Empowerment of Real Estate Developers in India." *Urban Studies* 53 (7): 1–44. https://doi.org/10.1177/0042098015585917.

Sabatier, P.A. and Weible, C.M., (2007) "The Advocacy Coalition Framework: Innovations and Clarifications." In: Sabatier, T.A. (ed). "Theories of the Policy Process". Boulder: Westview Publisher: 189–220.

Sanfelici, D. and Halbert, L. (2015) "Financial Markets, Developers and the Geographies of Housing in Brazil: A Supply-Side Account." *Urban Studies* 53 (7): 1465–85. https://doi.org/10.1177/0042098015590981.

Searle, L.G. (2014) "Conflict and Commensuration: Contested Market Making in India's Private Real Estate Development Sector." *International Journal of Urban and Regional Research* 38 (1): 60–78. https://doi.org/10.1111/1468242 7.12042.

UNCHS. (2003) "Slums of the World: The Face of Urban Poverty in the New Millennium." United Nations Human Settlements Programme. Nairobi: United Nations Centre for Human Settlements.

Chapter 3: Mutual Aid, Self-Management and Collective Ownership

Social Capital as a Housing-Finance Counter-Mechanism to Neo-Liberal Policies[1]

Marielly Casanova

INTRODUCTION

Cities around the world have experienced aggressive transformations mainly due to the speculative character of global capital. Global capital has been claiming urban centralities as arenas in which to place new global markets, thereby expanding new urban economies that are reshaping cities in a polarizing trend that has created conditions that exacerbate poverty and the marginalisation of urban populations (Sassen, 2011). Urban land and housing have become expensive commodities which are denied to a large majority of people in a system dominated by the politics of accumulation and the privatisation of essential aspects of life, including recreation, education and health care. This urban business model has been directed toward fostering financial profit while intensifying a process of the commodification of the city (see Rolnik in the foreword of this book for an elaboration on the commodification of land and housing). In turn, this has opened deep gaps in a society that constrains access to social services, infrastructure, facilities, and especially housing for the most vulnerable.

At the same time, new models of urban development have influenced the way governments conceive and implement housing policies in terms of how they

---

1 This paper is based on the dissertation "Social Strategies Building the City: A Reconceptualization of Social Housing in Latin America", by Marielly Casanova published by LIT Verlag Berlin, 2019.

affect affordability and accessibility to urban centralities where most social services and infrastructure are located. In this system, state investment in housing is reduced and state responsibility is replaced or dominated by market logic. Hence, the state is no longer the provider but the facilitator that supports market demand and promotes private ownership under a neo-liberal dogma (UN-Habitat 2012 – see also the elaboration on housing trends on a global scale in the first foreword by El Sioufi in this book). Therefore, housing and especially housing for the poor is built as an industrial product characterized by a mass production that is devoid of individual variation and social meaning as it has become completely disarticulated from its context (Ortiz 2011). These housing schemes are designed under principles of standardisation and mass production, emulating an industrial economy that has severe effects on the character of neighbourhoods (Calthorpe and Fulton 2001). This mass production acts against diversity and the human scale and denies the complexity of the community and its ties of solidarity; the spatial nature of this production neglects to include opportunities for encounters between neighbours, limits social control of the territory and reduces the feeling of security and comfort (Casanova 2019). These new private agendas provide no room for collective solutions. Instead, these industrial models encourage individualization in society by restricting participation, autonomy and self-determination. Social actors are not at all considered in the process of the conception, planning and/or construction of housing.

Additionally, the state's withdrawal from investment in economic activities and infrastructure has caused a weakening of the working class, which in turn translates into lower wages, higher unemployment and unfulfilled citizen rights in a system that neglects to accumulate social capital. Along with the individualization of problems, other negative outcomes result from the politics of exclusion in that any collective actions to solve these problems are excluded, such as in cooperatives, solidarity and mutual aid. However, in the past decades this situation has triggered a more structured resurgence from social movements and workers' unions that are active in popular urban sectors and that have been engaging in resistance to the new neo-liberal model and reacting in defence of their salaries, access to decent housing and services, and mostly advocating for the recovery of democratic spaces and decision-making processes.

In this sense, contemporary social movements have institutionalized the cooperative as the embodiment of one of the most effective forms of resistance in their struggle for access to employment and a dignified standard of living. Adopted by the early labour movements with an important precedent dating from the beginning of the industrial revolution in modern times the cooperative has become a mechanism for the construction of social capital. The cooperative movement operates mainly in spaces where the corporate system and the market cannot reach. Workers' cooperatives and social enterprises provide alternatives to people who would otherwise be unemployed and marginalised (Curl 2010). Housing cooperatives are using unconventional tools to empower people to access decent housing and also to build skills and capacities for their integration into their city and its systems.

In Latin America, the cooperative has been a response of organised collectives and socio-political actors whose aim is to counteract the consequences of neo-liberal policies. These cooperatives are based on three main pillars: self-management, mutual aid and collective property. Cooperatives in Latin America understand the interconnection between these three principles as being social capital. The aim of this paper is to provide another perspective to the concept of social capital and to describe in specific cases its implementation for the production of low-income housing.

APPROACH TO THE PROBLEM – NEO-LIBERALISM IN LATIN AMERICA

The end of the 1980s in Latin America was marked by a type of neo-liberalism that was the result of a radical transformation of the structures of capitalism; one that fractured the basis of the interventionist and benefactor state. This trend had already begun by the end of the 1970s when the global recession gradually concluded a debt-financed period of "apparent development" (Walton 2001).

The privatisation of public companies, productive areas and infrastructure in addition to the deregulation and cease of public subsidies for public goods and infrastructure were some of the rules imposed by the market. The right to the city was more than ever in dispute as neo-liberalism caused economic inequalities to increase. These were articulated within different forms of exclusion: physical, social and political (Samara *et al.* 2013; Casanova 2019). Neo-liberalism and globalisation encouraged the development of new centralities where corporate projects expanded. The consequences were new forms of city making that were mainly characterized by socio-spatial disintegration (Girola and Thomaz 2013), fragmentation and deep segregation.

Those economic measures along with the resulting austerity had high social and economic costs. Cities did not only host a growing number of poor people but were also becoming poorer in their capacity to provide basic needs. The neo-liberal ideas introduced in Latin America promoted and imposed the privatisation of public services and the deregulation of urban policy, which resulted in deficient or non-existent education, a lack of proper health care, the privatisation of public space, unaffordable "public" transportation and the commodification of housing (see for example, Boanada (Chapter 2), on the example of Brazil). In sum, it created a "disarticulated ill-equipped city" (Velásquez Carrillo 2004, p. 9) that was unfit to cope with emerging challenges and unable to provide a quality of life to its inhabitants.

The overall result of these measures was an increase in global poverty. Reduced salaries and the deregulated rents denied a majority of the population the possibility of accessing decent housing or even housing in general. The housing problematic translated into two general aspects: one aspect was the construction of new slums on occupied land in urban peripheries or the illegal occupation of empty buildings in inner cities. People in need of housing took into their own hands the role of housing producers without financial, technical or legal support. The second aspect relates to the transfer of responsibilities from the state to the market; this encouraged the mass production of low-quality housing, which was mostly built on cheap land far from city centralities. This typology of housing has increased the social gap and caused even more social and physical segregation. Low-income housing was and still is built in areas that are disconnected from cities; thereby, lacking cultural or social identity to root the inhabitants to the territory and also distancing them from social services and employment opportunities.

This neo-liberal crisis expanded throughout the territory, affecting countries and cities in Latin America, to different extents. Argentina was one of those countries where the state was severely affected; here, essential services were aggressively privatised while the state's planning role in the develop of infrastructure and social facilities was constrained. In 1998, Argentina began to advance toward a deep recession that culminated in a social crisis that exploded in 2001. As the country's international debt increased, social rights and social investment were reduced, especially in specific areas like public housing. These events together caused a national financial crisis (Fernández Wagner 2011) that shaped a process of social disarticulation and eroded the democratic basis of Argentinian society (Rodríguez 2009).

By 2001, all socio-economic indicators were showing the critical impoverishment of a population that was being influenced by an enormous qualitative and quantitative housing deficit. Poverty increased in Argentina over the next two years, so that 51.7% of the population in metropolitan Buenos Aires was living in poverty[2] and 25.2% of that percentage was homeless (Raspall 2010). The quantitative aspect of the problem shows that in 2001, the 'villas miseria' or the city's slums which were in constant and exponential growth housed 110,387 people while 55,799 people lived in tenement housing and 37,601 in hotel-pensions (Raspall 2010); none of those accommodations provided security of tenure or a minimum acceptable standard of living.

Figure 1: Accentuated occupation of land in the periphery of cities building new slums and densifying existing slums, Caracas.

Source: Daniel Schwartz, 2011.

One of the social solutions to (informally) solving the housing shortage was the squatting or illegal occupation of private and public buildings in the city. It is estimated that by 1991 there were 150,000 people involved in the occupation of vacant buildings in the city of Buenos Aires. This means that roughly 5% of the city's population (Rodríguez, 2009) that was living on the margins had taken this measure to meet their housing needs. However, the revalorization of the city's

---

2   Households in poverty present at least one of the following indicators of deprivation: Overcrowding (households with more than three people per room); poor quality of shelter (households that live in a dwelling of inconvenient type such as tenements, rooms in hotels or pensions not built for housing purposes); inadequate sanitary conditions (homes that do not have any type of toilet, etc.).

land between the 1990s and 2003 influenced the enactment of new urban policies (especially during the crisis of 2001-2002) that aimed to evict residents from illegally occupied buildings (Rodríguez 2009).

COUNTER-ACTION TO NEO-LIBERAL POLICIES

Throughout the decade of the 1980s, and more so during the explosion of the crisis in 2001, social movements were already organising themselves within the 'villas miseria', tenement housing, and illegally occupied buildings, so as to act in defence of citizen's rights and against the housing shortage, the inaccessible housing rents and the evictions. The decade of the 1990s marked the beginning of grassroots planning in which several grassroots organisations evolved into socio-political actors that later influenced public policy (Zapata 2013). During this period, these movements were performing independent from the state in their decision-making processes. In other words, the sense of autonomy that resulted from these participatory practices began to have an effect on state policy; thus, influencing urban policy as their own project for an alternative society (García-Guadilla 2018).

The contemporary cooperative movement is embodiment of those social organisations in the context of Buenos Aires. These cooperatives differ from traditional cooperatives due to the complexity of their fields of action, where they reject the traditional bureaucratic, vertical and clientelist structures (Ciolli 2011). Instead, they function through participatory democratic processes through which members advocate for solutions to the different problems that deeply affect Argentinean society (Rodríguez 2009). Self-management is one of the fundamental principles that enable these cooperatives to achieve collective goals. The first cooperatives achieved the collective renovation of occupied buildings, which they later formally acquired through public funding.

Since 2001, the cooperatives have been operating mostly with the public funds they have received through the Programme for Self-management Housing (a regulatory instrument formed under the framework of Law 341 for the allocation and monitoring of resources). Law 341 was conceived as a mechanism that would enable cooperatives to receive credits for the construction or purchase of affordable dwellings and also for the renovation of or construction work required on existing buildings. The main aspect of this law is the inclusion of social organisations as beneficiaries of loans or access to credit without their being subjected to income restrictions (Rodríguez 2009). The city government guides the lending process by providing financial and technical resources and the actual loans and also the later monitoring of the use of funds acquired through those loans. In 2003, the city created the Institute of Housing, which enabled it to sustain its self-management and participatory policies (Rodríguez 2009) and to support the cooperatives during the process of housing production. Despite being dependent on public money, the cooperatives and social organisations behind the programme have been able to establish clear boundaries between their capacities and responsibilities and those of the state; thus, ensuring the effective use of public resources to access decent housing, employment, education and health care, while investing in building capacities for their members.

'El Movimiento de Ocupantes e Inquilinos' (The Occupants and Tenant Movement (MOI)) is one of those relevant actors that emerged from the process of building occupations and subsequent forced evictions in Buenos Aires. This organisation was essential to the creation of cooperatives. It was also a major actor that, together with other pro-habitat organisations, achieved the enactment of Law 341 for housing cooperatives, in 2000, and supported numerous cooperatives before and after the law's enactment. The movement's main objective is to help process-oriented small-scale organisations access serviced urban land and gain legal tenure for housing production in the city's centralities. The MOI is composed of a combination of diverse professionals and academics from the University of Buenos Aires and La Plata, urban social movements (from the occupations and cooperatives) and workers from the 'Central de Trabajadores Argentinos' CTA.

The MOI has provided the necessary mechanisms for cooperatives' internal organisation; it has also supported self-management efforts that together with the public sector (co-management) have been instrumental in the development of housing projects. The cooperatives' affiliation to their structure is based on small-scale processes that build capacities for self-management and mutual aid. In addition, they incorporate their collective property as a powerful tool that contradicts the concept of a city that is structured as a speculative business; instead, they promote a democratic city where everyone has the right to reside.

The constitution of the MOI follows the values or three pillars that were adopted from successful experiences in Uruguay and which were institutionalized by the Federación Uruguaya de Cooperativas de Viviendapor Ayuda Mutua (FUCVAM).[3] These are self-management, mutual aid and collective ownership

---

3   The FUCVAM (Uruguayan Federation of Mutual-aid Housing Cooperatives) is an organization whose founding in 1970 was supported by the enactment of the National Housing Act 13728, in 1968. It functions as an umbrella organization in which the base cooperatives are federated.

which, along with the dimensions embedded within these pillars, constitute what the movement calls social capital.

SOCIAL CAPITAL AS AN ALTERNATIVE MECHANISM TO FINANCE LOW-INCOME HOUSING

Social organisations are constitutive producers of social capital (Kearns and Forrest 2000). Housing cooperatives hold a certain level of responsibility in that they are involved in the creation of social capital that is intrinsic in their ties to solidarity and their commitment to a collective effort. These organisations refer to social capital as the potential of human capital to encourage economic development; thereby, establishing a direct connection between mutual aid and social capital. Mutual aid is, in itself, both a social and economic asset due to the fact that the labour or working hours performed by the cooperative member and/or his/her family are translated into payments that complement the financing required for the construction of the member's house. Social capital can be transformed into financial capital (Putnam 1993); however, it cannot be used as capital (for exchange) as it is understood in the market economy but rather it is a value that can be accumulated and used as an asset for social benefit (Coraggio 2002); in other words, it is the constitution of a social economy.

The social economy is directly related to the theory of social capital; it represents the aggregate value of the steps housing cooperatives follow as social enterprises, steps that are vital to fostering economic development (Casanova 2019). At the same time, their organisation is shaped by self-managed practices and their governance system is based on direct democracy. These social enterprises have the capacity to manage social, economic and physical resources in order to produce income and social benefits for its members (Casanova 2019). Furthermore, self-management in combination with mutual aid are two principles that contribute to the generation of work value which is accumulated through individual and collective efforts. The two principles contribute to building personal capacities through the organisation and its logistics and also through management and construction-related activities.

Additionally, collective ownership adds another dimension to the concept of social capital. It creates a series of securities that protect the cooperative member from land speculation and the direct threat of eviction by third parties. Different from individual ownership, the family is the user and not the owner of the property they occupy. This means the cooperative members have the right to use and enjoy their dwellings and the cooperative's common spaces while the deed is registered under the cooperative as an organisation. This ensures both individual and collective tenure and benefits. Furthermore, collective ownership within this social-capital framework act as a financial guarantee so there is a reciprocal exchange between the cooperative and its members in the repayment of loans and debts. The collective act between these two entities is the guarantee for the debt incurred (Portes 1998).

This social-capital scheme also comes with some restrictions. Members as users cannot sell the dwellings, they occupy nor can they use them as capital for mortgages. If a family decides to move out of their dwelling, then they receive the value defined by the initial investment in labour and hours of work provided during the whole process (not limited to construction but also management, etc.) and any additional personal contributions. Due to the social nature of this arrangement, this compensation is not influenced by the market or the land value.

To understand the context of self-management, mutual aid and collective ownership depicted in social capital, it is essential to provide a closer look into the FUCVAM and its philosophy as it has influenced the configuration and functioning of the MOI in Argentina.

EXPERIENCES BASED ON SOCIAL CAPITAL – MUTUAL-AID HOUSING COOPERATIVES IN URUGUAY: THE MODEL FOLLOWED BY THE MOI

In Uruguay, participation in housing production has been institutionalized through the production of housing that is primarily based on the cooperative model. The first cooperative venture into mutual-aid housing dates back to 1966, with three pilot experiences supported by the Uruguayan Cooperative Centre (CCU) and funded through cooperation between the Uruguayan government and the Inter-American Development Bank. Inspired by these experiences, the National Housing Act was passed in 1968, and in 1970 the FUCVAM was founded as an essential actor for the organisation and consolidation of a growing number of cooperatives that included members of workers' unions and working-class dwellers.

The FUCVAM functions as a guild organisation in which member cooperatives are federated. These cooperatives manage and administer project funds, while the FUCVAM assumes a political role in providing support through technical assistance and capacity building. Furthermore, from 1984,[4] Montevideo City Hall created a land bank that allows the cooperatives to buy serviced urban land within the city's centralities. The FUCVAM is now the institution that allocates land for use by the cooperatives.

As mentioned in the previous section, social capital is defined as the combination of self-management, mutual aid and collective ownership; and the FUCVAM considers these factors to be a legitimate mechanism for financing low-income housing. This means that the government supported by the legal framework provides 85% of each loan and the families (or members that will inhabit the project) provide the remaining 15% in mutual aid along with other financial contributions. Before construction begins, first there is a contribution of two taxable units or Unidad Reajustable,[5] then during construction each hour of labour is recorded as an economic value, and when construction is over the members repay the loan through social quotas while continuing to self-manage the maintenance of the building. This format reduces costs in several ways: first the cost of intermediaries is avoided (construction profit, promotion, real estate); and second, the maintenance cost is also reduced as it is assumed through mutual aid (International Co-operative Alliance ICA). Cooperative members acquire considerable knowledge during the construction process and can therefore organise themselves to undertake this latter task.

After the construction is complete, the families distribute among themselves the responsibilities for the tasks and activities associated with self-management. This is a process that stimulates communication which, in addition to the constant consensus and decision-making, promotes solidarity among the community. This approach has enabled collective solutions for other social problems the community has faced (Rodríguez interview 2013). In the case of this project, those ties were behind the implementation of a series of community-oriented projects that have improved the quality of life for both the residents of the houses and of the surrounding neighbourhoods. Some examples of community interventions are: basic services and urban infrastructure, sports and recreation, culture, health care and other community-managed programmes.

Collective ownership in the context of the housing projects is an important aspect of development in that it prevents speculation since only the families involved in these projects have the right to use the housing units but not to sell them. Being a user means understanding that housing is a social asset and not an

---

4   In 1984, with the election of the left-wing government, democracy had been restored from the right-wing dictatorship that had ruled the country since 1973.
5   UR: 1021, 32, value in Uruguayan Pesos as of February 2, 2018.

asset for exchange or a commodity. In addition, being a user involves having two important characteristics: one is ideological as it ties people together in developing a sense of responsibility within the context of the project (the houses and the dwellings, the commons in the house, the community and the neighbourhood); the second factor, here, is more practical in that it has to do with the users' rights and the rights of their children to grow up in a healthy and safe environment (Rodríguez interview 2013). When a family is not able to pay credit instalments on their dwelling or is only able to partially pay them, then the case is presented to the cooperative. In turn, the cooperative presents the case to the state, which can provide subsidies to the family.[6]

Figure 2: Distribution of tasks and roles in FUCVAM cooperatives, Montevideo.

Source: Author, 2013.

Capacity building is an important principle that comes from the cooperative's social capital. Several economic activities emerge during and after the construction process. First, the cooperative goes through a process of education that helps the families understand the dimensions and complexity behind working and

---

6   These subsidies come from official programmes that are generally for low- and very low-income families; these subsidies also depend on the families' income and composition (Nahoum 2013).

living in cooperatives. Second, there is a strong process of training and the building of skills and capacities during the process of housing construction.

This model that has been working in Uruguay since the 1970s and has served as a solid base from which to replicate organisations such as the MOI in Argentina when it stepped in with support to navigate the severe social effects of the economic crisis in 2001. The FUCVAM provides a clear example of how social capital in its interpretation of the three main pillars could be incorporated in public policy and the implementation of social housing projects. Social capital is seen as a means not only to achieve the right to adequate housing but also as a platform for socio-economic development. It is strongly connected to the city's deployment of the right to allow vulnerable members of the population to access serviced urban land, social and cultural services and infrastructure, education, employment, and mostly to enable them to have a voice in decision-making processes.

The last point was a crucial characteristic from the point of view of the MOI and other cooperatives in Buenos Aires. These social organisations were able to boost political processes that promoted and achieved the redistribution of state responsibilities in the drafting of social policies and the provision and management of funds for housing. By following the FUCVAM model, the MOI was able to institutionalize its three main pillars: self-management, mutual aid and collective ownership, the bases for the functioning of mutual-aid cooperatives in Uruguay. Although the cooperative composition is smaller in scale in the case of the cooperatives associated with the MOI,[7] this organisation functions under a very similar structure that has ensured its success in the production of social housing in the centrality of Buenos Aires.

---

7   By 2007 (the period between 2002 and 2007 saw the highest number of loans under adjudication) the MOI had 180 housing units under construction (Rodriguez 2011) in a city of 2,890,151 (according to the National Census 2010; Rodriguez and Huerta 2016). On the other hand, from 1966 the cooperative movement in Uruguay has built 30,000 housing units in a country of 3.5 million people (Del Castillo 2015).

Figure 3: Housing units under construction by FUCVAM cooperatives, Montevideo.

Source: Author, 2013.

NEW VALUES – SOCIAL CAPITAL

From the late 1980s to today, capitalism in its most aggressive form of neo-liberalism has negatively influenced the development of cities and society in the Global South (especially in Latin America). It has affected the great majority of the population, especially in their capacity to access decent housing. Nevertheless, it has also provoked the creation and consolidation of movements whose proposals have contributed to the transformation of their societies. These movements have put forward measures that are not only pertinent to developing countries but that can also be discussed and transferred to other contexts in which crises are having impacts in similar ways.

One of the most important characteristics of the social movements that are behind the experiences of the MOI in Argentina and the FUCVAM in Uruguay is their understanding of the problems and their comprehensive approach to looking for solutions. Normally the solutions provided by governments are uni-dimensional. The social and urban fragmentation and segregation could not be solved by only providing mass housing. For social needs to be better clarified and understood, this has required social movements to point out how to better understand the problems and how to integrate essential solutions to basic social needs. These solutions would not only allow the poor and marginalised to access adequate housing but also to access education skills and capacities, culture, employment and social inclusion.

Using social capital as a mechanism to achieve these goals shows that housing and especially social housing cannot be seen through the logic of a market that expects to profit from its construction. But social capital can be conceived under the logic of the type of social investment that allows the population to have a dignified standard of living and a platform that supports social mobility and development.

Although the main ideology behind self-management, mutual aid and collective ownership is one that asserts that these principles belong to a socialist view and their application is intended to break with capitalistic structures (Rodríguez 2009), these elements of social capital also include the potential for society in general to undergo a great transformation. Beyond the present resistance to the dominant system, there is the possibility of incorporating this ideological approach within capitalistic systems so these two models can both coexist and cooperate in providing opportunities to the most vulnerable. However, the conservative bureaucratic models must change and acknowledge the capacities and responsibilities of social organisations. In this way, the democratic autonomy of these organisations could be ensured.

Additionally, the principles of social capital have not yet been completely explored. Thus, a complete assessment of their potential has yet to be deployed. The failure to do so might be related to the stigma attached to collective ownership and its association with socialistic stands; these are often rejected in certain contexts. Also, there is no official mechanisms for the regularisation and implementation of principles and policies that support social capital.

There are many alternative ways to introduce social capital mechanisms into democratic processes. A closer look at the functioning of these tools, and their evaluation and monitoring in existing proposals and implemented projects, would be necessary as a step to understand how to introduce them widely into public policy. Two concluding remarks: first, organisations that are working collectively for the defence of housing as a right and a social benefit should receive more legal, technical and financial support from the state, and, second, stricter controls and regulations should be imposed over land value and private property so as to avoid speculation and to allow these organisations to access urban land in city centralities with the support of legal, technical and financial mechanisms.

REFERENCES

Calthorpe, P. and Fulton, W. B. (2001) 'Designing the Region and Designing the Region is Designing the Neighborhood,' in Calthorpe, P. and Fulton, W. B., eds., *The regional city for the end of Sprawl*, Washington: Island Press.

Casanova, M. (2017) 'Social Strategies Building the City: A Reconceptualisation of Social Housing,'in Mantziaras, P., Milbert, I. and Viganò, P., eds., *Inégalités Urbaines: Du Project Utopique au Développement Durable*, Geneva: Metis Presse, 33–48.

Casanova, M. (2019) *Social Strategies Building the City: A Reconceptualisation of Social Housing in Latin America*, Berlin: LIT Verlag.

Ciolli, V. (2011) 'Cooperativaspopulares: Nuevoscaminos para re-articular democrácia y justiciasocial,' in Di Virgilio, M., Herzer, H., Merlinsky, and G., Rodriguez, M. C., eds., *La cuestiónurbanainterrrogada. Transformacionesurbanas, ambientales y políticaspúblicasen Argentina*, Buenos Aires: Editorial Café de las Ciudades, 355–384.

Coraggio, J. L. (2002) 'La economía social comovía para otrodesarrollo social', available: http://www.redetis.iipe.unesco.org/publicaciones/la-economiasocial-como-via-para-otro-desarrollo-social/ [accessed 11 Aug 2017].

Curl, J. (2010) 'The Cooperative Movement in Century 21', *Affinities Journal*, 4 (1).

Del Castillo, A. (2015) 'Una exposiciónsobre las cooperativas de viviendaUruguayas,' in Del Castillo, A. andVallés, R., eds., *Cooperativas de viviendaen Uruguay, medio siglo de experiencias*, Montevideo: Facultad de Arquitectura, Universidad de la República, 57–84.

Fernández Wagner, R. (2011) 'La Producción Social del Hábitaten la ciudad injusta,' in Centro Cooperativo Sueco, *El Camino Posible. Producción social del hábitaten América Latina*, San José: Trilce, 59–76.

García-Guadilla, C. (2018) 'The Incorporation of Popular Sectors and Social Movements in Venezuelan Twenty First Century Socialism,' in Silva, E. and Rossi, F., eds., *Reshaping the Political Arena in Latin America: From Resisting Neo-liberalism to the Second Incorporation*, Pittsburg: University Press, 50–77.

Girola, M. F. and Thomaz, G. (2013) 'Del derecho a la vivienda al derecho a la cultura: reflexionessobre la constitución del derecho a la ciudad en Buenos

Aires desdeunaperspectivaetnográfica', *Anuário Antropológico*, available: https://journals.openedition.org/aa/593 [accessed on October 9, 2018].

International Co-operative Alliance ICA. *Uruguay: Housing, Self-Management, Community Empowerment: The Coop Experience*. Montevideo: Federation of Mutual Aid Housing Cooperatives (FUCVAM).

Kearns, A. and Forrest, R. (2000) 'Social cohesion and multilevel urban governance', *Urban Studies*, 37(5–6). 995–1017.

Nahoum, B. (2013) *Algunas Claves. Reflexionessobreaspectoseseciales de la vivienda cooperative porayuda mutual*, Montevideo: Trilce.

Ortiz Flores, E. (2011) 'Producción social de la vivienda y habitat: bases conceptuales para unapolíticapública.' *El camino possible Producción Social del Hábitaten América Latina*, Uruguay: TRILCE, Centro CooperativoSueco.

Portes, A. (1998) 'Social Capital: Its origins and applications in modern sociology', *Annual Review of Sociology* 24, 1–24.

Putnam, R. D. (1993) 'The Prosperous Community. Social Capital and Public Life', *The American Prospect*, 4 (13).

Raspall, T. (2010) *Características del cooperativismo de viviendaen la Ciudad de Buenos Aires en el período 2001–2008*, Buenos Aires: Centro de Estudios de Sociología del Trabajo.

Rodriguez, D (2013) Director of the FUCVAM. Interviewed by Marielly Casanova on November 2, 2013 in Montevideo.

Rodriguez, M. C. (2009) *Autogestión, políticas del habitat y transformación social*, Buenos Aires: Espacio Editorial.

Rodriguez, M. C. (2011) 'Sobre la transformación de la significación cultural del espaciovivido,' in Rodriguez, M. C. and Di Virgilio, M. M., eds., *Caleidoscopio de las políticasterritoriales: Un rompecabezas para armar*, Buenos Aires: PrometeoLibros, 387–400.

Rodriguez, M. C. and Huerta, C. (2016) *Diagnóstico socio-habitacional de la Ciudad de Buenos Aires, Buenos Aires*: CESBA.

Samara, T. R., He, S. and Chen, G. (2013) 'Introduction: Locating Right to the City in the Global South', in Samara, T. R., He, S. and Chen, G., eds., *Locating Right to the City in the Global South*, New York: Routledge, 1–20.

Sassen, S. (2011) *Ciudad y globalización*, Quito: Olacchi.

UN-Habitat (2012). *El FuturoUrbano*, 1er ForoUrbanoNacional, Medellín.

Velásquez Carrillo, F. (2004) 'Presentación: Pensar la ciudad enperspectiva de derechos,'in Velásquez Carrillo, F., eds., *Ciudad e Inclusión- Por el Derecho a la Ciudad*, Bogotá: Gente Nueva Editorial, 7–24.

Walton, J. (2001) 'Dept, protest and the State in Latin America,'in Eckstein, S. *Power and Popular Protest. Latin America Social Movements*, Berkley, Los Angeles, London: University of California Press, 299-328.

Zapata, M. C. (2013) *El Programa de Autogestión para la Vivenda: El ciclo devida de unapolíticahabitacionalhabilitante a la participación social y del derecho al hábitat y a la ciudad*, Universidad de Buenos Aires: Instituto de Invetigationes Gino Germani, (36).

Part II: Housing and Migration

Chapter 4: Understanding the Housing Needs of Low-Skilled Bangladeshi Migrants in Oman
Case Study of a Labour Camp and Migrant-Dominant Neighbourhood

Shaharin Annisa

INTRODUCTION

The Gulf region has a long history of migration. Over the years, the patterns of migration and the demographics of migrants within cities in the Gulf have changed. Before the 20th century, the Middle Eastern countries indulged in 'intra-regional' migration, with members of the Arab-speaking population that migrated in and out of the Middle East specialising in administration and education (Choucri 1986). During the 1930s, the intra-regional migration of both skilled and unskilled migrants was evident within Middle Eastern countries. The 1960s saw an upsurge in extra-regional migration, with labour moving from the Middle East to the West. However, with the oil boom of the 1970s, the focus of migration shifted back to the Middle East, namely to oil-rich Gulf countries. With rising oil prices, infrastructural development became economically possible and this increased the number of new jobs available for low-skilled workers, especially in the construction industry (Choucri 1986). As a theoretical concept, Maslow and Lewis' (1987) needs triangle and migration theories were assessed in regards to the sustainable livelihood framework developed by the UK's Department for International Development (DFID) (1997), wherein each livelihood asset (human, financial, social and physical) was studied in depth to identify the basic and psychological needs that were not being provided to migrant labourers in Oman. Further, laws, policies and processes were assessed following DFIF framework so as to understand the social and spatial standpoints of these low-skilled migrants during their temporary stays in the country and to identify the possible causes of their temporary situation. Finally, this study takes into account Lefebvre's (1991) concepts of both the social production and appropriation of space so as to understand how and why low-skilled migrants undertake the temporary development of their own housing and the use of open spaces in order to provide for their basic needs.

This article aims to answer two research questions: First, what is the state of Oman's existing available housing provision for its migrant workers? Second, what are the basic spatial and social needs of low-skilled Bangladeshi migrants living in Oman?

A qualitative research approach was taken, starting with 174 interviews of Bangladeshi professional, skilled and low-skilled migrants who were living in different locations across Oman during the time of the study. The aim of these interviews was to understand the general wellbeing or livelihood status of the interviewees and to understand the selection of their housing typology. An attempt was made to identify the rental prices of these dwellings, but unfortunately, we were not successful. This limitation was due to the lack of trust between the interviewer and the interviewee, which made it impossible to obtain honest answers on rental agreements from among the respondents; there was also a lack of valid quantitative data on property/housing rents. The results of these interviews provided answers to the first research question and these are documented in this chapter under the title Housing typology of Bangladeshi migrants living in Oman.

In order to answer the second research question, 20 low-skilled migrants were interviewed using a narrative approach to the case study. Ten interviewees, each either from a labour camp or a migrant-dominant inner-city neighbourhood, were selected and interviewed. The results were recorded in a graphical representation that provides a life-history mapping; development of livelihood assets (in the form of an assets pentagon which provides information on the livelihood status of individuals by looking at their human, financial, spatial, and social situations); and the development of a livelihood strategy matrix (Annisa 2018). Furthermore, spatial mapping was used to understand the usage of indoor and outdoor spaces in labour camps and migrant neighbourhoods, respectively. This is documented as a housing typology map that includes floor plans of low-skilled migrant dwellings.

BACKGROUND

The Sultanate of Oman, being part of the Gulf Cooperation Council (GCC), has followed the region's trend of inviting temporary workers from Southeast Asian countries to work in low-paying jobs in the country. Oman is situated on the southeast coast of the Arabian Peninsula. It has a total population of approximately 4.6 million, of which 44% are expatriates and 56% are Omani nationals (NSCI 2018). From 1973 to the present, there has been a steady increase in the number of Southeast Asian migrants coming to Oman. The work of Birks and Sinclair (1978) (as cited by Choucri (1986)) shows that, by 1975, Oman had become the second highest preferred destination of Southeast Asian migrants (notably Indians and Pakistanis), after Dubai. According to the National Centre for Statistics and Information (NCSI), in 2013, fully 89% of all foreign workers in Oman were employed (the remaining 11% being family dependents) (NCSI, 2014), of which 87% originated from Southeast Asian countries, such as India, Bangladesh, Pakistan and Sri-Lanka (GLMM 2014). Furthermore, it was noted that, in 2014, Southeast Asians predominated blue collar jobs, with 74% having attained below a secondary level of education (GLMM 2014). These statistics also help us understand that the highest population of migrants in Oman are single, low-skilled Southeast Asian individuals. Until 2016, Indian workers took up the first rank, being the highest number of migrants in the country, with 39.4% of the total migrant population in that country (NCSI 2018). However, by 2018, the percentage of registered Bangladeshis in Oman had fallen to 34%, still surpassing the 33.6% of Indian migrant workers (NCSI 2018); this and the fact the Bangla language and connections within the Bangladeshi community in the city of Muscat are seen as a strength compelled the researcher to prioritise an investigation into the dominant Bangladeshi community for the selection of the case studies presented in this chapter.

THEORIES OF TRANSNATIONAL MIGRATION

Every migrant labourer entering Oman requires an employment visa. These are only valid for a limited period of time wherein every visa type ties these migrants to a certain employment status (ROP 2018). Furthermore, under the Gulf's unique employment system (Kafala system), every employee is bound by law to their employer, who takes financial and legal responsibility for them (Longva 1999). Thus, the employee is bound to their employer and is not legally permitted to work for any other employer/sponsor (Oman Labour Code, Article

18Bis). This effectively limits the options of low-skilled migrant workers in terms of both work and housing. In regards to the location of work, some migrants are housed in labour camps in proximity to work place. Residents of labour camps face this challenge as they are provided temporary housing in labour camps and are thus segregated from city centres and do not have the option of selecting the location of their stay.

Migrant labourers are recruited to the Gulf in a complex process that involves a number of stakeholders in both the home and host countries and which can be explained by institutional theory (Massey *et al.* 1993). Further, migratory networks theory explains these migrants' dependency on the social networks that provide them with personal connections to former migrants in the host country (Massey *et al.* 1987), where these networks prove to be "valuable adaptive resources" in an alien environment (Massey *et al.* 1987, p. 147). With the help of these networks, illegal channels of migration have given rise to a type of visa that is locally known as a "free visa", where the migrants are bound to an employer on paper but, in reality, have no connection to these employers (Rahman 2011). As these visas are not recognised by law, the employer is not bound by law to provide these labourers with acceptable housing or safe working conditions at legally established wages. Migrants that fit under this category are accepted by various employers who employ them either on contract or on hourly bases to perform short-term tasks. These poorly paid migrants seek out affordable housing close to city centres, where they rely on their social networks to find information on job opportunities. Migrant networks help migrants sustain themselves economically, making it viable for them to live and work in a host country, and they tend to accumulate in migrant-dominant neighbourhoods in order to benefit from the social capital that exists there.

In today's globalised world, the dual-market theory of Piore (1979) implies that low-skilled migrants become part of a secondary sector in the job market where they take up difficult, low paid, labour-intensive jobs that nationals refuse to do. In addition to the lack of integration schemes and nationalisation policies in the Gulf, this phenomenon not only creates a segmented employment sector but also waters down the concept of a parallel society, where residents of the host and home countries segregate themselves from each other by living in enclaves within the same city with each practising their own ethnicity, culture and traditions.

In his hierarchy of needs triangle, Maslow and Leiws (1987) identify three kinds of needs: basic, psychological and self-fulfillment needs, which contribute to the efficient functioning of the human mind and body; all of these aspects need to be touched upon. Basic needs are divided into physiological needs, such as food, water, and warmth; safety needs, including security and safety; and psychological needs, which are categorised into the need for belongingness and the need for love, and these are acquired through friends and intimate relationships; and esteem needs, which include prestige and feelings of accomplishment. It is evident that Oman's labour camps provide low-skilled migrants with basic needs; however, these camps fail to provide these people with opportunities to fulfill their psychological and self-fulfillment needs. Evidence shows that the latter two needs are seen to be fulfilled through the development of livelihood strategies in migrant-dominant neighbourhoods by the migrants themselves (Annisa 2018).

With an increase in the institutionalization processes of migration and in the technological advances that have taken place during our century, it has become easier for migrants to maintain connections between their home and host countries. Following this trend in migration, the term 'transnationalism' was coined in a new discourse in 1990 (Schiller *et al.* 1992). Schiller and colleagues define transnational migration as 'the process by which immigrants forge and sustain simultaneous multi-stranded social relations that link together their societies of origin and settlement' (Schiller *et al.* 1995, p. 48). Under this paradigm, '[f]amilial, economic, social, organisational, religious and political' connections and networks run effectively across physical borders (Schiller *et al.* 1992: ix). Transnational migrants have more than one location they refer to as 'home'. Their necessities and constraints are no longer bound to one region and, instead, expand over home and host countries. They develop strategies of adaptation on both an individual and communal level (Schiller *et al.* 1995). Their usage of space is affected by and developed as a product of their transnational relationships. In addition to Maslow's definition of basic needs, this paper concludes with a number of added aspects that can be considered as 'basic needs' for low-skilled transitory migrants living in Oman.

When considering the UN Sustainable Development Goals (SDG), focussing on Goal 11: To make cities resilient, sustainable and inclusive, the urgency of providing the basic, psychological and esteem needs of migrants becomes of high importance. Furthermore, taking into consideration Goal 3: Good health and wellbeing, it is essential for the Gulf countries to consider the living conditions of their low-skilled labourers working under a temporary state. Given that the GCC's large portion of low-skilled migrant workers continues to prove beneficial to the region's economic and infrastructural development, catering to these people's needs in relation to the efficient functioning of their wellbeing becomes important.

HOUSING PROVISION FOR OMANIS, GCC NATIONALS AND HIGH TO MEDIUM-SKILLED MIGRANTS

With the 1970s oil boom and a push to move towards Oman Vision 2020, the Sultanate of Oman began a period of rapid development that focused on infrastructure, housing, health and education. In 1980, as part of this development, the government of Oman initiated a land lottery system for Omani nationals; its aim was to provide and regulate the country's housing stock.

According to this policy, every Omani male citizen, from the 1980s on, and every Omani female citizen, from 2003, on, was eligible to enter into a draw to receive a plot of land in Oman (MOH 2009). This system encouraged Omani families to move to peripheries where larger plots were available. Furthermore, the social housing policy that was developed in 1973 offered three systems to aid low-income Omanis, who were earning less than 300 – 400 Rials (USD700 to 1000), to obtain housing (Al Shabia Housing law 1973). Under this program, the government provides residential units (a built dwelling) to households; further, the Ministry of Housing's housing assistance program provides 20,000 OMR (USD 52,000) to rebuild, construct, or restore a dwelling; and the housing loan programme provides loans to low-income Omanis for the construction of their dwelling (MOH 2009). In 2002, the government of Oman decided to permit GCC nationals to own real estate. In 2006, it permitted high-income expatriates (high-skilled migrants only) to own property in three locations within the Sultanate, under a programme that allowed them to own high-end dwellings in integrated tourism complexes (ITCs) where recreational facilities were available. Once this investment is made, the expatriate is eligible to apply for citizenship (OBG n.d.). While the news media have reported on various discussions about permitting long-term migrants to own property outside the ITCs, since 2016 nothing has yet been confirmed. Therefore, migrants are not permitted to own property outside the ITCs in Oman. Further, as the prices of these properties are high, they are far out of reach of Oman's low-skilled migrant population.

Figure 1: Prominent laws and policies in Oman regarding housing

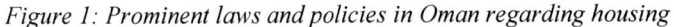

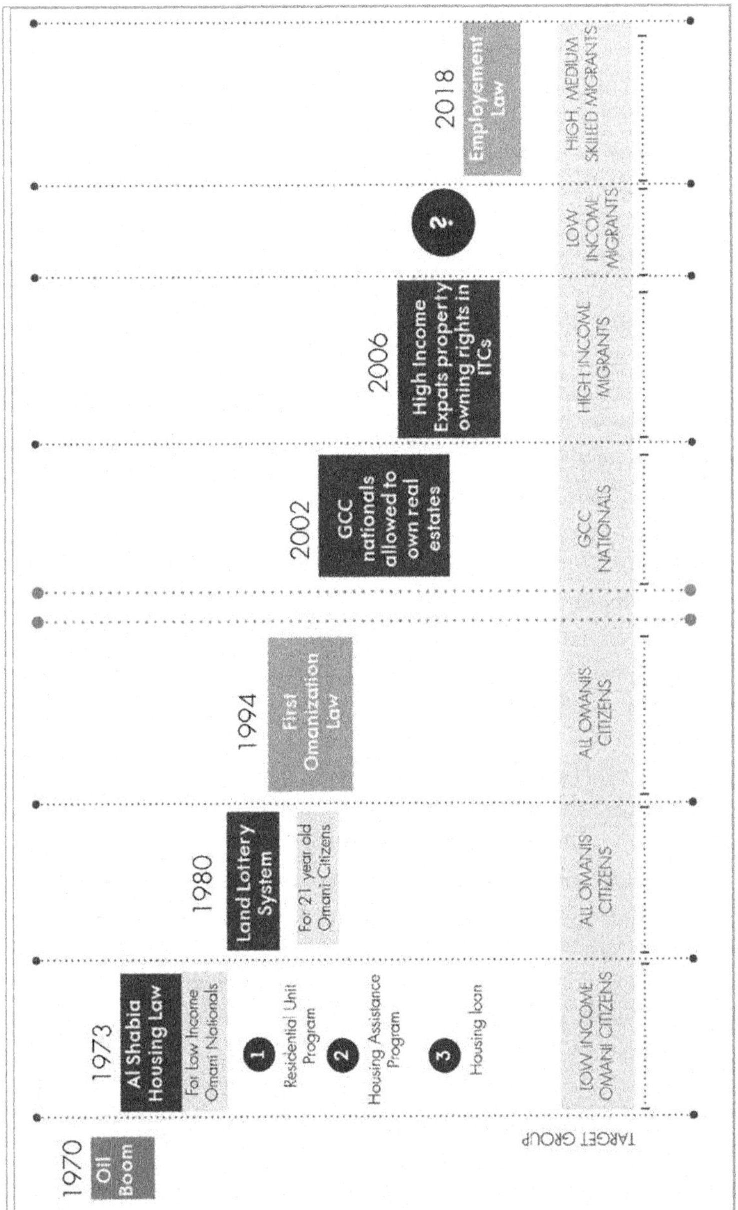

Source: Author, 2018.

The land lottery system has been heavily criticised by authors such as Al Gharibi (2014) and Nebel and von Richthofen (2016), who stated that this system has resulted in urban sprawl and has encouraged car-based mobility as the allocated lands are distant from economic centres. As such, the land lottery system and social housing policy have encouraged the movement of Omani nationals away from crowded older city centres and into the peripheries, causing an impact on inner-city neighbourhoods, such as Mattrah, Ruwi and Wadi Kabir. These neighbourhoods now consist of low-rent properties, largely rented to migrant families and individuals.

Housing provision for low-skilled migrants

A large number of low-skilled migrants are housed in labour camps that are situated in close proximity to their work sites; others live in apartment buildings or villas that employers rent out as shared housing to their employees (Gardner 2010). Each type of dwelling may differ in form and appearance but what they have in common is segregation. Notably, the most common deficiency in these spaces is any mode of recreation, open spaces and possibilities for informal activities. Being stripped away of basic necessities and living in camps that are located far from city centres often causes boredom, leading to mental health problems (Bruslé 2012). Further, these low-skilled (unmarried) migrant workers are perceived as a social threat to locals in terms of inappropriate social behaviours and are, thus, tucked away where they are not visible in what is perceived as the formal city (Elshashtawy 2008). Qatar, for example, goes so far as to plan mini "bachelor cities" for their migrant population in order to move them "out of public view" (Gardner 2010). Dubai's attempt at this is to create "luxury labour camps", which are strictly planned in a grid with housing and shopping facilities but are placed outside the city. Furthermore, Oman is currently working on plans for "bachelor colonies" and has delegated three plots for the development of large-scale housing for single migrant workers. Muscat municipality has located plots in Amrat, Bawshar and Mabella, which are known for being the city's industrial sites (Das 2017).

Housing typologies of migrants in Oman

However, these types of complexes are presently in the planning process and are not yet available for residents. But the question remains: how effective are these labour camps for the low-skilled migrants' livelihoods and wellbeing? This part of the paper analyses one such labour camp and documents the adaptations and modifications low-skilled migrants have created so as to provide for their own basic social and spatial needs.

Figure 2: Housing typology based on skill level and affordability.

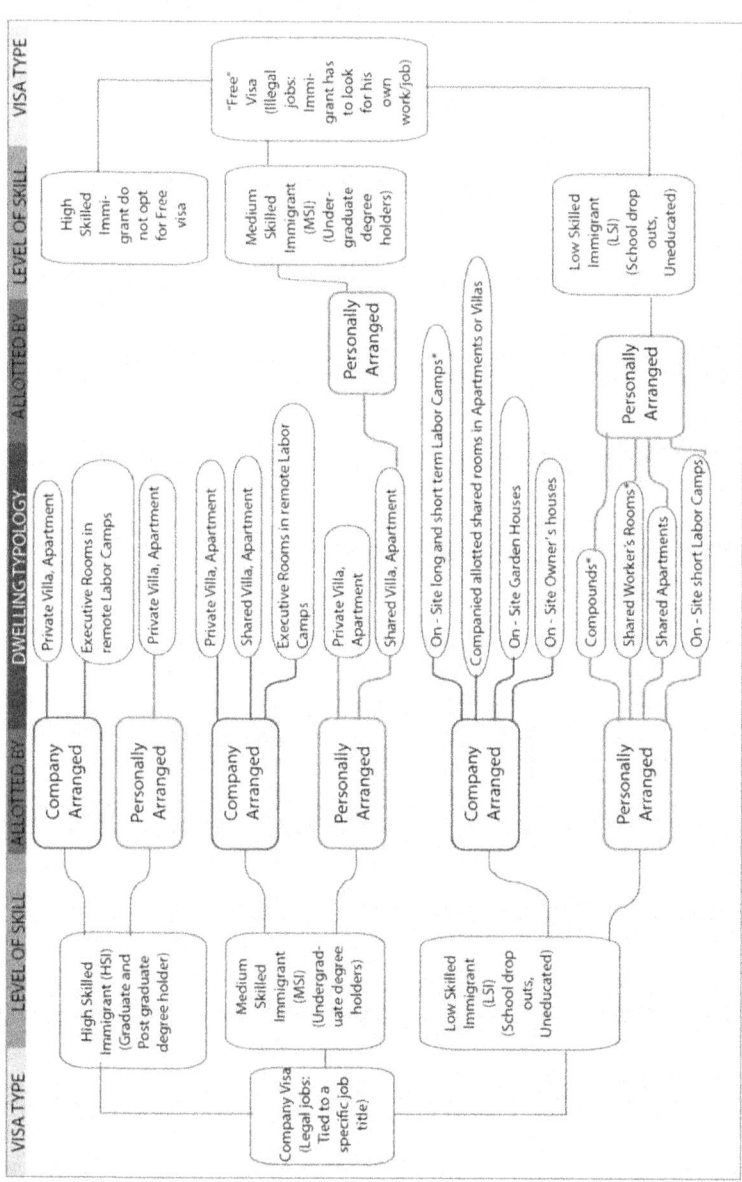

Source: Author, 2018.

A strong phenomenon was noted regarding low-skilled migrants' housing selection: Their visa type seemed to be corelated to their housing selection. The concept of a 'free visa' has given rise to illegal forms of work. On paper, migrants with these types of visas had employers and therefore automatically had job contacts but, in reality, their visa type placed them far from their skill level and, therefore, they lived on short-term free-lance jobs they found for themselves. These free visas were commonly used by low-skilled migrants who were in desperate need of migrating to Oman as a livelihood strategy. Therefore, low-skilled migrants who were on a free visa opted to live in migrant-dominant neighbourhoods where their social capital was high and it was easier to find short-term contracts for free-lance jobs. In these migrant neighbourhoods, they devised intensive shared housing typologies due to the lack of affordable housing.

Lessons learned from the case study of the labour camps

A case-study camp was selected whose name is withheld for privacy issues. Gaining access to labour camps is difficult; thus, for the purposes of the case study, the camp selection was done on the basis of successful access through the author's social networks. The camp in question has characteristics of a typical labour camp in the Gulf region but, in addition, has adaptive spatial and social features that the inhabitants had developed in order to fulfill particular dire needs.

The selected labour camp is situated on the periphery of the capital city, between Muscat and Barka, and it houses about 600 inhabitants. The closest town is 10 km away and the closest largest municipal area, Barka, is about 15 km away. The nearest mosque, petrol station and grocery store can be reached by car within approximately 30 to 40 minutes. The labour camp is situated inside a construction area and is closed off by a boundary wall and only accessible via its main gates. A typical labour camp consists of worker's cabins, executive cabins for management, a kitchen, a dining area, and toilets and a washing area; thus, catering to some aspects of Maslow and Lewis' (1987) basic physiological needs but failing to cater to psychological and esteem needs. With a combination of an empathetic camp manager and empowered inhabitants, the case-study labour camp has successfully developed adaptive features that cater to the needs of its resident migrant workers (Figure 3).

Figure 3: Case study labour camp.

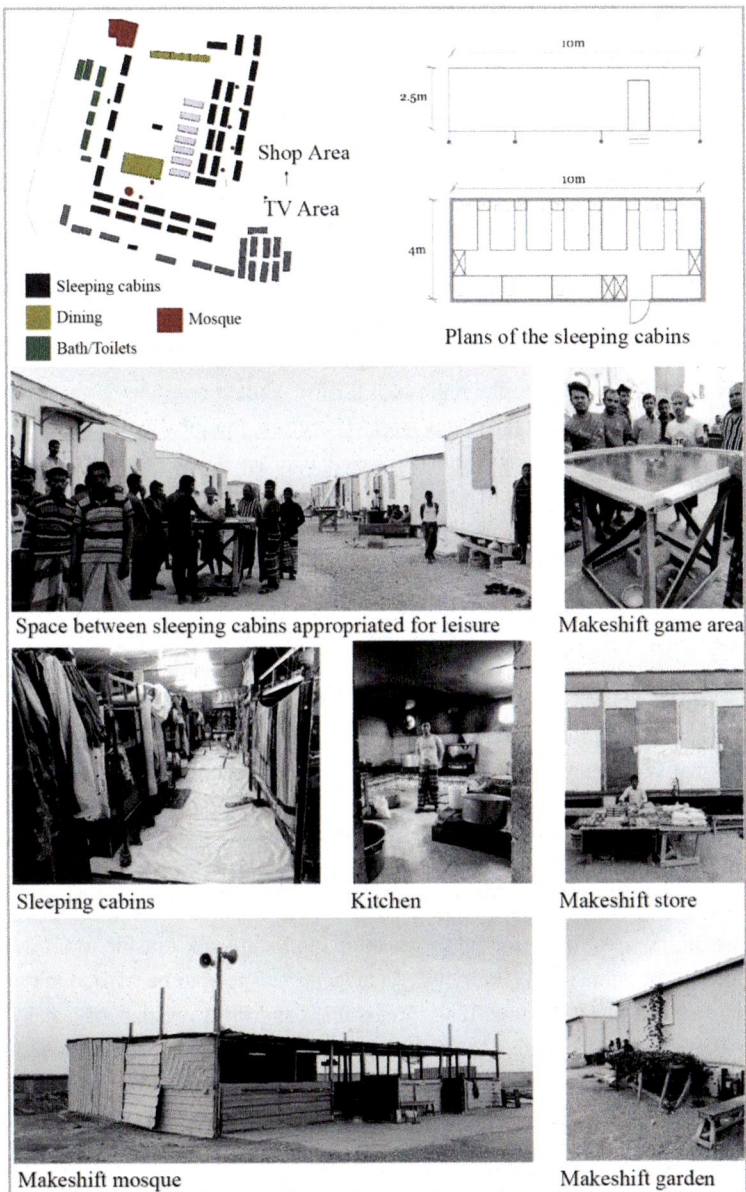

Source: Author, 2018.

Portable cabins of 40 square metres each were built with lightweight concrete walls, and cardboard and tin-plate roofs, mounted on concrete blocks that raise them half a metre off the ground. The two-by-one metre bunk beds and closed windows permits these cabins to accommodate the maximum number of inhabitants possible in such as small space (Figure 3). Small cupboards and spaces under the beds are used as storage for personal belongings and the structure of the beds means they can also be used for drying clothes. Thus, each cabin not only lacks optimum natural ventilation and daylight but also personal space. This increases the need for being outdoors. Mapping of the inhabitants' daily routines showed that they had nothing to do after work. A lack of gathering points, TV areas, and recreational activities was mentioned by 89% of the inhabitants. From the literature review and the interviews, it is evident that internet and news channels on TV are the main tool for low-skilled migrants in the Gulf to keep their transnational connections alive. Therefore, the inhabitants were not only segregated from their host country but were also separated from their home country. The camp had no on-site grocery stores, leaving the inhabitants dependent on car mobility to purchase food and other daily necessities.

Furthermore, 83% of the inhabitants of this labour camp are Muslims with a need to pray five times a day, but no mosque or praying area was provided. These conditions led the inhabitants of this particular camp to get together to cater to their own needs. They built a makeshift mosque within the camp for their use (fig 3, bottom left). They self-funded a TV for themselves as a free-time activity and to stay connected to the on-goings in Bangladesh. They developed informal vendors within the camp, where simple groceries and phone cards were sold during the evenings (Figure 3, middle left). They built makeshift game boards to gather around in their free time (Figure 3, top right). The informal vendors, makeshift game areas, and TV area are all located around one location which is close to the designated kitchen and dining area. 'Almost no one eats inside the dining area, they line up to get their food and walk outside to crowd around the TV or game area' (Interview: Manager). The need to be outside in the fresh air surfaced in many interviews. Vegetables and meat are part of a daily diet for Bangladeshis. In order to cater to this need, some inhabitants brought special seeds from Bangladesh and grow them inside the camp. Breeding chickens is also noted. For some of the camp dwellers, this and growing vegetables are also considered free-time activities as they were accustomed to doing these back "home" (Figure 3, bottom left). 'I am from a farmer's family. We live in the village. It is impossible for me not to grow my own vegetables. I do it for fun. I also like running behind the chickens. They remind me of home.' (Interview: Inhabitant). Thus, by catering to their own needs, these camp dwellers were able to increase their human, financial and social capital.

Lessons learned from migrant neighbourhood: Al-Hamriya

After careful analysis of different areas in the capital city Muscat, Al-Hamriya was chosen for this case study. This is because Bangladeshi migrants dominate its demography and it is also relatively easy to access.

Figure 4: Four different housing typologies found in Al-Hamriya show that the typology of the compound dominates the area.

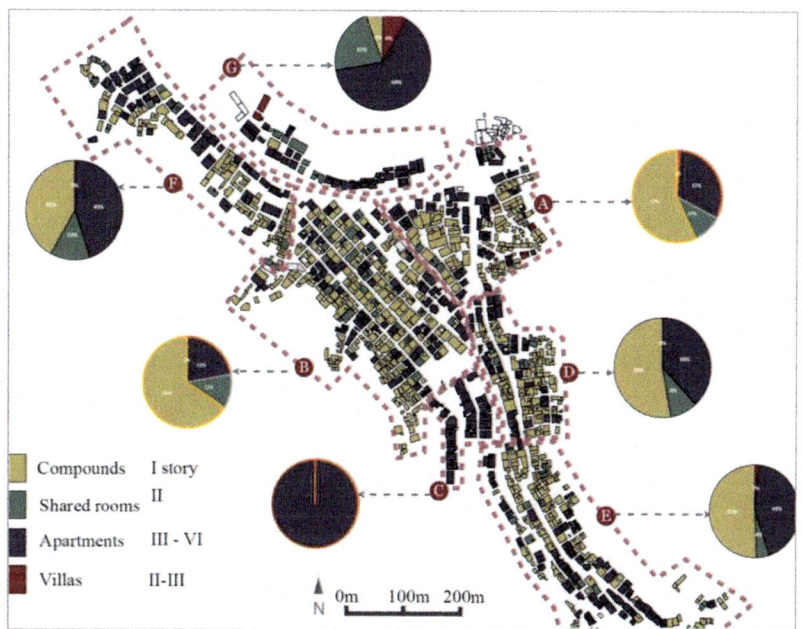

Source: Author, 2018.

Al-Hamriya is located in Ruwi, which is one of the oldest neighbourhoods in Muscat. During the 1980s, Ruwi's development focused on commercial, industrial and residential construction. Three types of residential categories were planned for: a high-rent area in the north, medium-rent districts located behind major commercial strips, and low-rent districts in the south. Development in Al-Hamriya fell under the last category (Scholz 1990), thus having a history of being inhabited by a low-income population. This area is homogenous in terms of the height of its buildings and the fact it mainly functions as a residential area with a strip of mixed-use buildings along one street. There were no planned recreational spaces owing to the fact that it was developed to house temporary residents. Today, Al-Hamriya is a preferred destination of absconders (Safar and Levelland 2015), free visa holders and runaways. This neighbourhood consists of a large number of financially vulnerable inhabitants who live and work there illegally. During our interviews, we found that these people selected Al-Hamriya because of the strong social networks within its Bangladeshi community; its proximity to the city centre; the availability of short-term contract jobs; and the ability to rent affordable rooms semi-legally (Annisa 2018).

Land and housing in Al-Hamriya can only be owned by an Omani national. Migrants are not legally allowed to do so. Omanis rent a large number of residential buildings to migrants (commonly referred to as migrant owners) and these migrant owners further sub-rent units in these building to other migrants (Tenant B, C, D…) without checking the legal residence or work status of these sub-tenants. These migrant owners' aim to make an optimum profit by renting units out to a large number of tenants. At the same time, the migrant tenants' aim is to minimise their living costs by minimising their rental space. These intensive shared-housing units in Al-Hamriya are commonly referred to as 'compounds'. The internal spatial organisation of a compound is very similar to that of the portable cabins in the labour camps. However, unlike in a labour camp, the migrants themselves opt for this spatial organisation, owing to their livelihood strategy of 'minimising living costs and self-developing shared housing' (Annisa 2018, p. 98).

A compound is a typology of housing where single rooms or units of rooms are clustered around a courtyard (Figure 5). Spaces within these compounds are used to the maximum possible efficiency and to accommodate basic needs. Each room contains from 6 to 18 single beds, depending on the size (Figure 5). On average, a person gets about 2.3sqm of personal space in a compound. Each compound contains a kitchen, a bathroom, a washing area and toilets, which all the inhabitants share. Internal walls are added to ease the flow and division of space between individuals. Often, additional holes are cut into the walls in order to install air-conditioning. Extra plumbing is added to create washing areas or toilets, and staircases are added to gain access to the roof. Additional floors are also added, depending on the need. Due to the shortage of space inside these rooms, residents often put a couch or a chair in the courtyard or store other things there. Within the courtyards of these compounds, migrants were noted to plant vegetables and fruits that are specific to Bangladesh and to take care of them. According to one interviewee, 'In my free time, I take care of my vegetables, it reminds me of Bangladesh. Not only me, there are other friends of mine who does the same. It's fun. (Interviewee, Inhabitant of a compound in Al-Hamriya). So often the courtyard substitutes as a living space, whereas the rooftops, streets and thresholds are often used as refuges from these people's crowded rooms (Figure 5). Even during warm evenings in the peak of summer, residents in need of personal space will climb to the roof. Owing to these migrants' livelihood strategy of maximising their modes of income (Annisa 2018), a large part of their daily life depends on networking and job-searching. Being visible in public gathering points is essential. These are primarily spaces that are situated between mixed-use buildings that provide higher chances of socialisation and thus are the main areas migrants are attracted to for such activities. A larger cluster of shops, restaurants and coffee shops provides seating opportunities in outdoor spaces. During the interviews, the inhabitants noted that, over time, these places have developed into hotspots, which recruiters and job-hunters refer to as "manpower supply points" or temporary informal markets where individual vendors sell vegetables, fruits and fish. Occasionally, fruit trucks enter these areas, also contributing to the informal activities that take place there (Figure 5).

Conducting an economic activity without a valid permit is illegal in Muscat. Therefore, vendors do not use furniture or stalls but sell their products out of trucks or cars; thus, they have developed quick ways to display their goods and to clear out on short notice. Intense social and informal economic interactions were documented within these spaces, such as conversations between multiple people, temporarily playing on makeshift game boards that are popular in Bangladesh, selling phone cards, drinking tea and enjoying snacks. The lack of parks and recreational spaces in Al-Hamriya has also encouraged residents to take over the larger spaces between buildings and parking lots for recreational activities, such as cricket and football (Figure 5). Makeshift game boards are developed (Figure 5). Drinking tea and chatting with friends are the most common activities noted. Conclusively, these communal spots are noted as the busiest locations, within Al-Hamriya, that are temporarily appropriated by the inhabitants themselves in response to their need to increase their financial and social capital, to respond to their need for esteem and to attend to their psychological welfare.

Figure 5: The housing typology of the compound dominates the area in Al-Hamriya.

Source: Author, 2018.

CONCLUSION

The temporary appropriation of indoor and outdoor spaces in both case studies can be taken as an indication of city management failing to provide basic social and spatial needs to low-skilled migrant workers in a system where members of this population are considered temporary and hosted in Oman for only short periods of time. However, this temporary situation has been reoccurring, most notably, since the oil boom of the 1970s. Therefore, more permanent infrastructure is called for, such as housing, mobility options and recreational spaces. Further, the development of compounds is illegal and must be enforced by law. If no other affordable housing options are legally available, then low-skilled and low-paid migrants will automatically be left to provide for their own needs. Thus, the need to provide legal affordable housing options should be a high priority.

Migrants who wish to maximise their incomes (Annisa 2018) need to be close to city centres or at least have adequate access to mobility options to travel to city centres. Policies that focus on these factors, in relation to migrant workers, tap into psychological and esteem needs in addition to respecting the SDGs Goal 11 of developing inclusive, safe, resilient and sustainable cities.

Both case studies show that migrants workers in Oman depend, live and function with the support of social capital, such as personal interactions, ties and trust. Communal gathering points, be they within labour camps or neighbourhoods, must be considered. The careful study of informal vendors in the labour camps and informal markets in neighbourhoods show the need for providing options for ethnic food and drink. Such activities should not be discouraged. It was also noted that transnational connections (economic or social) are established through access to television and telephones. Talking to their loved ones is an essential part of every interviewee's daily routine, and options for such activities are recommended regardless of whether these people live in a camp or a neighbourhood. Both of the case studies also show that recreational spaces are non-existent and temporary appropriation is strongly visible. Therefore, recreational spaces for playing sports or providing other options where migrants can spend time together, for growing vegetables and breeding chickens, for example, should be taken into consideration. The same goes for areas for praying and access to mosques. Religious rituals provide migrants with a strong connection to their roots, connections they value most when situated in foreign lands. Therefore, providing religious spaces is also recommended. A lack of indoor spaces has triggered the use of outdoor space, even during times of the day when it is extremely hot and humid. However, being present in outdoor spaces and increasing their social capital by interacting with others develops into a norm for this group of migrants; thus, outdoor sitting/gathering options are encouraged.

It is important to recognise that, while discussing the housing needs of a low-skilled migrant, the word 'house' for them does not necessarily mean a private space with four walls and a key to the front door but a place they willingly share and that is open to others. In a foreign land, these individuals are alone. And as they come from a family-oriented society, these individuals find family in the others around them and therefore prioritise social interaction. Thus, in addition to providing basic needs for sleeping, personal washing and cooking, the development of housing that includes spaces that encourage social interaction is highly necessary. The rooms can be small: the kitchen and bathrooms can be shared, but large living rooms, areas with TV or WiFi, areas for praying, courtyards and areas for planting are highly recommended. It is important to understand that housing should also incorporate the social and spatial needs of this group. Not everything can be planned. This group should take charge of their informal needs, themselves. Small informal vendors that undertake small economic activities seem to be highly successful in attracting a crowd. People gather near these vendors in search of something familiar, be it a product from Bangladesh or a chance to speak in Bangla. It is recommended that such spaces not be termed illegal; rather, they should be encouraged as they provide low-skilled migrants with opportunities to increase their financial and, more importantly, their social capital.

Finally, with the global agenda of working towards safe, resilient and inclusive cities, the status of low-skilled migrants within Gulf cities needs to be addressed (see also Mukaddim et al. in Chapter 7 for a discussion on addressing the status of migrants). While the countries of the Gulf region are assessing their sustainable development goals, policy-makers should not forget to include the high percentage of the low-skilled migrant population that lives and works there, paying special attention to Goal 3: Good health and wellbeing and Goal 11: Sustainable cities and communities.

REFERENCES

Al Gharibi, H. (2014) *Urban growth from patchwork to sustainability case study: Muscat.* (PhD Dissertation), Technical University Berlin.

Annisa, S. (2018) *Livelihood strategies of low-skilled Bangladeshi migrants living in Oman*, unpublished thesis (MSc. Thesis), University of Stuttgart.

Bruslé, T. (2012) What Kind of Place is this? Daily Life, Privacy and the Inmate Metaphor in a Nepalese Workers' Labour Camp Qatar, *Revisiting Space and Place: South Asian Migrations in Perspective*, 6.

Choucri, N. (1986) 'Asians in the Arab world: labour migration and public policy', *Middle Eastern Studies*, 252–273.

Das, R. (2017) 'Cities plan for single expatriates in Oman', *Times of Oman*, 16 Sep, available: https://timesofoman.com/article/117255 [Accessed 22 mar 2018].

Elsheshtawy, Y. (2008) 'Transitory sites: mapping Dubai's 'forgotten' urban spaces', *International Journal of Urban and Regional Research*, 32(4), 968–988.

Gardner, A. M. (2010) 'Labor camps in the Gulf States', *Viewpoints: Migration and the Gulf*, The Middle East Institute, 55–57.

Ghobash, M. (1986) *Immigration and Development in the United Arab Emirates*, Cairo: Al Wafa Press.

Gulf Labor Market Migration and population programm (GLMM) (2014) *Oman: Employed population by country of citizenship* [online], available: http://gulfmigration.org/oman-employed-population-by-country-of-citizenship-mid-2014/ [accessed 1st oct 2018].

Lee, S. M. (1996) 'Issues in Research on Women, International Migration and Labor', *Asian and Pacific Migration Journal*, 5(1), 5–26.

Mansour, S. (2017) Spatial concentration patterns of South Asian low-skilled immigrants in Oman: A spatial analysis of residential geographies, Volume 88, 118–129.

Martin, P. (2005) *Merchants of labor: Agents of the evolving migration infrastructure*. Geneva: International Labor Organization.

Maslow, A. and Lewis, K. J. (1987) *Maslow's hierarchy of needs*, Salenger Inco-rporated, 14, 987.

Ministry of Housing (MOH) (2009) *Residential land* [online], available at:https://eservices.housing.gov.om/eng/Pages/ResidentialLanding.aspx [Accessed 15 Sep. 2019].

Ministry of Housing (MOH) (2009) *Social housing services.* [online], available: https://eservices.housing.gov.om/eng/Pages/HS-Apply.aspx [accessed 15 Sep 2019].

Nebel, S. and Von Richthofen, A. (2016) *Urban Oman*, Münster: LIT Verlag.

National Centre for Statistics and Information (NCSI) (2018) *Population clock 2018*, [online], available:https://www.ncsi.gov.om/aboutus/Pages/PopulationClock.aspx [accessed 1 Oct. 2018].

National Centre for Statistics and Information (NCSI) (2018) *NCSI's home page*, available: http://www.ncsi.gov.om/NCSI_website/N_Default.aspx (English) http://www.ncsi.gov.om/NCSI_website/N_default [Accessed 22nd June2018].

Oxford Business Group (OBG) (n.d.) *Integrated tourism complexes have been a success in Oman* [online], available: https://oxfordbusinessgroup.com/analysis/complex-developments-integrated-tourism-complexes-have-been-success-sultanate-and-look-set-expand [accessed 1st Oct 10].

Scholz, F. (2010) *Muscat: Then and Now: Geographical Sketch of a Unique Arab Town,* Verlag Hans Schiller.

Safar, J. and levaillant, M. (n.d.) 'Irregular migration in Oman: policies, their effects and interaction with India', in Fargues, P. and Nasra, S., eds., *Skilful Survivals: Irregular migration to the Gulf*, glmm,115–3.

Chapter 5: Between Need for Housing and Speculation

Urban Expansion in the City of Tarija, Bolivia

Fabio Bayro-Kaiser

INTRODUCTION

By 2050, around two thirds of the global population will be living in an urban environment. Therefore, recent international agreements on the issue of sustainable development have centred the debate around urbanisation and the considerable challenges cities face (UN-Habitat 2017; WBGU 2016). Seventy per cent of the world´s economic activity takes places within cities; moreover, cities are responsible for 70% of worldwide greenhouse gas emissions, 70% of global waste, and over 60% of global energy consumption (UN-Habitat 2017). Furthermore, growing cities also consume large pieces of land as they continue to expand through rural-urban migration, migration between cities, and displacements through political conflicts or natural disasters, among other factors.

In recent years, the rate of urbanisation has become more critical in developing countries; in particular, Latin American trends in urbanisation are among the highest in the world and it is expected that the region's cities will continue to grow (UN-WUP 2018). In this context, informality is seen as a generalised mode of urbanisation (Roy 2005). The challenges posed by a development that often results in increasing social inequality and environmental damage have been widely discussed (Angotti 1995; Butterworth 1981; Rodgers *et al.* 2012). What comes to mind, here, is the often-used picture of a São Paolo favela that is segregated from the city's wealthier neighbourhoods. New approaches and agenda(s) where especially discussed in 2016, during UN-Habitat III (UN-Habitat 2017). Moreover, McGuirk`s (2014) comprehensive research around housing and settlement development in various cities in Latin America has shown the failure of politics, planning, and architecture to address this complicated issue, mainly due to the lack of success in linking formal and informal modes of urban development.

Not all cities have the same dynamic as mega cities such as São Paolo or Mexico City. Bolivia, for instance, has developed three metropolitan regions and 34 medium-sized cities; approximately five million people live in the metropolitan regions, which makes for almost half of the Bolivian population (PNUD 2015). And as research has mainly focused on the larger cities, dramatic changes in small- to medium-sized cities may have been overlooked. As mentioned before, cities are expected to grow due to migration. But is this the case for all cities? And what dynamic does their expansion follow? Furthermore, it is well-known that land markets will continue to play an important role in the future development of cities. But does a profit-oriented land market always act in the interest of the common good? How are planning institutions avoiding the negative side-effects of a speculative land market that benefits from a need-for-housing discourse? These initial reflexions address the issue of land speculation and challenge the common notion of the impact of an ever-increasing demand for housing; however, they can only be answered on a specific case-study basis. Therefore, building on the premise that densification in existing structures is a more economic and sustainable way of addressing the need for housing, this chapter analyses urban expansion in the city of Tarija, raising the question of whether urban expansion is triggered by migration and a demand in housing or whether it was promoted by land speculation.

BETWEEN NEED FOR HOUSING AND SPECULATION

Drawing from practical experience and various visits to the medium-sized city of Tarija, in Bolivia, this paper identifies a critical scenario: how a speculative land market, with few restrictions and constraints from the government, has dramatically expanded the city in terms of the surface area covered in recent years; large and fragmented settlements where produced on the periphery of the city, where basic infrastructure and services are lacking and the living conditions are not optimal. Figure 1 shows the gravity of this scenario, where the actual extent of the urban land the city occupies is around four times larger than its actual consolidated area[1].

Figure 1: The growing city of Tarija. The consolidated city in 1989, based on GAMT (2008) in relation to the consolidated city and the expanded surface in 2018.

Source: Images Digital Globe, Google Earth (edited by author).

In this context, two realities clash: the formal part of the city, which is within the urban radius, and the informal section, which continues to emerge outside of the urban radius. Moreover, dwellers who settle on the periphery lack property titles as they are occupying an area that is not properly defined and are, therefore, in a permanent legal argument with the municipal government. They remain in the hope of one day becoming the rightful owners of the pieces of land that were sold to them in an illegitimate market; at the time, they find themselves situated somewhere between the formal and the informal urban land (Vargas Gamboa 2014).

The process of the regularisation of property titles is not transparent and also extremely time-consuming. People are lost in a never-ending list of requirements and fees, while there exists a speculative land market nation-wide where actors continue to sell pieces of land, that lack basic services, at ridiculous prices (ibid.). Further, selling land situated in rural areas for urban uses is a lucrative business that has dramatic effects on the environment as it destroys the natural

---

1 Due to the informal nature of the urban periphery and the lack of official plans, this polygon was broadly defined, based on the authors' analysis and maps that have not yet been published.

landscape and valuable water bodies (Figure 2). Therefore, this chapter raises questions about the role of land speculation in the city of Tarija and reflects on the severe consequences of neglecting this issue. This research question is addressed by searching secondary sources that describe the city's urban expansion from a historical perspective and link it to the drivers of urbanisation and population density. Furthermore, through a literature review on local, departmental and national development plans, and through semi-structured interviews and discussions with local actors, this research reflects on the city of Tarija and Bolivia's urbanisation and housing strategies and makes the case for changes in policies and regulations related to land acquisition and development.

Five semi-structured interviews where held in Tarija in September 2018; they ranged from 30 minutes to 3 hours in length. Among the interviewees were representatives from the municipal secretaries of development, culture, and land-use planning and the environment; the departmental neighbourhood committee; and the departmental farmers' federation. Moreover, in the framework of a transdisciplinary approach a real-world laboratory two workshops where held to tackle the issue of land speculation and the consequent environmental damage: one in January 2018, and the other in September 2018. During both events, informal discussions took place with a wider range of actors, practitioners and scholars as well as peri-urban and rural dwellers. Above all, during these workshops, a conceptual framework was conceived for future development[2]; it was then presented to different residents of the various neighbourhoods so as to gain valuable feedback on the concepts of the framework. In particular, this approach served to fill gaps in the research due to the lack of official documents and plans on the topic of the impact of urbanisation and land speculation on the city of Tarija.

---

2 The framework focuses on three aspects of land development in the context of the case study: first, on reclaiming ravines vital water bodies and securing them legally through zoning plans in a regional open-space network; second, small-scale interventions on the main roads should secure risk-free transit for pedestrians. And later, this transdisciplinary approach should be institutionalized, in time, and thereby serve as a mediator between the municipal planning authorities and the National Institute of Agrarian Reform for the development of policies and regulations related to land development.

Figure 2: Left-over and degraded rural spaces waiting to increase in value. Land speculation has been the primary factor in the degradation of the natural environment in the city of Tarija.

Source: Author, 2018.

Urban expansion in the city of Tarija

The city of Tarija is located in a valley in the South of Bolivia, about 1850 metres above sea level, in an area that is defined by the South American Andes mountains. Founded in the year 1574 as a strategic city to support the expansion of the Spanish Empire towards the South, the city emerged next to the Guadalquivir River. It followed a traditional chequered urbanism, with a north-south and east-west orientation of its streets in the city centre. It is characterised by its traditional vineyards, its warm, charismatic and friendly people, and its rich folkloric culture.[3] From 1574 onward, the city expanded from its core towards the surrounding mountains, reaching its peak population density in 1977, as is shown in Figure 3. A description of the city's urban expansion can be divided into three historic time periods: the colonial period, from 1574 to 1825; the republican period, from 1825 to 1952; and the modern period, from 1952 onwards

---

3 For more information on the city's character, see Lea Plaza Dorado *et al.* (2003) and Trigo O'Connord'Arlach (2017).

(Lea Plaza Dorado et al. 2003; Trigo O'Connord'Arlach 2017; de Mesa Figueroa et al. 1998). In colonial and republican times the city grew in terms of population, increasing its density in the now historical city centre. Moreover, land tenure was not possible for the indigenous and farmers' community; thus, settlement development outside the city was constrained. In modern times, agrarian reform was introduced, making it possible to divide up the land in individual lots of property; thus, the development of settlements and the establishment of a land market (Urioste 2012). Moreover, regional economic development triggered migration towards the city, which led to its expansion from its core towards the surrounding mountains. New neighbourhoods and city districts were created by annexing existing villages into the city's structure (GAMT 2008).

Figure 3: Urban expansion of the city of Tarija, 1967-2006. An increase in surface area and a decrease in population and built density.

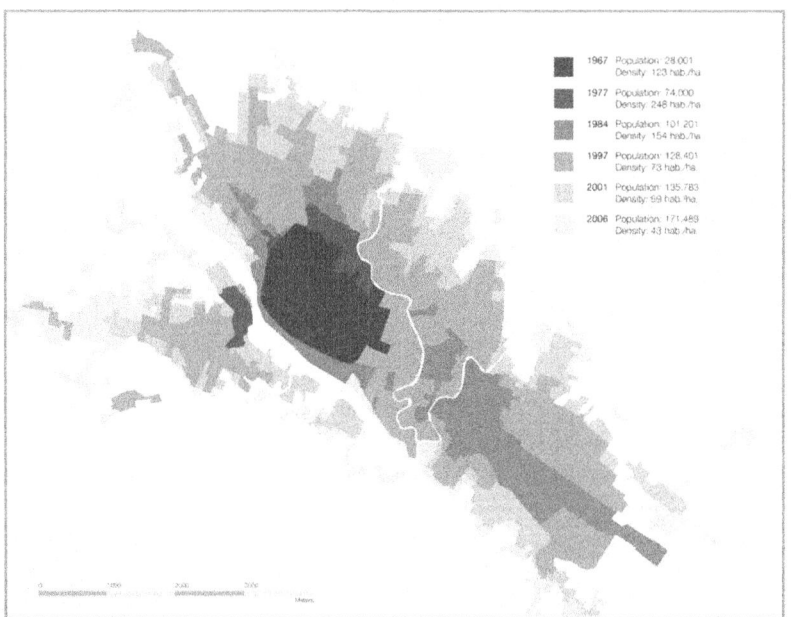

Source: Author's representation based on (GAMT 2008).

During colonial and republican times, city development was framed by the Spanish semi-feudal regime. Goods were produced in rural areas and traded in the city, and housing and political participation in the city was mainly reserved for aristocrats and wealthy members of society. In 1825, Bolivia proclaimed its independence from Spain and became a republic; however, its semi-feudal regime continued to define society (Trigo O'Connord'Arlach 2017). In rural areas, the form of land tenure was as in colonial times the hacienda, which is Spanish for a large productive estate. Natives lived on large estates owned by nobles; at the same time, they were exploited by these landlords and did not have the right to own property (Larson 2017). Urban expansion in terms of the surface area it covered continued to be extremely low as the boundary between urban and rural areas was protected through social exclusion. However, the city centre became slightly denser in terms of population as the casonas, Spanish for a big house with several inner courtyards, were subdivided primarily among growing families and through inheritance (Lea Plaza Dorado *et al.* 2003). In the early 1930s, this dynamic was slightly disrupted through migration, due to the Chaco War between Bolivia and Paraguay. The Gran Chaco region was thought to be rich in oil and, after the war, Bolivia lost a great part of the Chaco region to Paraguay. Since then, new neighbourhoods with lower population densities started to emerge around the centre of Tarija (GAMT 2008).

The revolution of 1952 marks a point of inflexion in Bolivia's history, its social structures and the subsequent urban development. This period of modernity accounts for one of the greatest transformations in citizenship, political participation, land distribution and state control of the national economy and the country's natural resources (Vargas Gamboa 2014; Urioste 2012). Moreover, the right to vote was universalised, which gave women, the country's indigenous population and farmers a new role in society. In 1953, the state promulgated agrarian reform through the National Institute for Agrarian Reform (Instituto Nacional de Reforma Agraria, INRA). This reform regulated land tenure and land uses in rural areas and protected indigenous and farming communities from being subjected to the earlier semi-feudal regime. Since the 1960s, the state, through the National Institute for Colonisation (Instituto Nacional de Colonización, INC), supplied on request between 20 and 50 hectares of physical land per family as non-transferable and indivisible private property. However, over time, these large properties where either sold to developers at low prices or divided up by the families, themselves. During the dictatorial military regimes of the 1970s and early 1980s, in particular, and the democratic neo-liberal governments of the early 1990s, land with no arable value was freely distributed to political supporters. This led to the establishment of a land market that freely operated on rural territory. (Urioste 2012, pp.61–64)

From 1996 to 2006, the main goal of the INRA was to regularise property titles for land that had been freely distributed since 1952. This was quite challenging as the INRA only provided titles to productive estates and many families had already transferred (or divided up) their lands to third parties that exclusively used it for housing. The process of regularising property titles was not transparent, extremely time-consuming and plagued by corruption as there were no records of previous transactions (Urioste 2012, p. 64). Since 2006 and the election of government of Evo Morales, Bolivia has seen profound socio-political changes (Lazar 2013). A new law of agrarian reform was promulgated to tackle the mistakes and corruption of the previous period; now the state had the ability to secure land for indigenous communities and to expropriate unproductive lands so as to avoid land speculation (ibid.). A government slogan is 'la tierra es de quien la trabaja', which is Spanish for 'the land is for those who work it'. However, corruption and the lack of transparency remain, thus making it difficult to address these issues. The distributed rural land is still being subdivided and speculation continues in a market for private land (as Figure 1 shows for the city of Tarija).

Moreover, in the mid-1990s, the election of a neo-liberal government led to the closure of state-owned mines in the city of Potosí. This, combined with the discovery of natural gas reserves in the Department of Tarija, led to a pattern of heavy migration throughout the country and especially into the Department of Tarija and its capital, Tarija (Vargas Gamboa 2014). People in search of employment migrated to Tarija from different cities and rural areas around the country. The existing regulatory frameworks and municipal capacities where overwhelmed by the influx and the compact structure of Tarija collapsed (PNUD 2015; GAMT 2016; GAMT 2008; GADT 2015; Vargas Gamboa 2014). Land speculators soon took advantage of the situation as, at this point, the pace of growth of Tarija became critical. However, the city did not grow as much in terms of population as the surface area covered, as is shown in Figure 3.

Furthermore, with the government of Evo Morales, the construction of social housing intensified and many informal settlements where formalised through Article 247, which was promulgated in order to address the demand for housing that resulted from strong migration. It was during this period that Tarija grew the most in terms of the surface area covered; however, as there are no official plans to measure the actual urban surface area developed, this remains the task of the author, based on an analysis of Figure 3.

LEVELS OF GOVERNMENT AND POLICIES ADDRESSING URBANISATION IN BOLIVIA

The year 2025 will mark the 200th anniversary of Bolivia's founding. In preparation for this occasion, and based on international agreements, the Ministry of

Autonomy of the Plurinational State of Bolivia proposes an agenda that includes thirteen pillars for development; it also identifies the role each level of government will play in the implementation of this agenda (Ministerio de Autonomías 2014, p. 13–14). At its centre is the promotion of an inclusive, participative and democratic society and nation; one that is without discrimination, racism, hatred or internal strife. Furthermore, the agenda proposes an inclusive and strategic collaboration between the country's four levels of government: central, departmental, municipal, and native indigenous farmers. The pillars of the 2025 agenda range from the eradication of extreme poverty through to securing basic infrastructure, the right to adequate housing and protecting the natural environment.

The role each level of government will play in the operationalisation of the above stated goals will then be quantified as a participatory percentage; that is, for each pillar and specific goal there is a clear statement of how responsible each level of government will be for the operationalisation of their part of the agenda. For instance, for pillar two, 'the socialisation and universalisation of basic services and infrastructure with sovereignty to live well',[4] the central government will have 31% responsibility, 25% will be carried out in collaboration between the central government and the autonomous territorial entity (ETA) (the remaining three levels of government), and 44% will be the exclusive responsibility of the ETAs (Ministerio de Autonomías 2014, p. 39). Overall, the ETAs will have 45% of responsibility for carrying out the agenda under pillar two and the central government, 33%, and the remainder will be carried out through collaboration. The main point of the document is for the ETAs to be the key to the future development of Bolivia (Ministerio de Autonomías, p. 65).

Pillar number two addresses urbanisation, and ambitiously aims to achieve 100% coverage of basic infrastructure and services, such as water, electricity, mobility and communication. Moreover, it particularly focuses on securing access to adequate housing that comes with basic infrastructure and services. A review of the participatory percentage responsibility for carrying out Bolivia's 2025 agenda shows that the roles and tasks of the various levels of government are distributed as follows: The central government is mainly in charge of policy development regarding human settlements in rural areas (through the National Institute of Agrarian Reform), planning and housing. The central government

---

4   To live well, in Spanish 'vivir bien', was formulated in the national law N°300, Art.1 and stressed by Bolivian foreign affairs minister David Choquehuanca. It describes a model for development in harmony with the natural environment based on traditional customs and believes of the indigenous communities. See: https://www.economia solidaria.org/noticias/vivir-bien-propuesta-de-modelo-de-gobierno-en-bolivia.

will work in combination with the ETAs in the planning and implementation of social housing projects. And the municipal governments will be mainly in charge of the development of land-use plans (framed by central policies), building codes, providing basic infrastructure, land for social housing, and property regulation in urban environments (MAEPB 2014, p. 40).

The issue of housing was also addressed through the (new) constitution of the Plurinational State of Bolivia (2009). Article 19 and Supreme Decree N°0986 state that everyone has the right to adequate housing and the state (through all levels of government) should promote adequate plans and financing for social housing, especially for the urban poor, the vulnerable and the inhabitants of rural areas. Moreover, Article 299 states that the central government in collaboration with the ETAs is responsible for housing and social housing, which is carried out through the National Housing Agency. Under Supreme Decree No. 0986, the National Housing Agency has been assigned the task of designing and implementing housing programs and/or projects. And although the ETAs are represented in this agency, the key decisions are made centrally. The municipal report for the city of Tarija, from 2017 and the departmental report for the Department of Tarija,[5] from 2015, point out this decision-making hierarchy (GAMT 2017; GADT 2015). The municipal government is not involved in housing projects as it is mainly in charge of basic services, infrastructure and property regulation in urban areas and for imposing building codes (GAMT 2015). Furthermore, in the departmental government report of 2015, addressing the issue of housing is not listed among the city's strategies for overcoming the economic crisis the department presently faces due to the dramatic drop in the price of oil in 2015 (GADT 2015).

In the 2016 HABITAT III report of the Bolivian Ministry for Public Works, Services and Housing (Ministerio de Obras Publicas, Servicios y Vivienda 2016 (MOPSV)), urbanisation is seen as an opportunity. Thus, the report proposed a definition of an urban area as being an urban environment that is quantitively defined as a human settlement of 2000 inhabitants or more, with buildings and spaces structured by a road system that is destined for housing development, and where economic activities are primarily those in the second, third and fourth sector (MOPSV 2016, p. 13–14). Furthermore, an urban environment must have access to basic services and infrastructure, such as water, electricity, sewage systems, schools, hospitals and areas for recreation and leisure. Urban environments can be sub-categorised according to their uses as intensive areas, exten-

---

5   Bolivia has nine departments, each with a capital city. The city of Tarija is the capital of the Department of Tarija.

sive areas and protected areas. Intensive urban areas can span from extensive high-density areas to areas of low density that include productive activities and serve as a belt to keep the city from expanding. Protected areas are meant to secure vital ecosystems. Furthermore, the document recommends that if there is a demand for housing then this should be accommodated in an intensive area (MOPSV 2016, p. 22). Regarding social housing, the government develops the policies and provides for the economic resources, and the municipal governments provide the land and basic infrastructure (MOPSV 2016, p. 30). In this positive vision of urbanisation, however, the issue of land speculation and its dramatic effects on the environment is presently being neglected. Although the purpose of agrarian reform is to avoid land speculation, the lack of a dialogue about and collaboration between this central government institution and the ETAs has hindered any progress in this regard.

The challenges for urbanisation in the city of Tarija

In recent decades, Bolivia has become predominately urban and almost half of its population is concentrated within the three metropolitan regions of La Paz, Cochabamba and Santa Cruz. The remaining population lives in small- to medium-sized cities, such as Tarija. Compared to the major Bolivian metropolitan regions, as of 2016 Tarija was relatively small with an estimated 247,000 inhabitants (INE 2017). Nonetheless, its spatial expansion and the dynamics along its periphery follow the same patterns as Bolivia's major cities. Firstly, as Figures 3 and 4 show, the city has expanded from its core, with few topographical constraints, as it has annexed villages and informal settlements in the process. Second, as was noted on the topic of agrarian reform, the lucrative business of selling rural land promotes the creation of settlements of an urban nature on rural land. This, combined with social pressure and corruption, promotes the expansion of formal urban areas, all to the benefit of land speculators who dramatically increase the prices of their land holdings, almost overnight. The actual urbanisation process occurs on a self-organised and incremental basis, as shown on Figure 4.

Nowadays, around 67.5% of Bolivia's population lives in an urban environment; the region with the highest urban population is Santa Cruz, where the urban proportion is an estimated 80% (PNUD 2015). It is estimated that Bolivia's urban population will continue to grow to 72% by 2025 and 53% of Bolivians will live in the three biggest cities. However, the censuses take from 2001 to 2012 show that small- and medium-sized cities have the highest urbanisation rates, making them also a force to reckon with in terms of the development and integration of the country's regions (MOPSV 2016, p. 34; PNUD 2015). So far, 34 intermediate cities with more than 10,000 inhabitants each have consolidated and their populations continue to maintain their agricultural customs and links to the rural hinterland. Consequently, the central government has proposed a multi-locality strategy for the 21st century (MOPSV 2016, p. 24). From 2006 to 2013, Tarija's urbanised area increased from 8,186 ha to 11,846 ha or by 45% (MOPSV 2016, p. 24). Over the same period, the population grew from 171,489 (GAMT 2008) to 212,856 inhabitants (INE 2012), and to an estimated 247,000 in 2017 (INE 2017), the latest year for which this data is available (INE 2017). This shows that the pattern of Tarija's development has been one of low-density in recent years because the population increase has not been as dramatic as the expansion that has occurred in urbanised areas.

Moreover, the urban expansion that has taken place has been informal, with inadequate municipal control and/or regulation. Land acquisition and housing construction took place without the approval of municipal planning institutions and urbanisation has mainly taken place on an incremental, self-organised basis (Figure 4). In this context, speculation accelerated and plots of land became over-priced. In response to this spontaneous growth and pressure from land speculators and social organisations, municipal governments expanded their cities' urban radiuses several times. This led to the creation of new settlements and neighbourhoods. These emerging neighbourhoods are not yet fully inhabited (Figure 2). However, they are self-organised and represented on local, departmental and national neighbourhood committees. According to the president of one departmental neighbourhood committees, since 2008, the neighbourhoods have increased in number from 60 to 170, nowadays. However, the exact number cannot be determined as not all of the neighbourhoods have been formally acknowledged by the municipality; doing so would imply the proper registration of land tenure, but this legal argument has not yet been settled. Therefore, the municipality refers to them as groups, and the number of existing neighbourhoods cannot be determined. Moreover, through an analysis of urban expansion, it also became clear that the new neighbourhoods are larger than the older ones in terms of the surface area they occupy; however, they also house significantly fewer people.

Addressing of the needs of Tarija's 170 neighbourhoods has proven to be a heavy burden for Tarija's municipal and departmental governments as more than half lack basic infrastructure. For many, expanding the urban radius may have solved the issue of property; however, it has yet to solve the issues of social disparities, lack of basic infrastructure and environmental damage. Land speculation has particularly benefitted from the expanding urban radius as the price of rural land has increased by merely being listed on paper as being urban land. This gave rise to a lucrative business where speculation and corruption steered development (Vargas Gamboa 2014). This has resulted in the growth in the number of vulnerable dwellers with no basic infrastructure, who then organise themselves through neighbourhoods committees that then put pressure on the government to appropriately develop their habitats (Figure 5).

Figure 4: Sequence of urban development. From the core towards the periphery, different stages of self-organised and incremental development can be observed.

Source: Author, 2018.

Figure 5: Vulnerable housing on a ravine. Migrants from the rural area who were deceived by land speculators.

Source: Author, 2018.

CONCLUSIONS

In recent years, the city of Tarija has seen a large expansion in terms of the surface area it occupies. This expansion has mainly occurred informally. However, there are questions as to whether this expansion was triggered by migration and the consequent demand for housing or by land speculation. An analysis of the city's urban expansion, from an historical perspective, in terms of surface area and population growth, has shown a dramatic decrease in both the built and population density in recent years. A review of policy and development agendas shows that efforts have been made to secure adequate housing for everyone in the city; however, those interviewed during the study noted the urgency of tackling land speculation and also voiced concerns over the lack of strategies to address this problem. Furthermore, the general public sees informal urbanisation as harmful for the consolidated city of Tarija; therefore, the general discourse around city development does not include these areas in their plans. Rather, legal efforts have been intensified to protect existing structures against encroachment from emerging informal surroundings.

I would argue that an informal mode of urbanisation does not harm the development of a city. Further, this type of development provides opportunities to develop cities in new and more inclusive ways, as informal urbanisation is more capable of adapting to new socio-economic circumstances than the generalised formal bureaucratic mode of urbanisation. Different innovative approaches throughout Latin America offer examples of successful informal modes of development (McGuirk 2014). Moreover, discussions on this topic have raised a whole new set of questions that will challenge planning institutions in the future. But what will happen to the lands that are not yet inhabited? Which constellation of actors is needed to oversee the development of these areas? And what strategies are needed to accomplish development here? Reforestation and agricultural land use were also discussed in the study interviews; however, densification through social housing or privately developed forms of housing could also be topics of discussion. For these types of initiatives, it is crucial to understand site-specific circumstances, discuss them in a transdisciplinary manner, and integrate them into development plans that recognise the need to find a median between top-down and bottom-up approaches.

Addressing the overall question of land speculation in the city of Tarija is quite challenging. First impressions argue that the expansion that took place due to speculation was out of proportion in relation to the influx of migrants, as the city's low population density has shown. Further, the question of whether migration will increase or decrease remains an open one. Moreover, there is a clear consensus between those interviewed for the study and the discussions around land use that assert that land speculation has deprived the city of valuable natural land, has destroyed important water bodies, and has been the main driver behind urban expansion in terms of the amount of surface area used. This was, thus, a highly inefficient way of achieving urbanisation, the severe consequences of which are shown in Figures 2 and 5. Therefore, it is crucial to prioritise this issue in local development plans and to tackle it with the same intensity as the issue of land ownership is currently addressed. To continue neglecting this critical issue would only promote even more uncontrolled and unjustified expansion, where the main victims are those who dwell on the periphery of the city.

To conclude, three important points can be raised that are relevant to a general understanding of the issue of land speculation. First, the centralised housing policy and programmes in Bolivia makes it difficult to put development agenda(s) into operation, as centralised programmes cannot respond to site-specific circumstances and, in a way, disagree with the key role of the ETAs. This highlights the importance of establishing a median between top-down and bottom-up approaches. Second, there is the issue of land ownership. In the context of the case study, land for social housing must be provided by the municipal government; however, the municipalities often do not own land in housing-intensive areas as this land is mainly privately owned. Thus, the land provided is mainly in extensive areas, thereby promoting the type of low-density urban expansion identified in Figure 3. Last, the State of Bolivia has made great progress in developing financing systems for housing and social housing at very low interest, making housing available to an increasing number of people every year (AEVIVIENDA 2018). However, this serves and promotes the land market as people who previously did not have the resources are now are able to buy land for housing. Land speculators then take advantage of this situation (Vargas Gamboa 2014). The need for housing and low-density development creates conditions for a profitable land market; therefore, different actors involved in land speculation and development have promoted this type of model. However, from a planning and environmental perspective, the densification of existing structures is a more economical and sustainable way of urbanisation. It is, therefore, crucial to challenge the existing discourse around the demand for housing and to propose urbanisation strategies and policies that are based on site-specific circumstances and trade-offs between institutions, actors, and future dwellers.

REFERENCES

Agencia Estatal de Vivienda (AEVIVIENDA) (2018) *Solucioneshabitacionalesc onlcuidas (2006-2017)* [online] available: http://aevivienda.gob.bo/ [accessed 17.02.2019].

Angotti, T. (1995) 'The Latin American metropolis and the growth of inequality', *NACLA Report on the Americas*, 28(4),13–18.

Butterworth, D. (1981) *Latin American Urbanization*, Cambridge: Cambridge Univ. Press.

de Mesa Figueroa, J., Gisbert, T. and Mesa Gisbert, C. (1998) *Historia de Bolivia*, La Paz: Gisbert.

Estado Plurinacional de Bolivia (2009) *ConstituciónPolítica del Estado*, La Paz: Estado Plurinacional de Bolivia.

German Advisory Council on Global Change (WBGU) (2016) *Humanity on the move: Unlocking the transformative power of cities*, Berlin: WBGU.

GobiernoAutónomoDepartamental de Tarija (GADT) (2015) *Un nuevo rumbo para salir de la crisis: Informe de Gestión Junio-Diciembre 2015*, Departmental development report.

GobiernoAutónomo Municipal de Tarija (GAMT) (2008) *PMOT y POU Municipio de la Ciudad de Tarija y la provincia Cercado*, Tarija: GAMT.
GobiernoAutónomo Municipal de Tarija (GAMT) (2015) *Plan de Desarrollo Municipal 2015-2019*. Tarija: GAMT.
GobiernoAutónomo Municipal de Tarija (GAMT) (2017) *Informe de Gestión del OrganoEjecutivo 2016/2017*. Tarija: GAMT.
Instituto Nacional de Estadística (INE) (2012) Ficha Resumen Censo de Población y Vivienda 2012 [online], available at: http://censosbolivia.ine.gob.bo/censofichacomunidad/ [accessed 17.02.2019].
Instituto Nacional de Estadística (INE) (2017) *Censos Nacionales 2017: XII de Población, VII de Vivienda y III de comunidades Indígenas* [online], available: https://www.inei.gob.pe/media/MenuRecursivo/publicaciones_digitales/Est/Lib1437/libro.pdf [accessed 17.02.2019].
Larson, B. (2017) *Colonialismo y transformación agraria en Bolivia: Cochabamba, 1550-1900*. La Paz: Vicepresidencia del Estado Plurinacional.
Lazar, S. (2013) *El Alto, ciudad rebelde*, La Paz: Plural editores.
Lea Plaza Dorado, A., S., Vargas Guardia, X. and Paz Ramirez (2003) *Tarija en los imaginariosurbanos*, La Paz: Fundación PIEB.
Ministerio de Autonomías Estado Plurinacional de Bolivia (2014) *Agenda Patriótica 2025 ¿Quiénhacequé?* [online], available: http://vpc.planificacion.gob.bo/uploads/recursos/AGENDA_PATRIOTICA2025_QUIEN_HACE_QUE.pdf [accessed 17.11.2019].
McGuirk, J. (2014) *Radical Cities: Across Latin America in Search of a New Architecture*, New York: Verso.
Ministerio de ObrasPublicas, Servicios y Vivienda (MOPSV) (2016) *ConstruyendoComunidadesUrbanas para Vivir Bien el Siglo XXI. Informe del Estado Plurinacional de Bolivia para Hábitat III*, La Paz: MOPSV
Programa de Naciones Unidas para el Desarrollo (PNUD) (2015) *Informe Nacional sobre Desarrollo Humano en Bolivia. El nuevo rostro de Bolivia – Transformación Social y Metropolización*, La Paz: PNUD.
Rodgers, D., Beal, J., and Kanbur, R. (2012) *Latin American Urban Development into the 21st Century*, Hampshire: Palgrave Macmillan.
Roy, A. (2005) 'Urban Informality. Toward an Epistemology of Planning', *American Planning Association*, 71(2),147–158.
Trigo O'Connord'Arlach, E. (2017) *Tarija en la Independencia del Virreinato del Río de la Plata*, La Paz: Vicepresidencia del Estado Plurinacional.
United Nations Human Settlements Programme (UN-Habitat) (2017) *New Urban Agenda*, United Nations New Urban Agenda [online], available: http://habitat3.org/wp-content/uploads/NUA-English.pdf [accessed 17.11.2019].

United Nations World Urbanization Prospects (UN-WUP) (2018) *Key Facts*, United Nations world prospects [online], available: https://population.un.org/wup/Publications/Files/WUP2018-KeyFacts.pdf [accessed 17.11.2019].

Urioste, M. (2012) 'El caso de Bolivia' in Soto Baquero, F. and Gómez, S., eds., *Dinámicas del mercado de la tierra en América Latina y el Caribe: concentración y extranjerización*, UN-FAO, 59–104.

Vargas Gamboa, N. (2014) 'El asentamiento irregular como principal Fuente de crecimientourbanoen Bolivia: Entre ilegalidad y constitucionalidad,' *América Latina Hoy* (68), 55–78.

Chapter 6: Influence of Migrants' Two-Directional Rural-Urban Linkages in Urban Villages in China
The Case of Shigezhuang Village in Beijing

Shiyu Yang

INTRODUCTION

China's urbanisation can be understood as an in-situ process where rural areas gradually become urban (Zhu 1999). This process is characterised by the informal growth of urban villages situated on the periphery of large cities and the huge inflow of rural migrant workers into these cities due to the better chances of finding employment (Hao *et al.* 2011; Liu *et al.* 2010; Zheng *et al.* 2009). Under the dual urban-rural land system, indigenous villagers are allowed to extend the houses that have been built on their own plots and rent out rooms to the migrant population. Because of the low living costs and prime location, migrants prefer to settle down in urban villages in their destination cities. In certain urban villages in metropolitan cities like Beijing, the number of migrants can be more than ten times that of indigenous villagers (Feng 2010). As such, urban villages have been identified as migrant enclaves (Friedmann 2005; He *et al.* 2010; Lin *et al.* 2011; Liu *et al.* 2017; Liu *et al.* 2018; Wu *et al.* 2013; Wu 2016). Much literature has described urban villages as settlements that are 'chaotic', 'unplanned', 'congested' and 'substandard' (Chung 2010; Tian 2008), arguing that this situation is attributed to the informal mechanisms of land development and the rational rent-seeking decisions of (urban) villagers who wish to maximise profits from their assigned housing plots (Ma 2006; Wu *et al.* 2013). In the development and redevelopment process of urban villages, villagers, governments and developers are identified as key stakeholders and the negotiations that take place among them have been investigated and analysed (Herrle *et al.* 2014). Nevertheless, even though migrants are the largest group living in these locations, their interests are often neglected in these negotiations (Liu *et al.* 2018). Although there is some literature that focuses on migrants' housing conditions and the inequalities that exist in the housing market (He *et al.* 2010; Zheng *et al.* 2009), it mainly observes the issue from a top-down, institutional interpretation. Given the fact that migrants have no property rights and tenancy security (Liu *et al.* 2018), they are seen as only passively adopting the space they inhabit. The impacts of migrants' decision-making and daily activities on housing conditions in urban villages remain unclear.

Many studies have proved that in traditional Chinese society blood bonds (xueyuan) and place bonds (diyuan) play a central role in people's decision-making, and migrants coming from the same rural origin (tongxiang) tend to agglomerate so as to be spatially close within their new urban destinations (Fei 1985; Zhang 2001). Researchers have examined the socio-spatial pattern of migrants' networks and their attachment to and engagement with both their rural places of origin and their urban destinations (Fan 2002; Fan *et al.* 2011; Liu *et al.* 2012; Liu *et al.* 2018; Saunders 2011). Therefore, this paper conceptualises migrants' two-directional linkages as being invisible ties between their rural hometowns and their arrival cities, in terms of personal, economic and social perspectives. The research question in this enquiry focuses on how this two-directional linkage influences migrants' decision-making processes and activities upon their arrival in urban villages. The primary aim of this paper is to contribute to a better understanding of housing conditions for migrants in urban villages by highlighting their bipolar relationship with both their rural places of origin and their urban destinations. It also seeks to shed insight on the conceptualisation of temporary migrants by examining the relevant factors, including migration time and family size. Moreover, it critically analyses the effects of social networks and neighbourhood attachments among migrants who come from the same place of origin. Due to the informal status of the migrant population in China and the lack of quantitative data on their everyday activities, this research uses qualitative analysis that is mainly based on interviews and investigates the village of Shigezhuang, in Beijing, as a case study.

This chapter is presented in five sections. The following section gives a brief overview of the literature on China's internal rural-urban migration and migrants' perceptions and activities concerning their rural origins. It also provides a conceptual framework for the empirical research. In section three, the research method is explained and the village of Shigezhuang is introduced as the case study. The fourth section provides insight into the migrants' current housing conditions and backgrounds and the factors they take into consideration when decision-making; it does so by analysing their demographic profiles and by reviewing and analysing the interview transcripts. Discussions are interwoven into the data analysis. Concluding remarks are drawn in the final section.

MIGRANTS' LINKAGE TO THEIR RURAL ORIGINS

Since the late 1980s, China has witnessed a surge in the rate of internal rural-urban migration (Hao *et al.* 2011) and those workers coming from rural areas or small cities to large cities are referred to as the migrant population. These migrants maintain constant links to their rural origins, both as individuals and as members of families. Splitting up households is identified as a strategy migrant workers use to benefit the most from working in cities (Fan *et al.* 2011). A split-household family refers to a situation 'where family members who under normal circumstances would be living in the same place are in actuality living in separate places' (Fan *et al.* 2011, p. 2166). Migrant workers straddle the city and the countryside as they circulate between the two locations and send money back to their hometowns as a major source of income and savings for the family members who are left behind (Fan 2002; Fan *et al.* 2011; Yang 2000). However, the study is limited as it categorises split households into forms of sole migration, couple migration and family migration, thereby overlooking the traditional Chinese culture of including three generations in this culture's conceptualisation of a family.

There has also been a debate on migrants' perceptions of urban villages and their intention of settling down in the established city. Some scholars have argued that most migrants consider urban villages as temporary places of arrival and are eager to transit into the nearby urban area and become a permanent residents there (Saunders 2011). In contrast, other findings indicate that migrants are unlikely to have long-term plans to settle down in the city (Fan 2002; Yang 2000). However, migrants merely view the destination city as a place of work instead of a place in which to live, and they have no intention of staying. Determinants that include the period of time spent working in a certain city and family size have been examined and proven to have little influence on migrants' interpretations and decision-making. Another argument is that it is better to focus on migrants' 'attachment to and engagement with the origin and destination' rather than interpreting these factors according to a 'go or no-go' dichotomy (Kaufmann 2007). The system of classifying 'temporary migrants' and 'permanent migrants' was adopted when differentiating migrant workers from those who attain a relatively high educational level and benefit from institutional welfare (Fan 2002). Two explanations account for this unsettled situation. The first and most widely discussed reason concerns China's hukou system, which prevents migrants from accessing many public services in destination cities, including health care, education, housing and other social benefits (Lin *et al.* 2011). Another reason is that migrants are more likely to invest money in their rural hometowns out of a sense of social and economic security and also of belonging (Fan *et al.* 2011; Liu *et al.* 2018).

Besides the fact that migrants or migrant families' decision-making is influenced by their two-directional linkage between their rural origins and their urban destinations, certain communities are informally set up in the established city because of the migrant inhabitants' linkages to their hometowns. Research shows that there is a long history of migrants who come from the same origins, settling in the same urban villages. Extreme cases are those urban villages where the majority of migrants come from the same province and where that village has been given the name of that province, such as Zhejiang Village and Xinjiang Village (Chung 2010; Friedmann 2005; Zhang 2001). However, there are many urban villages that accommodate heterogeneous migrants and where there are not necessarily strong community ties among these residents (Chung 2010). A shared finding is that migrants tend to cluster in particular locations within a city, based on their shared sense of identity (Ma and Xiang 1998). This sense of identity is based on kinship and geographic relations to their place of origin rather than to their place of arrival. Those migrants having the same place bonds (diyuan) call each other tongxiang and their place of origin can be flexibly and differently defined according to contexts, which vary between village, township, city and province (Zhang 2001). For migrant workers, tongxiang is the main source of labour market information (Fan 2002). Although new-generation migrants probably rely more on 'non-territorial' networks, 'hometown-based bonds' still play a key role in their social networks (Liu *et al.* 2012, p.192).

The fact that migrants rely on social networks and have uncertain feelings about their arrival cities can be understood best when reviewing the recent massive demolition of urban villages and the evictions of migrant workers. For city governments, urban villages are blamed for the inefficient and chaotic land use that hampers the process of 'modernisation' (Wu 2009). This negative characterisation of urban villages is used to justify large-scale demolitions under the auspices of urban development. A growing body of literature argues that migrant workers, as the tenant class in urban villages, have an inferior status and are often neglected by municipalities and academia (Liu *et al.* 2018; Wang *et al.* 2009). Migrant workers are treated as a 'means of production' rather than a 'social asset which contributes to the identity and culture of the city' (Hao *et al.* 2011, p.223). With no property rights or legal protection, migrants have no discourse in bargaining over rental prices and are not compensated when faced with displacement. When they are evicted from their original enclaves, migrants tend to make short-distance moves that are dependent on their social ties because of the lack of information on and access to other neighbourhoods. In addition to investigating these migrants' physical evictions, researchers have also looked into their economic displacement (Liu *et al.* 2018). Whereas direct economic displacement means migrant renters are priced out by rising housing costs and are forced to relocate to other urban villages, indirectly, one can understand how they become displaced in situ where they tend to remain in the same neighbourhood and must accept unreasonable rental increases because of the other potential loss, which is in their social ties.

The above literature review provides the study with a conceptual framework that guides its empirical analysis. To identify the impacts of Chinese migrants' two-directional linkages on their living conditions in urban villages, this research was approached from three perspectives: the case of a migrant or a migrant family, migrants as members of the migrant community, and the migrant community as a whole. First, migrants' individual linkages to their rural origins influence their activities in their urban destinations and their decisions as circulators between these destinations is a superficial reflection of this linkage. In this case, a migrant or a migrant family is analysed as an individual subject. Second, migrants gather in urban villages, based on their bonds of place, and form a tongxiang community, which is a collective reflection of their two-directional linkages. As such, two more types of subjects are identified a migrant or a migrant family as a member of the community and the migrant community as a whole. Therefore, the specific research question is how the two-directional linkage acts on these three subjects and also on migrants' overall housing conditions in urban villages. Based on this conceptual framework, the case of the village of Shigezhuang was selected and examined in the research.

RESEARCH METHOD AND DATA

Historically, Beijing's periphery has been dotted with hundreds of village communities (Jeong 2011), but there are almost no urban villages left within the city's fourth ring road because of the large-scale urban redevelopment of recent years. The village of Shigezhuang is located to the east of the central business district and just beyond the fifth ring road. Shigezhuang is one of the most centrally located villages among those that remain in Beijing, which means it has existed for a long time in the form of an urban village.[1] Further, it has a high migrant-to-native ratio of around eight-to-one and a large percentage of these migrants come from the province of Sichuan. Therefore, Shigezhuang was chosen as the case village for this field research, based on the need to investigate migrants' activities and decision-making processes as they relate to their rural origins.

Figure 1: Location of Shigezhuang village in Beijing.

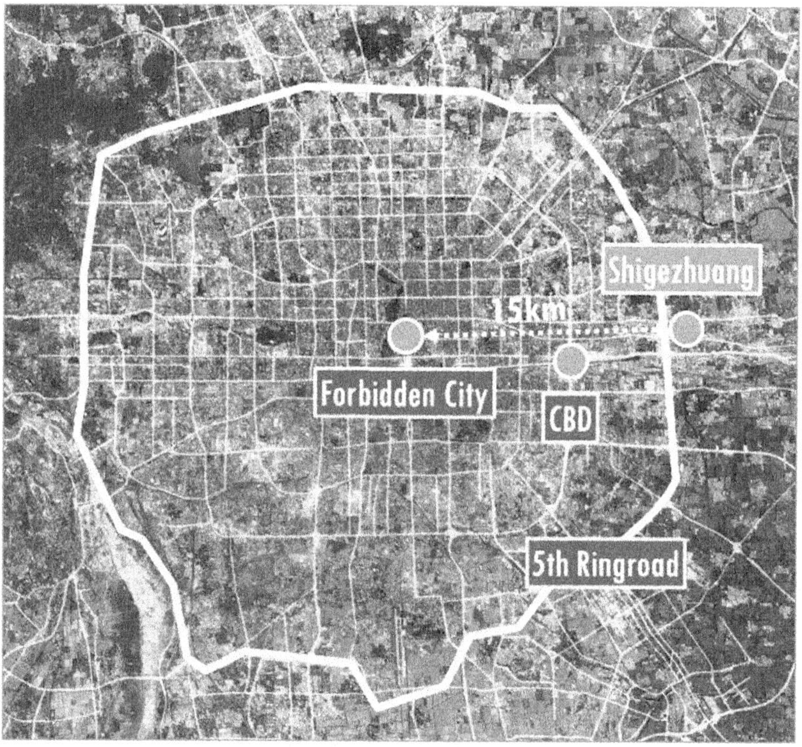

Source: drawn by author based on Google map.

The data were collected from various sources during the field research, including from interviews, a questionnaire survey, field observations, photographs and

---

[1] The statement in this paragraph is based on an early round of overall field research on urban villages in Beijing. In addition, the research of Fan *et al.* (2011) is also an important reference.

mapping. The period of the study was from September to October 2017. Due to the fact that urban villages are considered informal settlements and migrants are usually not formally included in the urban economy, information about migrants' demographics is not officially publicly available. Therefore, the aim of this research was not to enrol a representative sample of migrants but to examine the individualized experiences and choices of housing that are linked to these migrants' two-directional linkages.

First, a face-to-face survey was conducted with 58 residents who were randomly selected from different parts of the village so that they were relatively evenly distributed, spatially. The subjects were asked to provide information on their demographics (including gender, age, hukou province and occupation[2]), as well as to give profiles of their dwellings (including the size of their rental rooms, the number of dwellers per room and whether there was an in-room toilet). Subsequent to the survey, semi-structured interviews were conducted with some respondents. Respondents were each assigned a number, which was used for anonymity in the following discussion. A number with a suffix means that these people were interviewed together as one household. Although the sample is not big enough for a reliable quantitative research, the appropriate saturation was achieved after 58 surveys and the subsequent interviews; that is, no new information concerning the main aspects of the migrants' activities and decision-making related to their rural origins could be collected by undertaking more interviews.

MIGRANTS IN THE CASE OF SHIGEZHUANG VILLAGE

In this section, detailed interview content and data analyses are presented in combination with discussions. Based on the aforementioned conceptual framework, the research findings concerning the two-directional linkages were structured from three perspectives: migrants as individuals, migrants as tongxiang, and a migrant community as a whole.

---

2   In the surveys, each person was asked about the details of the tasks they performed at their work. Occupations such as construction worker, electrician and decorator were mentioned as different categories of jobs in the construction industry. Men who worked as hourly laborers are often referred to as those workers who do not specialize in a certain type of work but mainly work on a construction site. Women who work as hourly laborers often work in different occupations, such as in cleaning.

As an individual migrant perceiving the arrival city as a place for work

Among all of the respondents, five were residents with Beijing hukou and 53 were migrants. All the Beijing residents were over 60 years of age. A majority of the migrants were in their 30s (25%) or 40s (36%), while only 13% were younger than 30 and 13% were in their 50s. As for dwelling profiles, for the Beijing residents the average living space per person was 21.8 square metres, while that for the migrants was 5.1 square metres. One family of three migrants did not travel to Beijing for work. When they were excluded, the average living space per person for the migrant workers was 3.6 square metres and only three of these 50 migrants had an in-room toilet. The majority of these migrants had to use public toilets, which were substandard, and they had to bath in an outdoor shelter by temporarily setting up plastic tents. The rent for these rooms without toilets was around 80 yuan (11.4 USD) per square metre per month. For example, for the family of Interviewee 10, their 9-square-metre room costs around 750 yuan (107.0 USD), and the 4-square-metre room of Interviewee 4 cost 300 yuan per month (42.8 USD).

During the interviews, some interviewees were invited to answer a hypothetical question:

'I know there is a room, in the nearby urban village, that is the same size as the one you live in now but that has a toilet, but the rent is 200 yuan higher. Would you be willing to move to that room' (Author, September 2017).

Interviewee 5's answer represents most respondents:

'There is already enough space within our room for my family to live. Why would I pay extra money for the rent? We don't need an in-room toilet' (Interviewee 5, September 2017).

This is a surprising answer because these migrants earned a fairly high salary compared to the rent they paid. Taking Interviewee 5 as an example, he and his wife had worked in Beijing for more than 15 years and had lived in Shigezhuang for more than 10 years, until 2017. He worked as a construction worker and his salary was 500 yuan per day. When he worked for 22 days per month, on average, his monthly income was 11,000 yuan. His wife worked as a cleaner and her salary per month was around 4,000 yuan. In this case, if this family worked for 11 months a year in Beijing, their yearly income would have been 165,000 yuan, which is higher than the 2017 annual income per capital of the residents in Beijing, which was 57,230 yuan (Beijing Municipal Bureau of Statistics 2018). In this case, their 8.5-square-metre room, with a monthly rent of 750 yuan, only took up 5% of their combined income.

Figure 2: 2(a) Street in Shigezhuang village; 2(b) A 9-square-metre room of Interviewee 48.

Source: Author, 2017.

Besides expressing an unwillingness to spend money on rent, more evidence can be seen that these migrants considered the city of Beijing only as a place for work:

'The shopping mall within ten minutes' walk and I have never been there. That is not for us. Why would we go there?' (Interviewee 5, September 2017).

'I drive my car from Sichuan to here for more convenient transportation to my work place. I know that cars without a Beijing licence are not allowed inside the 5th ring road. But most of the construction sites are in the outskirts. Sometimes, I need to drive even 1 hour to a more peri-urban area for work. I don't need to drive my car to the city centre' (Interviewee 1, September 2017).

'I will go back home when I can't work anymore. We peasants don't have rent insurance. The living cost here in a city is much higher than that of our countryside. I don't think we can afford this when we are old' (Interviewee 48, September 2017).

'My son is a young soldier in the army now. I don't need to give him money every month like in his university times, but we need to save money from now on to help him buy an apartment when he gets married in the future' (Interviewee 5, September 2017).

This indicates that for these migrants the destination city only means better opportunities for finding a well-paid job; they are not interested in the city life. These migrants seldom consider the established city as their home nor do they intend to permanently settle down there. The term 'temporary migrants' mentioned in the literature review does not refer to the time period but rather to their 'floating' situation and intention of moving back to the rural countryside. For example, interviewees 5 and 48 are in their 50s and are certain about their intention to return to their rural hometowns when they are no longer able to work. The fact they have been working in the city for more than 10 years has not influenced their plans. Besides, the idea of saving money in case of an emergency or to provide a better future for their children is also a traditional idea that is deeply rooted in the minds of Chinese rural peasants.

Prior studies have categorised forms of migration into sole migration, couple migration and family migration (Fan *et al.* 2011). Compared to these stereotypes, this field research has identified another type of migration, that of three generations migrating together. Over 90% of the migrants that come to Beijing travel with other family members with whom they share one or two rooms when settling in Shigezhuang. As interviewees 9, 24, 25, 26 and 45 reported, each of their families had five or six members living in Shigezhuang; these might have included a couple of older migrants, their son or daughter along with his or her spouse and one or two small children. In this case, the family rented two rooms that were situated close to each other. The young couple worked during the daytime, while at least one of the elderly migrants stayed home to care for the children. So instead of leaving their children behind in the rural place of origin, parents and children could see each other daily and the young couple could take care of the elderly couple when needed. Therefore, when economic conditions allowed, this was the preferred mode of temporary migration for most families with children younger than 6 years of age. However, no significant differences were found between these migrants and those who came to the city alone or only with their spouses. Having more family members in the destination village did not mean a willingness to invest more to obtain better living conditions. The average living space per person of the aforementioned four families was only 2.5 square metres. The choice of this type of family migration can be seen as a compromise between saving the most from working in an urban area and enjoying the best of family life.

When the children reached school age (6 years old), most parents sent them back to their rural origins because the city did not provide migrant children with access to public education. In most cases, both the mother and the father continued working in the city and let the grandparents take care of their children in their hometowns, in a situation the interviewees described as being an annual bi-directional circuit. Here, parents visited their children in the winter time when celebrating the spring festival in the countryside, while the children visited their parents during summer vacations in Beijing. As some respondents reported, the average living space per person was even less when taking the temporary visiting children into account.

To summarise, most migrants were reluctant to invest in rental housing. In the case of these migrants, indigenous villagers preferred to build rooms that only satisfied basic sheltering needs when they developed their housing for rental purposes. In this specific rental market, rooms with more decent conditions, like those that included a toilet, did not receive more attention from migrants.

As tongxiang: Relying on social networks for survival

Among the 53 migrants who responded to the survey, 58% were from the province of Sichuan, 15% from Henan, 7% from Shandong, 6% from Hubei, 6% from Hebei, and 8% from other provinces, including Shanxi, Gansu and Jiangsu. Of these migrants, 53% were female and 47% were male. Excluding the 11 migrants who did not work (including two housewives, three students, two unemployed people, and four people who were visiting), all of the men from Sichuan worked as labourers in the construction industry, while all but one woman (from Sichuan) were cleaners. Interestingly, when it came to migrants from provinces other than Sichuan, only one man worked as a decorator and two women were cleaners. Others worked as salespersons, company staff and cooks, or were self-employed. According to the interviews that went further in-depth, this interesting phenomenon that migrants from the same province tended to take on the same occupations can be attributed to their informal access to employment information.

During their interviews, the 31 of the migrants from Sichuan introduced more information to this research about the lives of other tongxiang. Some of them had been invited by an acquaintance who had already been a migrant worker living in Beijing, while some had moved to Shigezhuang by chance after coming to Beijing. These tongxiang did not necessarily have blood bonds or know each other before coming to Beijing but they tended to form a strong community once they settled down in Shigezhuang because of their similar dialects and life styles. These Sichuan tongxiang were mostly low-skilled migrants who had not been trained for any specific occupation. Therefore, their occupations were not decided by their ability but by their access to information on opportunities for work.

As the majority of these migrants did not have steady jobs, they needed to keep searching for new job opportunities. In such fields as construction or cleaning, little information was available online or via a formal platform and migrants needed to rely on their relatives and social networks in their job-search processes.

'When a familiar construction team leader calls me and tells me that they need four or five construction workers on their sites for a week, I will say I can help him to find all these people. Then I often call my relatives or go to knock at the doors of my neighbours and ask if they have time for that one-week work. We will also drive a car together to the construction site. This is very common and other people will also do so. The man with much job information is highly respected' (Interviewee 5, September 2017).

'Sometimes I am busy when the household that I often work for asks me to do the cleaning. I will recommend my friends from the villages and guarantee the household that they can do the cleaning as well as I do' (Interviewee 11.1, September 2017).

In this case, migrants tended to remain in Shigezhuang even when the housing prices were steadily increasing and the conditions were not ideal, as they took into account the possible loss of working opportunities should they opt for resettlement. Some scholars refer to this as economic displacement, as mentioned in the literature review. Dependence on a social network that was attached to their bonds of place indirectly led to these migrants' economic displacement.

As a community: Negotiating with other stakeholder groups

Although there was an observed strong neighbourhood attachment in sharing information and undertaking everyday activities, such as cooking, playing cards and taking care of each other, it is important to point out that this established social network among the tongxiang did not help the migrants in their negotiations with indigenous villagers.

Figure 3: Tongxiang playing cards after work.

Source: Author, 2017.

During the field research, several interviewees reported that conflicts took place between migrants and indigenous villagers and the main concern was rent:

'You want to interview my landlord (the villager who rents a room to the interviewee)? I know his family lives in that courtyard house, but I have never been inside. They keep a fierce guard dog and it will bite us. You could go for a try. Maybe the landlord will be more friendly to a university student' (Interviewee 47, October 2017).

'They (indigenous villagers) are all very bad. They keep raising our rent unreasonably, especially after the government's demolishing of the nearby villages. If we don't agree to the high rent, they will force us to move out. There are plenty of people waiting to rent their house' (Interviewee 1, September 2017).

Despite being dominant in number, these migrants were still in vulnerable positions when agreements needed to be reached with indigenous villagers. This was not only because of the informality of the rental market but also because these migrants lacked the necessary resources for undertaking these negotiations. Although some scholars, such as Zhang (2003), suggest that in some urban villages there are leaders, among these migrants, who can gain the right to enter into a discourse because of their wealth and thus are able to represent other tongxiang who are fighting for their rights in the negotiation process, what happens in Shigezhuang is common in most urban villages. A migrant group, which typically consists of those with low social status and education levels, has few back-up resources with which to fight for the right to discuss their issues. Further, members in the established tongxiang community support each other in everyday life but few people are willing to represent their common interests:

'Last month the villagers decided collectively to raise our rent by an average of 200 yuan. We are so angry because they just raised the rent once at the beginning of this year. We had a big fight with them. However, the village committee leaders who were supposed to administer justice always stood by the villagers' side. The rent still rose despite the fight' (Interviewee 48, September 2017).

'Of course, there is no leader for our tongxiang community. Nobody dares to be the leader. Leaders are always the first to suffer. Those villagers can at any time kick us out of their room' (Interviewee 5, September 2017).

All of the migrants knew that their primary reason for staying in the city was to earn money and few people wanted to bear a possible loss by taking responsibility for this 'temporary' community. Therefore, as long as these people remained migrant workers with few resources in such an informal setting, their inferior statuses would not have changed with the addition of more tongxiang in one urban village. Indigenous villagers always dominated the negotiations as they had resources in their own legal tenancy and the village agency would always back them up in any negotiations.

CONCLUSION

Urban villages have been identified as migrant enclaves of which migrant workers make up the largest but most inferior group. This study examined the impacts of these migrants' two-directional linkages between their urban destinations and rural origins on their housing conditions in urban villages. The village of Shigezhuang was chosen as a case study and surveys and interviews with 58 residents were conducted during the field research. There are three major findings related to the conceptual framework of investigating the influence of this two-directional linkage from the perspectives of migrants as individuals, migrants as members of a tongxiang community, and the migrant community as a whole.

First, temporary migrants as circulators between their rural origins and urban destinations consider the city as a place for work rather than a place to live and, thus, are reluctant to invest money to live in the city and only seek out substandard housing. Migrants have these attitudes regardless of the period of time spent working in the city or the number of family members living there. Migrants' decision-making on their choice of housing and indigenous villagers' decision-making on developing housing for the rental market have mutual impacts on each other. Second, migrants' limited access to job information in the city makes them rely on social networks that are based on their bonds of place. Besides the physical or direct economic displacements evictions cause, migrants' dependence on having informal access to employment information may lead to indirect economic displacement, which means they may have to endure high prices and inequality in the rental market. Third, although the neighbourhood attachment among the tongxiang is strong in the sense of sharing information or taking care of each other, without strong community leadership, being a member of the tongxiang is of little help when entering into a negotiation process with other stakeholder groups in the city. To conclude, this study argues that migrant workers' constant linkages to their rural origins and the social networks based on bonds of place may contribute to more employment opportunities, a better sense of belongingness and strong neighbourhood attachments; however, at the same time, these bonds might exacerbate their inferior and vulnerable status in their urban destinations.

REFERENCES

Beijing Municipal Bureau of Statistics (2018) *Ju Min Ren Jun Ke Zhi Pei Shou Ru Qing Kuang [The per capita disposable income of residents]* [online], available at: http://www.bjstats.gov.cn/tjsj/yjdsj/jmsz/2017/ [accessed 16 Feb 2019].

Chung, H. (2010) 'Building an image of villages-in-the-city: a clarification of China's distinct urban spaces', *International Journal of Urban and Regional Research*, 34(2), 421–437.

Fan, C. C. (2002) 'The elite, the natives, and the outsiders: Migration and labour market segmentation in urban China', *Annals of the association of American geographers*, 92(1), 103–124.

Fan, C. C., Sun, M. and Zheng, S. (2011) 'Migration and split households: a comparison of sole, couple, and family migrants in Beijing, China', *Environment and Planning A*, 43(9), 2164–2185.

Feng, X. (2010) 'Transformation of "urban village" and cooperative governance of the floating population concentrated communities in Beijing', *Population Research* (06), 55–66.

Fei, X. (1985) *Xiang Tu Zhong Guo [Earthbound China]*, Beijing: San-Lian Publisher.

Friedmann, J. (2005) *China's urban transition*, U of Minnesota Press.

Hao, P., Sliuzas, R. and Geertman, S. (2011) 'The development and redevelopment of urban villages in Shenzhen', *Habitat International*, 35(2), 214–224.

He, S., Liu, Y., Wu, F. and Webster, C. (2010) 'Social groups and housing differentiation in China's urban villages: An institutional interpretation', *Housing Studies*, 25(5), 671–691.

Herrle, P., Fokdal, J. and Ipsen, D. (2014) *Beyond Urbanism: Urban (izing) Villages and the Mega-urban Landscape in the Pearl River Delta in China (Vol. 20)*, Münster: LIT Verlag.

Jeong, J. H. (2011) 'From illegal migrant settlements to central business and residential districts: Restructuring of urban space in Beijing's migrant enclaves', *Habitat International*, 35(3), 508–513.

Kaufmann, F. (2007) *Emigrant or sojourner? Migration intensity and its determinants*, Political Economy Research Institute, University of Massachusetts, Amherst, MA.

Lin, Y., De Meulder, B. and Wang, S. (2011) 'Understanding the 'village in the city' in Guangzhou: Economic integration and development issue and their implications for the urban migrant', *Urban Studies*, 48(16), 3583–3598.

Liu, Y., Geertman, S., van Oort, F. and Lin, Y. (2018) 'Making the 'Invisible' Visible: Redevelopment-induced Displacement of Migrants in Shenzhen, China', *International Journal of Urban and Regional Research*, 42(3), 483-499.

Liu, Y., He, S., Wu, F. and Webster, C. (2010) 'Urban villages under China's rapid urbanization: Unregulated assets and transitional neighbourhoods', *Habitat International*, 34(2), 135–144.

Liu, Y., Li, Z. and Breitung, W. (2012) 'The social networks of new-generation migrants in China's urbanized villages: A case study of Guangzhou', *Habitat International*, 36(1), 192–200.

Liu, Y., Tang, S., Geertman, S., Lin, Y. and van Oort, F. (2017) 'The chain effects of property-led redevelopment in Shenzhen: Price-shadowing and indirect displacement', *Cities*, 67, 31–42.

Ma, H. (2006) *"Villages" in Shenzhen-Persistence and Transformation of an Old Social System in an Emerging Megacity*, (PhD), Bauhaus-Universität Weimar.

Ma, L. J. and Xiang, B. (1998) 'Native place, migration and the emergence of peasant enclaves in Beijing', *The China Quarterly*, 155, 546–581.

Saunders, D. (2011) *Arrival city: How the largest migration in history is reshaping our world*, Vintage.

Tian, L. I. (2008) 'The chengzhongcun land market in China: Boon or bane? A perspective on property rights, *International Journal of Urban and Regional Research*, 32(2), 282–304.

Wang, Y. P., Wang, Y. and Wu, J. (2009) Urbanization and informal development in China: urban villages in Shenzhen', *International Journal of Urban and Regional Research*, 33(4), 957–973.

Wu, F. (2009) 'Land development, inequality and urban villages in China', *International Journal of Urban and Regional Research*, 33(4), 885-889.

Wu, F. (2016) 'Housing in Chinese urban villages: The dwellers, conditions and tenancy informality', *Housing Studies*, 31(7), 852–870.

Wu, F., Zhang, F. and Webster, C. (2013) 'Informality and the development and demolition of urban villages in the Chinese peri-urban area', *Urban Studies*, 50(10), 1919–1934.

Yang, X. (2000) 'Determinants of migration intentions in Hubei province, China: individual versus family migration', *Environment and Planning A*, 32(5), 769–787.

Zhang, L. (2001) *Strangers in the city: Reconfigurations of space, power, and social networks within China's floating population*, Stanford University Press.

Chapter 7: Urban Environmental Migrants

Demands for a Unique Category of Refugees
to Ensure their Right to Land and Resettlement

Syed Mukaddim, Md. Zakir Hossain, Sujit Kumar Sikder

INTRODUCTION

Environmentally induced migration is quite an old phenomenon, yet its recognition as a distinct category remains a topic of debate (Myers 2005). Along with it, persons displaced chiefly due to the consequences of climate change do not hold an important place on the agendas of the relevant international organisations (e.g. International Organization for Migration (IOM), United Nations High Commission for Refugees (UNHCR)) so as to be treated with the attention they need. In his publication 'Environmental refugees: myth or reality', Black (2001) argues that the phenomenon of such migration is evident and supported by scholarly literature yet, unfortunately, the concerned organisations do not address this issue with the gravity that it merits. Lambert (2002) argues that even though the problem of environmentally induced migration exists, its lack of recognition among political organisations makes it more troublesome to address. The lack of political will to acknowledge this problem is the root cause of the failure to create any framework to assist environmental migrants or displaced persons. Furthermore, the literature on environmental risk management (e.g., Mallick and Akter 2013; Etzold and Mallick 2016; Roy *et al*. 2017) reports the increased risk among socially and economically vulnerable communities located in tropical coastal belts, due to the adverse effects of environmental disruptions.

Very few steps have been taken to bring these people into an institutional framework. Some studies, for example, Kolmannskog (2008), point to the fact that applying the term 'refugee' to such displaced groups is inaccurate and thus needs to be addressed separately. This author suggests that closer consideration should be made for the prevailing policies of prevention and protections before bringing in new measures to deal with this issue. Further, various scholars and authorities have offered draft conventions to address people who have been displaced by climate change, in an effort to enclose them within an international regime of status and treatment in accordance with the challenges these people face due to the climate effects of rising global temperatures (Aylett 2014). Finally, the literature shows that a significant number of people are in need of protection and thus deserve attention at both national and international political levels. Even though the number of such displaced persons is not yet known, Myers (2005) suggests that by 2050 an estimated 200 million people will fall under this category. Hence the time has certainly arrived for all actors to take necessary action on this critical issue.

Keeping all of these issues at the forefront, the main focus of this research is to address the problem of recognising that environmental migrants should have a separate identity. In addition, when the typology of such migrants gains considerable ground in the arena of policy support, it will then become necessary to prepare a policy framework for their protection and, more so, for their right to land that has not incurred environmental degradation, which appears to be the most significant and troublesome issue for these migrants. Therefore, the main problem this research focuses on and is about identifying 'environmental refugees' with a clear understanding of what this term actually refers to (Black 2001). Preferably, this would be treated as a separate category of migrants rather than adding them to the long list of political or economic refugees or the like. Along with this, another issue that has been largely ignored is the lack of a clearly acknowledged identification for these people and this has led to the problem of how to provide this migrant group with adequate structural support and assistance. The remainder of this chapter provides a literature review, the research strategy, some discussion, the findings and some conclusions.

"ENVIRONMENTAL MIGRANTS": AN IDENTITY IN THE MAKING?

The hurdle in linking environmental degradation to human migration is that the victims of such consequences are nowhere when it comes to the devising of policies and initiatives that would ensure they are accorded the basic rights they are supposed to be entitled to. However, scholars have acknowledged that the terminologies used to indicate this group are not only confusing but also insufficient to incorporate the totality of such migrants. Thus, a distinctive categorisation of this population bears utter significance, both in terms of recognising them as the most vulnerable group when environmental calamities strike and in formulating policies to integrate them into a support-and-assistance framework.

It is undeniable that population displacement mainly caused by environmental changes (that eventually trigger other driving factors behind migration and displacement) must be recognised as a distinctive identifiable category beyond those identified under risk management strategies (Dun and Gemenne 2008; Etzold and Mallick 2016). With this recognition comes the necessity of establishing an identity base for those who are the victims of such displacements. Therefore, a definition that separates this particular group from other types of migrants is of utter importance. Very little space in the contemporary literature has been assigned to defining those forced to migrate due to environmental disasters. Most of this literature focuses on policy gaps and how to mitigate this deficit. The urgency of a clear definition and, hence, a particular identity for these migrants has attracted even less attention from policy makers and academics, mainly because there are already quite a few terms one can refer to when it comes to writing about this population; for example, 'environmental migrants' (Boano et al. 2008); 'climate refugees' (Berchin et al. 2017); 'people displaced by climate change' (Hodgkinson et al. 2009). Nonetheless, attempts have been made to find a concise definition for this group of migrants. Dun and Gemenne (2008, p.10) clearly state that 'without a precise definition, practitioners and policy-makers are not easily able to establish plans and make targeted progress'. They also indicate that the current definition of refugee set out in the 1951 Refugee Convention has helpful elements with which to create an identity for these migrants. The literature also brings forward the fact that even though the definition might have some elements of creating an identity, the migrants or displaced people who fall under this definition remain unrecognised and, thus, non-recipients of proper assistance.

In an attempt to define 'environmental migrants' Kolmannskog (2008) mentions two well-known definitions, one of which is that of El-Hinnawi (1985) and another of Myers (2002). El-Hinnawi (1985) clearly stated that people who are forced to migrate due to environmental factors, be it permanent or temporary, are to be labelled as such, given that their natural habitats have been seriously compromised to such an extent where the normal possibility of a livelihood is next to impossible. Even though El-Hinnawi's definition gives some clarity to a separate group of people who are suffering from environmental disruptions (Kolmannskog 2008), it still is not inclusive of all of the situations under which people are forced to relocate. Myers and Kent (1995) offered yet another definition, when they stated that, when people are faced with being forced from their traditional habitats, due to various environmental changes, notably, soil erosion, water shortages, deforestation and the like, and the challenge of securing a livelihood whether on a semi-permanent or permanent basis, inland or out, this group of people falls under the definition of 'environmental refugee'. Furthermore, these authors considered the fact that people living under such conditions have no other alternatives but to migrate within or outside the country and that environmental disasters eliminate the chances of their returning home when things got back to normal, if ever. Thus, the crucial question is one of status and whether these people should be recognised as environmental/climate migrants and be granted proper treatment.

Boano et al. (2008) argued that the existing terminologies used to identify environmental forced migrations are problematic as these terminologies often represent a more subjective classification and the decision to migrate is being made mostly by the refugees themselves (El-Hinnawi 1985; Berchin *et al.* 2017). Taking a look at Zetter (2017), however, terms like 'environmental refugees', 'tsunami refugees', 'development refugees' and so on, offer an initial identification of a group of people who have been forcefully displaced from their habitats; further, these terms provide insights into and interpretations of the actual causes and consequences of the real situation this group finds itself in. Keane (2004) suggested that these terms do not fall under the definition of refugees as set out in the 1951 Refugee Convention. On one hand, the absence of a proper definition makes the term unsuitable and hence unacceptable by most. On the other hand, there is a consensus, in the literature, that not all people who are displaced by environmental degradation, such as climate change, which can be caused by either rapid- and slow-onset events, will migrate or relocate outside their national borders; hence, it is crucial to avoid referring to them as refugees (Boano *et al.* 2008). Yet from another definitional perspective, since the status of refuge assumes a 'persecutor' whom people fear, unless the 'environment' or 'nature' is seen as such, it is not authentic to label as 'refugees' people who are forced to migrate due to environmental causes (Keane 2004).

All of this literary evidence hints at the two-fold aspect of a need for an identity for this population and the inadequacy of the existing terminologies and also the real need for a distinctive identity base for this migration type and population. Amidst the discussion about whether the term 'climate refugees or 'forced climate migrants' (Berchin *et al.* 2017, p. 148) should be used, the former has gained popularity over the latter. This label provides the public with an emotionally sensitive and open approach to the issue (Brown 2007); it also helps differentiate environmentally induced migrants from the other types of migrants. Due to severe climatic events, people continue to leave their homes or countries and seek asylum in other regions or countries. As such, they are left in situations of insecurity and hopelessness (Berchin *et al.* 2017). However, the general category of 'migrant' has an adverse implication, since these people had decided to move spontaneously in search of a considerably better future (ibid.).

CONCEPTUAL FRAMEWORK

This chapter aims to focus on people who are forced to relocate to new places due to environmental events and it also addresses their sense of being around new localities, which is a consquence of their having to relocate due to environmental impacts. This relocation or displacement takes place mainly due to severe environmental events that seriously disrupt their everyday lives and damage their livelihoods; in most cases, these former lives and livelihoods are not repairable. Therefore, these people are either forced to change their usual earning strategies or their place of living or both. Making the decision to migrate does not rely only on the event that forced people to move; rather, it triggers other hurdles that in themselves are difficult enough to overcome. Hence, the construction of the conceptual framework for this research is based on perceptions gathered from the preliminary or initial fieldwork and literature reviews. This investigation took place in three interconnected phases. Figure 1 (below) shows the relational diagram of the phases that served as a conceptual framework for this research. All three phases were intertwined and played crucial roles both during the migration decision and in the post-migration identity-making process.

The effects of upcoming climate-change events on livelihood strategies are expected to be significant (Black *et al.* 2013). Phase one describes the principal drivers for migration. Being one such driver, environmental events contribute to people making migratory decisions either directly or indirectly due to other aggregating factors (Sikder *et al.* 2015). This phase shows the initial thrust environmental factors and other drivers provide. This thrust also serves to agitate the existing environmental degradation and helps accelerate the process of displacement. For example, during the fieldwork, one of the interviewees described how her family survived Sidr, one of the deadliest cyclones on record, and avoided migration. Two years later, she was forced to migrate to her current location due to being a victim of an even deadlier cyclone, Aila. The latter event intensified the gravity of the catastrophic situation cyclone Sidr had created.

Figure 1: Conceptual framework for identity making of the 'environment migrants'.

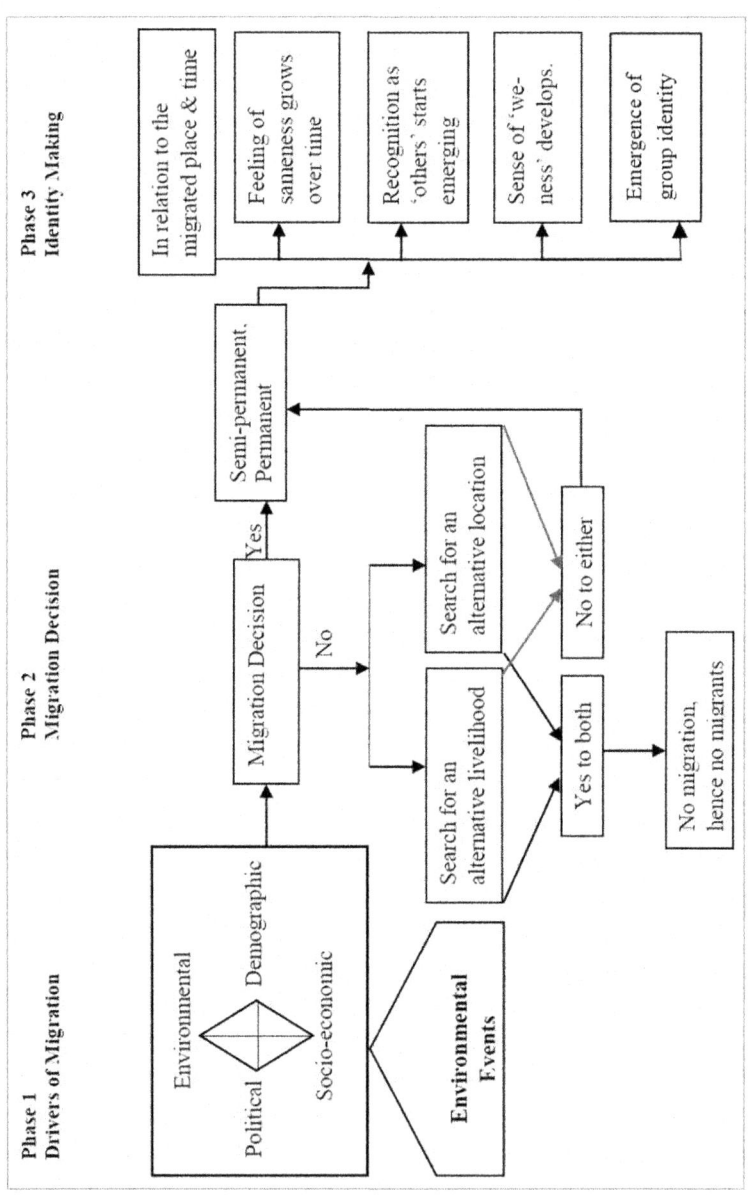

Source: Authors' own draft, based on secondary literature survey.

The number of displaced persons due to environmental disasters is not insignificant. The United Nations Development Programmes (UNDP) Human Development Report suggests that, as of 2009, there were approximately 740 million internal migrants due to circumstances related to climate change (UNDP 2009). The process of migration takes place in two phases. The decision-making process begins during phase one and can speed up, depending on the context and severity of the events. Phase two describes the actual migration decision-making stage; this migration decision could be to migrate internally, externally (transboundary) or to not migrate at all. It also shows the relationship between the decisions taken in favour of or against migration. In this phase, migration may or may not take place, depending on the success of finding a suitable location in which to live and in securing another means of livelihood around the location where these people had lived prior to the event. If the latter occurs, then migration is unlikely to take place. Phase three shows the building of a sense of self among the people who took the necessary steps to move away from their original living place of habitation. Once the displacement is completed over time, these people become aware of the fact that their livelihood pattern and the meaning of their lives have both changed in relation to the place in which they currently reside. This building of sense also gives them an understanding of how and why they are different than those who are native to the place. This phase is where the research focuses greater concentration.

RESEARCH STRATEGY

This research adopted the case study method, through fieldwork and analysing secondary literature. Being inductive in nature, it focused on understanding how environmentally displaced people gain a distinct sense of identity. This study aimed to find the probable link between environmentally induced migration and identity. Simply put, it argues for the need of an identity base for those who are displaced internally or internationally due to environmental events. In so doing, it is important to consider whether there is a connection between the two processes through which the displacement decision must be made in the first place. For this study, three slums were selected, namely Khora *Bastee*[1], Labanchara Bastee and Rupsha Bastee located in Khulna city in Bangladesh. A high percentage concentration of internal migrants due to climatic events was a priority when selecting these slums.

---

1   *Bastee* is a local term for slum.

Data collection methods for this research included in-depth interviews; non-participant observations, followed by informal discussions; and an analysis of secondary literature. As the migrant households were dispersed throughout the slums and sometimes were found in some pockets of these slums, this research first identified the pockets and locations of these migrants. Then, households were randomly selected from the listed locations, using an unbiased view of the perceptions that people held about these slums. A total of 20 households were considered for the in-depth interviews. Interviewees were selected regardless of gender, age, educational qualifications or professional standings. For this study, unstructured interviews (Bryman 2008) were used so as to keep the data-extraction process close to a regular conversation. Respondents talked freely and in an informal tone, since the focus was to grasp the perceptions and understanding of the people being interviewed.

This study also heavily depended on an analysis of the literature on identity and migration as they related to environmental factors. Both phenomena are complex and are driven by multiple factors. The aim was to find a functional link between the two so as to provide a basis for the groups that were displaced and hence bound to migrate due to environmental degradation (Warner 2010). Therefore, the literature was reviewed from both arenas to find similarities and differences. Investigating the literature also provided an understanding of people's perceptions regarding both the causes of their migration and the subsequent identity-making processes. Moreover, the literature review helped reveal the existing bridges and gaps between the two phenomena under discussion. One form of observation is a non-participant one that permits the researcher to observe while remaining aloof. Here, the aim was to grasp an understanding of what people from and around a particular age group thought about themselves and how they perceived their existence. Thematic analysis was adopted as a data analysis method; here, themes were validated by evidence found in scholarly literature. The next section reports the results of a case study of Khulna. The empirical study was conducted in three distinct large slums/informal settlements in Khulna city. The discussion on the key findings include a review of the conceptual framework that was introduced in an earlier section.

THE CASE OF KHULNA CITY

Migration decision

This section addresses why and under what contexts people migrate once an event takes place. Migration decisions are based on multiple concerns that each act in conjunction within a particular situation. After a climatic incident, people may decide to either migrate immediately or gradually, depending on the type and intensity of the incident, the extent of the damage it caused and the sources available to restore these people's livelihoods within the shortest time possible. A climatic event has impacts on both social and economic factors. The extent to which these factors are affected determines the decision to migrate. Figure 2 shows the relational links among the various factors that influence the migration decision.

Depending on the situation, migrants vary by type, and this is mainly a reflection of their pre-migration condition and how this had been altered during or after an event or calamity. The three slums selected for the fieldwork are settlements of migrants who had moved mainly due to environmental events. Among the three slums, Labanchara had the largest population of these types of migrants and Rupsha slum had the least number of environmental migrants. Findings from these three slums are not exactly the same; while some of the data and information obtained were identical in relation to migration and identity-making, other data on these migrants differed. When struck by a climatic shock, the people in the affected areas tended to relocate to ensure they could continue to carry out their primary livelihoods. This tendency was found throughout these three slum areas.

In most cases, it was found that cyclones Sidr and Ailahad caused the environmental degradations that had resulted in migrations. Jahanara Begum, a migrant living in Labanchara slum (interviewed on 8th April, 2016), described why she had to migrate after cyclone Aila. She lost her source of income due to the damage caused by this cyclone. She expressed her helplessness and inability to support her family after the event, when she said, 'sob jhoree nei gaeilo', which literally means that everything was destroyed during Aila. She noted that she had run out of options to care for her family. Better employment opportunities influenced her to make the decision to migrate to the nearest city. In their theoretical model on migration patterns, Maurel and Tuccio (2016) provide similar perspectives on the impact of environmental events on migration decisions. The aforementioned model highlights climate shocks, such as floods, cyclones and so on, that push the transition of labour from agriculture to modern manufacturing and the service sector, causing the migration of rural people to urban-centres.

Figure 2: Links among various factors that influence the migration decision.

[Figure 2: A flowchart showing climatic events such as cyclone, storm, flood etc. affecting Social Factors, Economic Factors, and Other Factors (environmental, demographic, etc). Social Factors interact with Economic Factors, leading to Reduced level of protection, Increased insecurity, Reduced level of stratum e.g. loan defaulter. Economic Factors lead to Loss of livelihoods, capitals, resources, which causes social issues and Interruption of other economic activities. All contribute to the Migration Decision.]

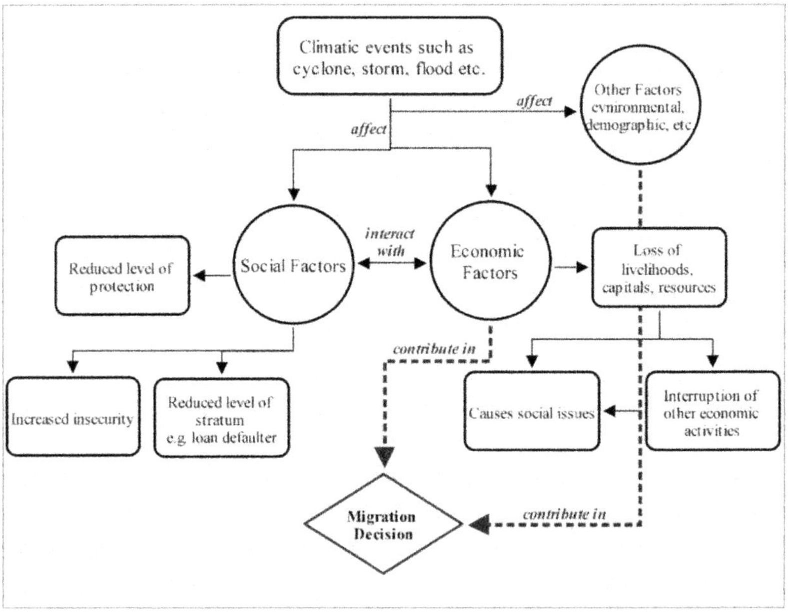

Source: Authors own draft based on findings from field survey and secondary literature.

People also make migratory decisions for socio-economic reasons. But then again, an area's socio-economic conditions often worsen due to climatic shocks, whether sudden or gradual. For example, interviewees found in the slums Labanchara and Sonadanga expressed how they had been forced to migrate to their current location due to cyclone Aila and the consequent irrecoverable losses in economic activities. They noted how they had taken out loans from local money lenders so as to establish and carry on their main sources of income. Borrowing from local moneylenders is quite a normal scenario in rural areas of Bangladesh, due to the availability of this type of financing and the fact there is less paper work than there is in banks and other financial institutions. However, when Aila caused irreparable damage to their primary sources of income, these people were no longer able to repay the moneylenders and had no choice but to 'escape'. In the words of the interviewees, 'ki koire mukh dekhabo, taka diti parini', which means that they were ashamed of being a loan defaulter. When people become loan defaulters, this adds social pressure to the economic ones, since their status quos have been interrupted. Both factors contributed equally to making the decision to migrate, to escape both social and economic pressures, and these factors were largely influenced by Aila a climatic event.

In addition to socio-economic conditions being intensified by environmental ones, many other factors also heavily influence the migration decision. For example, the demographic pressure exerted on people who are victims of a climatic event pushes them out of their places of origin. At the same time, they are mainly pulled by the availability of work and support from relatives who live in nearby cities. Both of these factors work in conjunction to influence the migration decisions of populations affected by environmental events. While migration may be 'one of the fundamental choices to be made' (Collins 2013, p. 113), the reasons for so doing are complex and interconnected. Thus, the decision to migrate depends on the contexts and the intensity of the primary drivers.

Identity making

Identity is an abstract reality; the concept of 'the self' is the generic definition of the term. Identity evolves and takes on various roles in people's lives, in relation to particular points of reference. Being a perceived sense of existence, identity is fluid in nature and thus changes in form. The displacements that take place chiefly because of environmental shocks can create a unique base of identity for a migrant population, and this is the main premise of this study.

The need for a distinctive identity

Environmental events can trigger displacements, either internally or across borders. Fieldwork shows similar traits of human mobility, as discussed earlier. While scholars, such as Myers (2002), emphasise that there is growing concern for a group of people around the world who face forced displacements due to environmental problems, findings from fieldwork suggest that environmentally induced migrants identify themselves as being different from the slums' non-migrants, who are mostly land owners. When asked if he felt any different here, one of the respondents replied,

'Where will we go? We have lost everything there [previous living place]. Now this has become our home. They [the land owners] help us more or less, we survive this way' (Interview with Abdul Momin, Rupsha slum, 30 October, 2016).

In another interview, one of the interviewees, Shefali, expressed how she felt different from the native dwellers. She also expressed how she felt 'connected' to those who migrated from *Koyra* (a sub-district of Bangladesh), her native land, due to cyclone Aila. She said,

'We are all the same. Most of us [tenants] have come here after the 'big storm' [cyclones like Aila, Sidr etc.]. They [native dwellers] helped us live here, but we have to pay them. We live here but they own it' (Interview with Shefali, Rupsha slum, 30 October, 2016).

Such case studies show how people develop an understanding of their existence in relation to those who are not subject to the same challenges, in these cases being forced to migrate due to environmental events. Climatic events are by no means the sole drivers of displacement, be it internal or external; rather, these events work as catalysts that aggravate existing problems and, hence, cause mobility (Kartiki 2011). Likewise, in Bangladesh, people who are internally displaced, due to various environmental catastrophes, are a cause for concern.

Table 1: Sense of the self: present and level of concentration.

Slums	Sense Type: Strong » Less	Concentration of Migrants
Rupsha	Individual	Least
Labanchara	Group » Individual	High
Sonadanga	Individual » Group	Moderate

Source: Authors, 2016.

Table 1 shows that in, Rupsha slum, migrants were inclined toward feeling a sense of the individual. In Labanchara slum, interviewees noted a strong prevailing sense of feeling togetherness as a group and a weaker sense of the individual. Migrants in Sonadanga slum felt more individualistic in type and had a more moderate awareness of sameness, but their group feeling was still somewhat prevalent. One of the reasons for the interviewees expressing such a differentiation of senses was the concentration of migrant groups in those slums. Whereas in Labanchara slum, there was a high concentration of homes of such groups, it was obvious that the sense of being the same as a group was stronger than for being part of another type. The opposite was true for Rupsha slum, while respondents in Sonadanga slum showed a varied view of leaning toward both descriptions. These findings also suggest the growing need to recognise the movements of these migrants so it becomes easier and less confusing to conceptualise and identify them. In a personal communication, Mitu Akter, a 19-year-old girl living in Sonadanga slum, expressed her feelings toward people her same age and explained why she liked to spend more time with those who had migrated from the same place of origin as she had. Here, she showed a feeling of sameness that was based on the migration context and the similar locality of origin. She termed these migrants as 'nijer lowk' to point out the type of connection she felt toward them. This is a unique finding that shows why identity creation for such groups is significant.

Table 2 presents an overall picture of migrant's understanding of the type of senses people hold in terms of whether they are the same or different in relation to their different contexts. This is a manifestation of the types of identity group or individual found among the migrants in the study. The relational references here play a role in the elements of identity that are described in the study's conceptual framework.

Table 2: Differences in perceptions and related cause, according to age group.

Age groups	Perception type	In relation to
> 20	Mostly collective	Same age group
20-30	Individual, if not undecided	Income opportunities, employment
30-40	Overlaps; ⟷ Collective Individual	Social networking, relatives
40<	Mostly individual, overlaps	Sources of income, assets, social strata

Source: Field Survey, 2016.

Sense of place and the self

The empirical findings from the three slums within the city area of Khulna suggest that Khulna is the first choice among coastal residents because it is the nearest urban area in the event of a climatic disaster, such as cyclones Aila and Sidr. While conducting the fieldwork, these particular city slums were chosen based on the concentration of migrants who had faced such displacements. The fieldwork findings show that most of the migrants who had to relocate to these slums, due to environmental catastrophes such as a cyclone, flood, excessive salinity and such, wished to remain in their current dwelling locality and had developed a 'sense of place' (Relph 1976). One of the interviewees showed his sense of connectedness when he said:

'We have lost everything there. This place has become our home now' (interview with Abdul Momin, Rupsha slum, 30th October, 2016).

In terms of the findings in the literature, similar observations were also made during this study's fieldwork. The sense of place grows over time. Abdul Momin referred to himself in relation to his current locality. His social identity became centred around that place of living. At the same time, when asked, he noted that the place provided him with a point of recognition. Thus, in nature, the interactions are two way. Similarly, scholars such as Hauge (2007) emphasised that the interdependent relationship between the place and the people narrates as a unit that centres the reciprocal influence between the people and the place. Place is also seen as a product of its physical attributes, human conceptions, and the activities that take place there, as termed by Canter (1997). The migrants' feelings of being at home, otherwise known as rootedness (Hauge 2007), which they had developed over time in relation to their current dwelling places and the local environment indicated that their had taken on a sense of place a positive feeling for the locality they were currently in. Scholars have termed this positive psyche as having a place identity (Proshansky et al. 1983). When people show signs of recognising themselves in relation to the physical place they are located in, they are in fact manifesting one of five central functions of place identity (Hauge 2007). Thus, they attach a socio-cultural meaning to their physical environment. Figure 3 shows that after migration, interactions between the people and the place become significant to the process of identity-making. Over time, these interactions help migrants grow attachments and assign significance to the places to which they have migrated. The place refers to the socio-cultural meanings people attach to it in relation to the physical environment and then there emerges the identity people attach to the place or the place identity they establish (Proshansky et al. 1983).

Figure 3: Identity-making process through interactions between place and people over time.

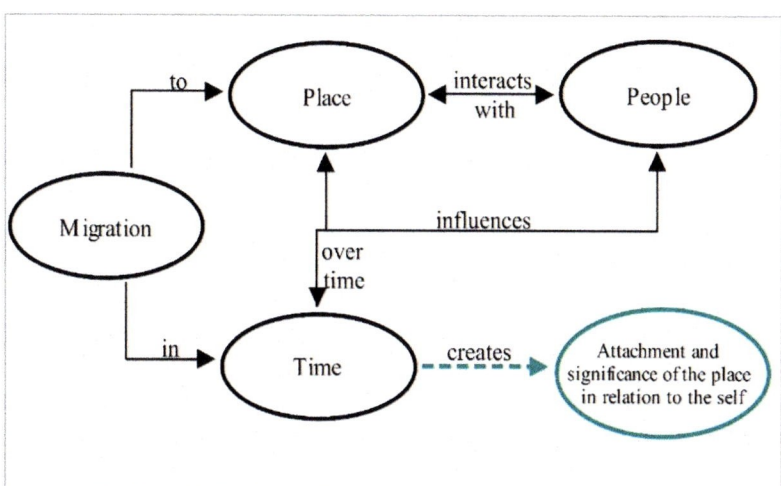

Source: Authors own draft, based on findings from a field survey and secondary literature, 2016.

Migrants also develop a sense of sameness that is based on various criteria. These criteria include similar migratory conditions, places of origin, the similarity of events for which they had chosen to migrate, and so on. During informal conversations in the fieldwork, informants noted how their relocation had changed their lifestyles and livelihoods, along with how they had been treated once they had migrated after the two climatic events. One such respondent, Motahar, age 33, had owned land and run a business back 'home' (he referred to his original location as the home from where he had to migrate to the current location). After Aila which was a devastating cyclone he and his family were forced to relocate because of decreasing business conditions and being trapped by loans. In the slum where he was residing, he had relatives who had been living there for a long time prior to his and his family's relocation. After the environmental event, he got in touch with these relatives and made the decision to relocate to secure his family's livelihood and children's education and, thus, their future. He felt at home there, at the time of the study, after having lived there 'all these years'. He also felt a connectedness to those who had also migrated under similar conditions to his. In his words, his relatives made it feel more like home for him, since he mentioned them as 'nijer jon'.

Migration experts, such as Massey et al. (1993), point out that social network theory is one of the prime theories of migration used to describe different aspects of migration. In the cases discussed in this study, this theory seems to have served more significantly over the other theories presented in the literature. In the above case, the family had sought social networks in an urban area, with a view to migrating from the affected zone. Once they were settled, they began the process of blending in with the original non-migrant slum dwellers. Yet, there remained a clear distinction between these two groups migrants and non-migrant slum dwellers. When asked, a non-migrant household could easily pinpoint a migrant household by referring to the event that had forced them to migrate. Even though the two groups did not hold to any noticeable identity crisis, during the informal interviews it would be interesting to know whether this came from the migrants themselves or whether the original community members sensed this need. In addition, the forced migrants also recognised themselves as a unit against the 'other' and had developed a sense of being a group-self, which indicates the internalisation of a distinctive categorisation process taking place in their psyches.

'PEOPLE OF FORCED DISPLACEMENT'

During the fieldwork, it was evident that the migrants that had been displaced mainly due to environmental factors were in a disadvantageous position relative to the local (non-migrant) inhabitants. This does not mean that there were no interventions in local and international forms of assistance; rather, the issue for these migrants was the insufficiency in the lack of a proper and distinctive identity. Dim and Gemenne (2008) urged for a need for a definition of a term that could be used to conceptualise the issue of identity in an effective way. Another insufficiency was housing and land or homeownership. For such migrants, housing is particularly challenging. In informal discussions with the slum dwellers, it was made clear that their right to land had been degraded due to being treated as 'homeless', as being seen as such by the land and homeowners of the localities they had migrated to. In general, this homelessness status may be implicit in nature but it becomes evident when it comes to receiving any aid, especially from non-governmental organisations. This also creates a sphere of political power where the landowners play the deciding role in determining who gets what type of facility. The senses of insideness and outsideness (Relph 1976) are simultaneously functional in the psyche of both groups of inhabitants. Landowners generally have an influential presence over those to whom they rent their houses but more so if the tenant is a migrant. Regarding tenants, even though they are seen as being in the same group, they heavily differ in relation to their stay time and migratory status. Therefore, tenants who are not migrants seem to enjoy greater status in the social hierarchy. In any case, the findings of this study note that migrants were the least-preferred group to be sanctioned assistance. For example, some of the migrants (who wished to remain unnamed) stated that they were not accepted for reasonably sized loans because they did not own any land or a house. 'Bariwalarai sob pabi. Amager to bari nei, tai hreen daei na', which translates to 'people of such forced displacement within or across a boundary, are mostly left with the fewest number of opportunities to return to their original homes' (Myers and Kent 1995). Hence, they encounter higher degrees of social discrimination, which in the case of housing and land-owning, becomes more visibly noticeable. They seem to belong to no eligible group (Keane 2004) of migrants that can receive specialised assistance after being forcefully displaced and have no clear identifiable term with which to be labelled.

Migration scholars heavily contest environmentalists' use of the term 'environmental refugees' for dislocated groups of people; they argue that in international law the term 'refugee' is specifically defined to include a group that does not fit the group under discussion (Martin 2013). Dun and Gemenne (2008) argue that this recognition is an unavoidable fact in the case of providing such migrants with appropriate assistance. The conceptualisation of such migrants also requires that a crucial step be taken to establish a precise identity (Dun and Gemenne 2008). This study finds likewise: there is a need for a distinctive categorisation for people who are displaced due to environmental events. The literature indicates the necessity of expanding the existing definitions (Dun and Gemenne 2008; Kartiki 2011; Martin 2013) and of incorporating these terminologies into a policy framework that prioritises and identifies those in need of adequate and appropriate assistance. To effectively address the future flow of such migrants, scholarly works should also signify the need for a distinctive identification both for migration and for policy-making. Despite the absence of a full-scale manifestation of the impact of climate events on migration, many argue for the prediction of migratory behaviour, to some degree, by analysing the impact of the effects of past environmental events on human migration (Reuveny 2007). Drawing on instances of mobility cases in Bangladesh, Joardar and Miller (2013) show that the type of migration, whether permanent or temporary, depends on many factors, such as migrants receiving appropriate assistance immediately after an environmental event as these migrants are more likely to be permanent in nature. McMillan (2015) argues that as climate change is thought to have substantially contributed to increasing human mobility, it will influence the scale and nature of future human displacements. Fieldwork findings suggest similar traits.

CONCLUSION

This research has contributed to a deeper understanding of how environmentally induced migration takes place and how the people who migrate perceive the process in line with where they stand in the conceptual framework of environmental migration. Two principal factors are the key points of focus here: the migration decision and the identity of an environmental migrant. On one front, the migration decision that is due to environmental shocks or hazards is hardly a separate event; rather, it is a complex mixture of interrelated variables that are socio-economic, demographic, political and environmental. On another front, once the migration decision is taken and the movement has been completed, the new place and people act as points of comparison and recognition for these migrants. These points give them a meaning that is one of both outsideness and insideness (Relph 1976). Eventually their interactions with the entire environment define what they understand about themselves and help them form new identities. Experts are concerned that the environment and its changes are playing significant roles in creating a type of human mobility that will become more complex than it already is. Findings from the study's fieldwork, though limited in context, also show this fact. People who face this type of mobility must undergo numerous changes and adjustments on various levels, starting from socio-cultural to individual ones. Nevertheless, until policy-makers properly recognise and acknowledge this group (Arnall and Kothari 2015), these migrants will always be in a constant situation of deterioration, given the catastrophes that are expected to be brought about by future environmental events. This study acknowledges the fact that the spatial scope for this study makes it difficult to get an overall idea on the questions being searched for, since the fieldwork was conducted locally. Despite the limitations, scholars have agreed on and note that the number people affected by climatic events is big enough to count as a separate migratory process, though it is not yet being added. Therefore, this study could also be conducted in some other countries so as to cross-check and validate the responses and overall scenarios pertaining to the research questions. Moreover, a transboundary research may reveal even more interesting aspects of this study in relation to how migration shapes identity in reference to place and time.

REFERENCES

Arnall, A. and Kothari, U. (2015) 'Challenging climate change and migration discourse: Different understandings of timescale and temporality in the Maldives', *Global Environmental Change*, 31, 199–206.

Aylett, A. (2014) *Progress and Challenges in the Urban Governance of Climate Change: Results of a Global Survey*, Cambridge: ICLEI and MIT.

Berchin, I.I., Valduga, I.B., Garcia, J. and Guerra, Baltazar S.O.de.A.J. (2017) 'Climate change and forced migrations: An effort towards recognising climate refugees', *Geoforum*, 84, 147–150.

Black, R., Kniveton, D. and Schmidt-Verkerk, K. (2013) 'Migration and climate change: Toward an integrated assessment of sensitivity', in Faist, T. & Schade, J., eds., *Disentangling Migration and Climate Change*, Netherlands: Springer, 29–52.

Black, R. (2001) 'Environmental refugees: Myth or reality? new issues in refugee research', *Working Paper* No. 34, UNHCR, United Kingdom: University of Sussex.

Boano, C., Zetter, R. and Morris, T. (2008) 'Environmentally displaced people: Understanding the linkages between environmental change, livelihoods and forced migration', *Forced Migration Policy Briefing 1*, Refugee Studies Center, United Kingdom: Oxford Department of International Development-University of Oxford.

Brown, O. (2008) 'Migration and climate change', *IOM Migration Research Series*, Switzerland: International Organization for Migration.

Brown, O. (2007) *Fighting Climate Change: Climate Change and Forced Migration: Observations, Projections and Implications. Human Development Report*, Switzerland: International Organization for Migration, available at: https://www.iisd.org/pdf/2008/climate_forced_migration.pdf [accessed 2nd Feb 2019].

Bryman, A. (2008) *Social Research Methods*, 3rd ed., New York: Oxford University Press.

Canter D. (1997) 'The facets of place', in Gary T.M., Robert W.M., eds., *Toward the Integration of Theory, Methods, Research, and Utilization. Advances in Environment, Behaviour and Design*, vol 4, Boston: Springer, 109–147.

Casey, E.S. (2001) 'Body, self and landscape: A geographical inquiry into the place-world', in Adams, C.P., Hoelscher, S. and Till, E.K., eds., *Textures of Place*, Minneapolis, MN, USA: University of Minnesota Press, 403–425.

Collins, A.E. (2013) 'Applications of the disaster risk reduction approach to migration influenced by environmental change', *Environmental Science & Policy*, 27 (S1), S112–S125.

Dun, O. and Gemenne, F. (2008) 'Defining environmental migration', *Forced Migration Review*, 31, 10–11.

Etzold B., Mallick B. (2016) 'Moving beyond the focus on environmental migration towards recognising the normality of translocal lives: Insights from Bangladesh', in Milan, A., Schraven, B., Warner, K., Cascone, N., eds., *Migration, Risk Management and Climate Change: Evidence and Policy Responses*, Global Migration Issues, vol 6, Switzerland: Springer, 105–128.

Hauge, Å.L. (2007) 'Identity and place: A critical comparison of three identity theories', *Architectural Science Review*, 50 (1), 44–51.

Hodgkinson, D., Burton, T., Young, L., Anderson, H. (2009). 'Copenhagen, climate change 'refugees' and the need for a global agreement', *Public Policy*, 4, 155–174, available at: http://www.hodgkinsongroup.com/documents Copehagen_And_CCDPs.pdf [accessed 18th Nov 2016].

Hugo, Graeme J. (1981) 'Village-community ties, village norms, and ethnic and social networks: A review of evidence from the third world' in De Jong, F.G. and Gardner, W.R., eds., *Migration decision-making: Multidisciplinary approaches to micro-level studies in developed and developing countries*, New York: Pergamon Press, 186–225.

Hugo, G. (2011) 'Future demographic change and its interactions with migration and climate change', *Global Environmental Change*, 21(S1), pp. 21–33.

Joarder, M.A.M. and Miller, P.W. (2013) 'Factors affecting whether environmental migration is temporary or permanent: Evidence from Bangladesh', *Global Environmental Change*, 23(6), 1511–1524.

Kartiki, K. (2011) 'Climate change and migration: A case study from rural Bangladesh', *Gender & Development*, 19 (1), 23–38.

Keane, D. (2004) 'Environmental causes and consequences of migration: A search for the meaning of environmental refugees', *Georgetown International Environmental Law Review*, 16, 209-223.

Kolmannskog, V. (2008) *Future floods of refugees: A comment on climate change, conflict and forced migration*, Norway: Norwegian Refugee Council.

Lambert, M. (2002) 'Politics, patriarchy and new traditions: Understanding female migration among the Jola', in Hahn, P.H. and Klute G., eds., *Cultures of Migration*, New Burnwick, USA and London, UK: Transaction Publishers, 129–148.

Mallick, B. and Akter, S. (2013) 'The poverty-vulnerability-resilience nexus: Evidence from Bangladesh', *Ecological Economics*, 96, 114–124.

Massey, D.S., Arango, J., Hugo, G., Kouaouci, A., Pellegrino, A. and Tylor, E.J. (1993) 'Theories of international migration: A review and appraisal', *Population and Development Review*, 19 (3), 431–466.

Maurel M. and Tuccio M. (2016) 'Climate instability, urbanisation and international migration', *The Journal of Development Studies*, 52 (2), 735–752.

Martin, S.F. (2013) 'Environmental change and migration: What we know', *Migration Policy Institute*. 2, 1–12.

McMichael, C. (2015) 'Climate change-related migration and infectious disease', *Virulence*, 6 (6), 548–553.

Myers, N. (2002) 'Environmental refugees: A growing phenomenon of the 21st century', *Philosophical Transactions of the Royal Society B*, 357, 609–613.

Myers, N. (2005) 'Environmental refugees: An emergent security issue', *Paper presented in 13th Economic Forum, Session III – Environment and Migration*, 23–27 May, Prague.

Myers, N., & Kent, J. (1995) *Environmental Exodus: An Emergent Crisis in the Global Arena*, Washington, DC: The Climate Institute.

Proshansky, H. M., Fabian, A. K. and Kaminoff, R. (1983) 'Place-identity: Physical world socialization of the self', *Journal of Environmental Psychology*, 3, 57–83.

Relph, E. (1976) *Place and placelessness*, 1st ed., London: Pion.

Renaud, F., Dun, O., Warner, K. and Bogardi, J. (2011) 'A decision framework for environmentally induced migration', *International Migration*, 49(S1), 1–25.

Reuveny, R. (2007) 'Climate change-induced migration and violent conflict', *Political Geography*, 26(6), 65–673.

Roy, K, Gain, A., Mallick, B. and Vogt, J. (2017) 'Social, hydro-ecological and climatic change in the southwest coastal region of Bangladesh', *Regional Environmental Change*, 17(7), 1895–1906.

Sikder S., Asadzadeh, A., Kuusaana, E. D., Mallick, B., and Koetter, T. (2015) 'Stakeholders participation for urban climate resilience: A case of informal settlements regularisation in Khulna city, Bangladesh', *Journal of Urban and Regional Analysis*, 7(1), 5–20.

Smith, A. D. (1991) National identity, London, England: Penguin Books.

United Nations Development Programme (UNDP) (2009) *Overcoming barriers: Human mobility and development Human development report 2009*, New York: UNDP.

Warner, K. (2010) 'Global environmental change and migration: Governance challenges', *Global Environmental Change*, 20, 402–413.

Zetter, R. (2017) 'The politics of rights protection for environmentally displaced people', in Martikainen, T., Sainio, K. and Heikkilä, E., eds., *Siirtolaisuus-Migration Quarterly,* Finland: Migration Institute of Finland, 5–12.

Part III: Housing and Climate Change

Chapter 8: Heat-Stress-Related Climate-Change Adaptation in Informal Urban Communities

Reflections on Socially Inclusive Approaches in Cairo, Egypt

Franziska Laue

INTRODUCTION

Climate change is affecting human settlements, worldwide, to different degrees of severity. The mutual relationship between climate change and urban forms and urban development are subject to scholarly and applied discourse. Heat stress, in particular, is understood to be aggravated by non-climatic stresses that are linked to urbanisation and those that make cities hotspots of risks and disaster (Wamsler 2008), thereby intensifying the existing vulnerabilities of urban populations. Hence, this chapter's main question: What are the connections between adapting to climate change and housing and community involvement, particularly in informal urban areas?

This chapter aims to shed some understanding on how knowledge adds up and becomes beneficial for co-beneficial interventions. To achieve this objective, the chapter focuses on a recent theoretical discourse on the type of heat stress that is linked to housing and informal settlements. The chapter[1] opens with a section dedicated to the impacts of climate change that are linked to housing,

---

1 This chapter draws its initial motivation and ideas from the author's master's thesis research from 2013, which is linked to the discourse on community-level climate-change adaptation in urban areas, particularly in informal settlements in arid regions (Laue 2013). The discussion builds on selected reflections from the author's dissertation and an additional literature review.

including some findings and conclusions of the Working Group II (WGII) of the IPCC's 5th Assessment Report (AR5) 2014, on risk and adaptation in urban areas.

Recent conclusions on an ongoing Egyptian discourse on climate adaptation and housing are referred to, followed by reflections on climate risks within the GCR. Here, the phenomenon of urban informality in Egypt is discussed alongside how an increase in knowledge has linked climate-change adaptation in the context of housing to the possibilities for dealing with heat as one climate-related stress. More precisely, a case study of the settlement of Ezzbet El-Nasr will illustrate efforts to introduce adaptation measures into an informal urban community, based on descriptions of a project undertaken by the German development agency GIZ's[2] participatory development programme (PDP 2017). Then the chapter will present complementary findings from the author's semi-structured interviews, mappings and observations in the community as part of the post-graduate findings from a 2013 case study of Ezzbet El-Nasr. The final section of this chapter will briefly look into the questions of participation and transferability.

CLIMATE-CHANGE ADAPTATION AND HOUSING

Climate adaptation is identified as one response to the impacts of climate change and is complementary to mitigation[3] (IPCC 2007; WBGU 2016). The International Panel on Climate Change (IPCC) defines climate adaptations as a 'process of adjustment to actual or expected climate and its effects' (IPCC 2014, p.1758). In order to pinpoint adaptive options and capacities, vulnerabilities are identified via three factors: exposure, sensitivity, and adaptive capacity to a climatic stress (Dreyfus 2015; IPCC 2014). The German Advisory Council on Global Change (WBGU) notes that adaptation to climate change is one of the five fields with the 'biggest potential leverage effects for urban transformation toward sustainability' (WBGU 2016, p.11).

Adaptation is achievable across scales and through varying strategies that can contribute to resilience. However, one strand of scholars regard adaptation as 'intensely local' (Huq *et al.* 2007, p.1), thus potentially playing a crucial role along with national and regional strategies. The scope and extent of climate-

---

2 GIZ refers to the German development cooperation entity, Deutsche Gesellschaft für Internationale Zusammenarbeit, which is active in Egypt.

3 Mitigation refers to reducing harmful anthropogenic emissions (IPCC 2014, p.1769).

adaptation measures depend on their size and focus. Moreover, the ability to adapt is highly dependent on financial and administrative capacities, which vary significantly (Moser and Satterthwaite 2008).

Intensive research on climate-change adaptation evolved between the 1980s and the 2000s. Before the Brundtland Report (1987) was released, adaptation was a secondary subject on the international climate-change agenda (Ayers and Forsyth 2009; Klein 2002; Smit et al. 2000), yet it gained "standing within the international climate change arena" (Ayers and Forsyth 2009, p.25) with each subsequent assessment report the IPCC released. The IPCC's 2007 Working Group II report (WGII) intensively reviewed the subject of adaptation and its interrelations with mitigation (IPCC 2007; Klein 2002). With regards to cities and urbanisation, strategic and scholarly discourse on adaptation has become increasingly relevant (Dreyfus 2018), yet the authors of WGII for the AR5 synthesis report on climate change stress the persistent lack of attention being paid to urban adaptation (in contrast to mitigation) by national governments (IPCC 2014). Moreover, for some cities, adaptation seemingly remains an unclear model and the knowledge gap between decision-makers and scientists is notable (IPCC 2014).

Housing and climate-change adaptation are increasingly relevant, crosscutting topics within academic (Dodman 2009; Hunt and Watkiss 2010; Huqet et al. 2007) and strategic discourse. Concerning the latter, the authors of WGII on 'Impacts, Adaptation and Vulnerability' within the IPCC's 5th Assessment Report (AR5), dedicated chapter eight in particular to urban areas (IPCC 2014, pp. 535-612). This chapter compiles analyses, case studies, and definitions of probabilities of benefitting from a more nuanced understanding of these linkages, based on the increased availability and diversity of the relevant literature (Dreyfus 2015; IPCC 2014). A large scientific community has validated the report's conclusions (e.g., Beattie and McGuire 2019). Chapter eight not only comprises subsections on urban risks associated with housing but it also mentions extreme heat as a particular challenge for housing (IPCC 2014, p. 569). Hence, housing is referred to as being 'often the major part of the infrastructure affected by disasters' (IPCC 2014, p. 559). Yet, simultaneously, housing is mentioned as a key sector for adaptation (IPCC 2014, p. 568).

When looking at case studies on adaptations to extreme heat, however, the report acknowledges that the literature and examples still predominantly refer to high-income nations and consequently calls for more discourse and practice in low- and middle-income nations (IPCC 2014). Furthermore, urban settlements in low- and middle-income countries, especially those facing a combination of rapid urbanisation and migration (Dreyfus 2015), are expected to face climate-change impacts more immediately and severely (Moser and Satterthwaite 2008). Housing's exposure to climatic stresses, whether rapid or slow onset, creates sensitivities and vulnerabilities at the local level (Figure 1), yet differ across communities as the impact of climate change on housing is tendentially linked to socio-economic constraints (Bazrkar *et al.* 2015). Particularly neglected or contested are historical areas, informal settlements, and low-income communities, which may face higher vulnerabilities (Dreyfus 2015). Accordingly, more attention is given to evidence-based research, vulnerability studies and the identification of adaptation measures as the topic of discourse moves toward identifying adaptive capacities and adaptation measures (IPCC 2014) on social, physical and urban scales.

Climate change and urban informality

The intersection between climate change and informally developed urban areas over the past decade is becoming the subject of research, development cooperation and local initiatives. Moreover, two global agendas, the 2015 'Paris Climate Agreement' and the 2016 'New Urban Agenda' recently and explicitly intersected with regard to climate action. In its chapter entitled 'Urban Areas', the IPCC's AR5 WGII refers to informal settlements as being particularly vulnerable to amplified climate risks (IPCC 2014, p. 538; Moser and Satterthwaite 2009) and as having some or 'very little adaptive capacity or resilience/ "bounce back" capacity' (IPCC 2014, p. 546). Climate issues related to informal settlements are also mentioned within the key risk matrix for urban settlements, under 'livelihoods' and 'poverty and access to basic services' (IPCC 2014, p. 562).

The increased vulnerability that is linked to the causes and effects of rapid urbanisation (Bazrkar *et al.* 2015) is also correlated with the 'changing dimensions of migration' (IPCC 2014, p.552). For instance, increasing temperatures are discussed in relation to the changing availability of local resources and economic (agricultural) activities; i.e., in rural areas, temperature increases result in migration (Raleigh *et al.* 2008) toward more economically advantageous locations, typically toward cities (see also Mukaddim et al. in this book on climate-related migration). This forces individuals to permanently relocate, thereby gaining access to affordable housing mainly in underserviced and informal neighbourhoods and communities. This is communicated by the IPCC's AR5 as part of a discussion on 'spatiality and temporal dimensions' (IPCC 2014, p.551), creating a 'dynamic quality of risk' (IPCC 2014, p.552) for housing and urban informality. As recommended by the IPCC (2014) and Magali Dreyfus (2015), adaptation strategies will need to consider the impact of climate on migration and the consequent stress on housing. Consequently, AR5 continues to refer to informal settlements being locations where adaptive strategies and measures can be linked to the above-mentioned key risks, with the help of community-based case studies (Pelling in IPCC 2014, p.566); the IPCC also suggests stakeholders in informal areas engage in risk assessment and in fostering adaptive action (IPCC 2014), as is briefly elaborated below.

Community-Based Adaptation

Community-based adaptation (CBA) refers to a localised and people-centred approaches to adaptation (Dreyfus 2015) in responses to climate risks that capitalise on local and social capital so as to build adaptive capacities (IPCC 2014). Moreover, the CBA approach is considered the 'only means of responding to risk' for a significant part of households living in informal urban areas (IPCC 2014, p.563). The IPCC AR5 WGII elaborates on CBA, recommending that a broad range of community actors and planners engage in the planning and implementation process for adaptation (IPCC 2014, p.580). Here, the IPCC is referring to experience gained in previous practice and also to scholarly work throughout the past decade, for instance by Satterthwaite, Dodman, Pelling, Mitlin, and Jabareen (IPCC 2014, p.581). References were made to successful CBA cases in Africa and Asia (see for example IPCC 2014, p.566). The case study in this chapter will illustrate the initiation and work of the CBA inside an informal urban community in the Greater Cairo Region.

CLIMATE-CHANGE ADAPTATION IN URBAN EGYPT AND THE GREATER CAIRO REGION

Egypt's decision-makers have acknowledged climate change on both national and regional levels (EEAA 2016) and within development cooperation agencies and local communities (PDP 2018). Climatic stresses and sensitivities affecting the country are complex and linked to the following particular geographical settings. Egypt's most fertile areas stretch along the Nile and its tributaries, which cover 45 (OECD 2004, p.14) to 56% of the total land mass, mainly Egypt's desert land area. Yet, this land provides about 95% of the country's entire water needs and most of its agricultural production (EEAA 2016, p.112). All of Egypt's major urban centres, with their industries and commercial activities, are located along a narrow strip of land that runs along the banks of the Nile, thus, putting stress on the country's water resources and its coastal zones

(Agravala *et al.* in OECD 2004, p.14; OECD 2010). The IPCC's AR5 states that Egypt will face further reductions in rainfall amounts (IPCC 2014, p.1210).

Figure 1: Sensitivities and vulnerabilities on the city and community levels – the example of Cairo.

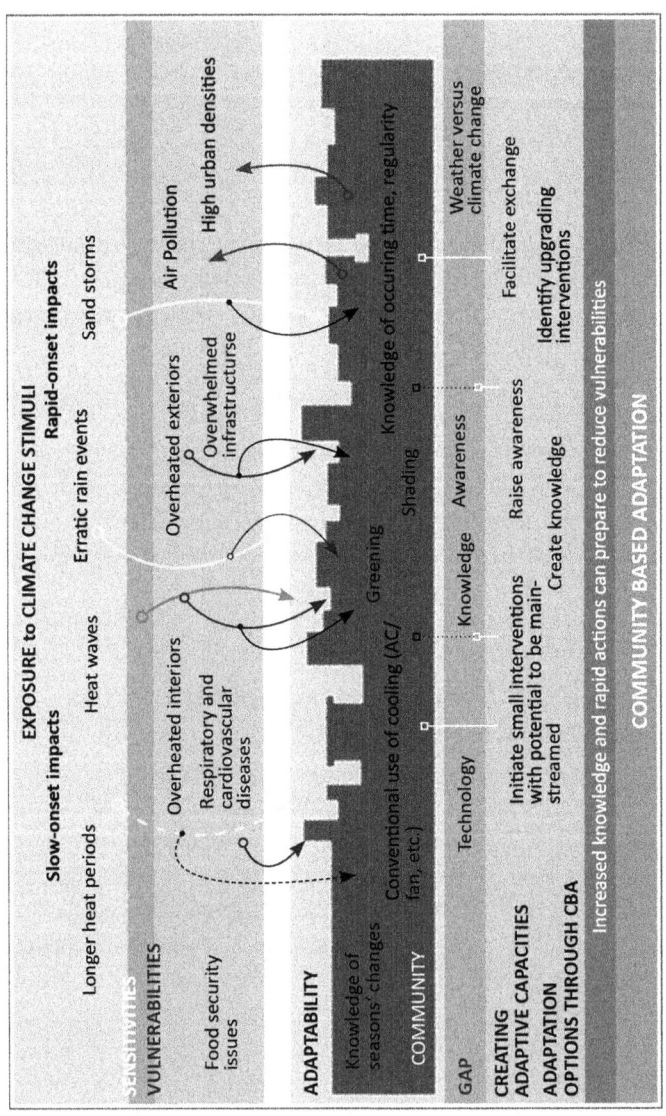

Source: Author, 2019, based on Author, 2013, p.46.

To deal with climatic stresses in Egypt, identifying the country's vulnerabilities to climate change and the need for adaptation has been part of the national policy agenda since the early 1990s. With its national communications that comprise both mitigation and adaptation (EEAA 2010a, 2016; IDSC 2011, Egypt acknowledges that the urban sector is among an increasing number of sectors[4] that are vulnerable to climate change (EEAA 2016).

On the topic of housing and human settlements, the Egyptian Information and Support Centre (IDSC) acknowledges that Egyptian cities are affected by extreme heat that is linked to climate change; moreover, this is intensified through hot air that is being emitted by buildings that use energy inefficiently (IDSC/UNDP 2011, p.92). In Egypt's Third National Communication, it was noted that heat in urban settings is associated with the phenomenon of urban heat island (UHI) effects or to a slow-onset heat threat. Particularly concerning is the projection of a temperature increase of an average of 3°C by the year 2100 (EEAA 2016, p.156). This will become a growing burden, particularly in dense neighbourhoods (CSC 2013; UNDP 2013); and these will contribute to increased energy demands and deteriorating air quality all of which can be exacerbated by environmental challenges (Dreyfus 2015).

This combination will continue to directly affect not only the functioning of urban areas but also their residents. Consequently, besides erratic winds and rain occurrences (EEAA 2016), (extreme) heat (IPCC 2007) that is linked to impacts on human health[5] (Chapman *et al.*, in and Strengers 2011, p.493) requires adaptation. However, differing prioritisations may occur, based on a settlement's geographical location. For instance, while Egypt' surban coastline (including Alexandria, Port Said) is considered the most vulnerable to climate-change impacts (EEAA 2016; IPCC 2014),[6] climate exposure in the GCR, which is located along the Nile Delta, is considered to be 'less dramatic, but nonetheless serious' (Huq *et al.* 2007, p.1), with its equally complex combination of slow- and rapid-onset effects and direct and indirect risks, all of which are centred around heat (Figure 1). summarizes the various sensitivities (affectedness and responsiveness) to heat in the GCR, the specific vulnerabilities city-wide and in neighbourhoods and communities (susceptibility to harm), and some existing adaptive

---

4   Sectors include water resources, tourism, health, bio-diversity (EEAA 2016, p.150 et sqq.).
5   Hotter periods contribute to heat-related mortality (IPCC 2014; Maller and Strengers 2011; McMichael and Githeko 2001, in McCarthy et al 2001).
6   Climate change impacts refer to sea-level rise and flooding as a result of erratic weather events.

capacities (Laue 2013). Combined analyses of climatic and non-climatic stresses in cities like the GCR are essential to comprehending the burden on infrastructure, services, quality of life, and how to contain the potential for increased poverty.[7]

Housing and climate adaptation in urban Egypt and the Greater Cairo Region

In the context of Egypt, housing and climate change are closely interconnected. In contrast to previous National Communication Reports[8] of the United Nations Framework Convention on Climate Change (UNFCCC), the Egyptian Environmental Affairs Agency (EEAA), in its Third National Communication (2016), elaborated on housing and took a broader perspective, first, with housing being a basic human right (EEAA 2016) and, second, by acknowledging the gap between housing demand and delivery for low- and middle-income groups, which has resulted in an informal housing market. In the adaptation section of the EEAA's updated report,[9] housing is associated with both housing policies and formal and informal urban development (EEAA 2016, p.150). By adding the link between housing and climate-change-related exposures (ibid., p.171), it has become recognised that low-income and informal communities of the GCR are especially affected (CSC 2013).

URBAN INFORMALITY IN GREATER CAIRO: CATERING TO A MAJORITY

This section looks at informal housing in urban areas in Egypt, particularly in the GCR, which developed alongside policy shifts and transformation dynamics throughout the 20th century (Wodon *et al.* 2014). The GCR grapples with complex realities. Historically, it has been an attractive destination for both workers and residents, over decades (Madbouly 2009; Batran 1998). It has also experi-

---

7   Non-climatic pressures are administrative centralization, rural-urban migration, high natural population growth, changing housing policies, and particularly the liberalization of the housing market.
8   The Second National Communication Report (2010) links housing and climate change with increasing temperatures exacerbated by energy emissions, spatial orientation, and façade design (EEAA 2010, p.91).
9   Mitigation measures also refer to housing (EEAA, 2010, p.107 et sqq.).

enced natural population growth, declining mortality rates, and increasing pressure on the local housing market, land availability, and natural resources. With continuous migration toward urban centres (World Bank 2014), urban and rural settings have been dramatically transformed since the 1950s (UNDP 2004). Ever-growing urbanisation rates have materialised mostly in the formation of informal settlements (Madbouly 2009), such that the formal housing market has struggled to meet the demand for affordable housing.[10] Madbouly (2009) describes how housing in Egypt, in particular, has been a dichotomic topic for decades.

The gradual formation of Cairo's informal urban areas, predominantly termed as 'ashwa'iyat' in the Arabic language, can be traced back to at least the 1960s (UN-Habitat 2003, p.206). Their development is a result of complex and historic policy decisions, a dynamic housing market and population growth over decades, and economic and regional pressures. Whereas new cities were built within Cairo's greater metropolitan region, informal settlements significantly extended the existing urban fabric to accommodate the city's growing population and to contribute to an anticipated stable economic situation or to improve incomes. In 2000, informal urban settlements in and around Cairo covered over 94 square kilometres (UN-Habitat 2013, p.3) of the GCR's approximately 600-700 square kilometres (UN-Habitat 2011, p.xix ff.), or 13.4 % of the city's land mass.

These informal urban areas constitute a considerable and undeniable part of the GCR's[11] urban reality, both economically and spatially. The first recognition of informal communities and the initial reactive measures took place from 1974 to 1985 (UN-Habitat 2003), mainly through policies aimed to prevent encroachment on and the urbanisation of agricultural land. Since then, Egypt's informal settlements were the subject of various reports, action guides and international exposure (UN-Habitat 2003, 2015; PDP 2011; Davis 2006). The UN-Habitat report 'The Challenge of Slums' includes Cairo as a case study (UN-Habitat 2003). Furthermore, the Egyptian uprising of January 25, 2011, augmented inhabitants' call for improved quality of life "for deprived people who were suffer-

---

10 Egypt continuously suffers less from an overall undersupply of affordable housing but more from a mismatch between the demand and supply of affordable housing and locations, thereby resulting in inhabitants missing out on the security of property rights (EEAA 2016).
11 About 65% (Al-Gohari 2010, p.5; UN-Habitat 2011, p.xx] to 70% (GTZ 2009, p.15) or around 18 million (GIZ 2018) of Cairo's inhabitants lived in informal settlements in 2006.

ing from bad living conditions" (Hassan 2012, p.9). Some communities, such as Miit 'Uqba (2011), developed initiatives to improve their communities, based on self-mobilisation and creating networks to external non-governmental actors. Informal areas[12] progressively became subject to rights advocacy and support from urban activists and organisations, which contributed to adjusted responses in policy revisions and administration, resulting in the creation of urban upgrading units within the Cairo government and a shift from 'prevention' to 'upgrading' (Abouelmagd 2014). With their great socio-economic and morphological complexity, these informal areas continue to be the subjects of researching graduate and post-graduate work and in design projects across a number of disciplines (e.g. Khalifa 2011; Kipper and Fischer 2009; Shehayeb 2009). Consequently, these areas provide illustrations of increased knowledge, changing practices and ongoing, decades-long exchanges on topics related to housing and climate change (Cluster 2018a; Kipper and Fischer 2009; Singerman 2006). The related contemporary housing and planning discourse (Madbouly 2009) remains a topic of interest to scholars in the Global North and South, urban practitioners, advocates, and artists throughout the past decade.[13]

The research on environmental and climate action gained momentum during the 2000s and 2010s, becoming linked with informal urban settlements and, particularly, with community mobilisation (Miit 'Uqba, Tadamun – Cairo Urban Solidarity Initiative 2013) and cultural exchange (i.e., newly created art space like El-Lewa community). Around 2012, the particular connection between heat (including urban heat islands, UHI) and informal urban development became not only the subject to research (German Egyptian Research Fund / Science and Technology Development Fund – GERF/STDF)[14] but was also assessed to become subject to an innovative approach within development cooperation, with GIZ dedicating a strand of its local PDP programme in the GCR portfolio (PDP 2018; Verner 2012). After an extensive vulnerability study and participatory needs assessment, a number of affiliated consultants (Plan + Risk Consult) developed an initial catalogue of suggested interventions (Lückenkötter et al. 2016) – these are illustrated below. Subsequently, a number of projects were commis-

---

12 Along with deteriorated central urban areas.
13 This includes the continuous work throughout the decade by Manal Batran, Yehya Shawkat, Marwa Khalifa, and Nezar Al Sayyad.
14 In the context of dry urban areas, three to nine areas became the subjects of research (German Egyptian Research Fund / Science and Technology Development Fund – GERF/STDF) and the locations of projects for adaptation (UNDP, GIZ PDP).

sioned for up to six informal urban communities, some of which were implemented between 2016 and 2018.[15]

FROM ADAPTIVE CAPACITIES TO ADEQUATE MEASURES IN EZZBET EL-NASR, GREATER CAIRO REGION

This case study briefly illustrates efforts that were linked to identifying adaptive capacities and community adaptation measures in an informal community, namely Ezzbet El-Nasr, which is located in the GCR. GIZ and its partners from the EEAA, and the Ministry of Housing, Utilities and Urban Communities (GIZ 2017) selected this urban community to be one of the first to implement community-based adaptation measures under the PDP programme's sub-component 'Climate-Change Adaptation in Informal Settlements Physical Change (retrofitting) for Adaptation to Heat Stress' (PDP 2017).

Ezzbet El-Nasr evolved in 1977 and consolidated as a community with a population of approximately 60,000 inhabitants (UMP 2010, p.31) through people continuously squatting on state-owned land and the increasing influx of residents throughout the subsequent decades (Figure 2). Since then, the legal status of the land has been pending, leaving the area underserved. Being located in no particular disaster-prone area, the community struggles particularly with heat stress and the UHI effect. Ezzbet El-Nasr faces non-climate-related pressures within its built environments as it lacks basic urban services and faces ecological challenges due to nearby tanneries and a waste disposal site. Along with economic and social challenges, these contribute to the lack of adaptive capacities and, hence, the community's potential overall vulnerability toward the impacts of climate change. During the initial assessment, in 2012, the community's limited awareness of any climate-change impacts was reported in the Participatory needs Assessment (PNA) by CDS, consultants commissioned by GIZ. In interviews with some of the inhabitants, no specific associations were made with the term "climate change", yet those interviewed[16] referred to the increasing heat

---

15 The Egyptian platform 'Cluster', commissioned by GIZ in partnership with RISE/AUC, implements urban interventions, including urban shading, façade painting, and green roofs in Saqiyat Mikki, MasakenJazirat al-Dahab and Giza (Cluster 2018b).

16 About 62% of respondents in the baseline study (2013: 146) and all interviewed households.

and the sun's intensity as the strongest overall weather-related pressures on the area (CDS 2013, p.48).

An initial assessment of Ezzbet El-Nasr identified the community's susceptibilities and adaptive capacities. Following this, vulnerability studies, (on-site and desktop) baseline studies, and a participatory needs assessment were conducted so as to formulate community-based interventions.

In 2013, the author of this chapter complemented these findings with semi-structured interviews, visits to the interviewees' dwellings and conversations with household members about the level of thermal comfort inside different rooms of their homes. Accordingly, household members had previously altered parts of their houses to improve the microclimate (see Figure 3), taking various forms of pragmatic action on a smaller scale.

Figure 2: Location of Ezzbet El-Nasr inside the Greater Cairo Region.

Source: Author, 2013.

Climate Change Adaptation in Informal Communities | 201

Figure 3: Pre-project coping and adaptation measures in Ezzbet El-Nasr inside the Greater Cairo Region.

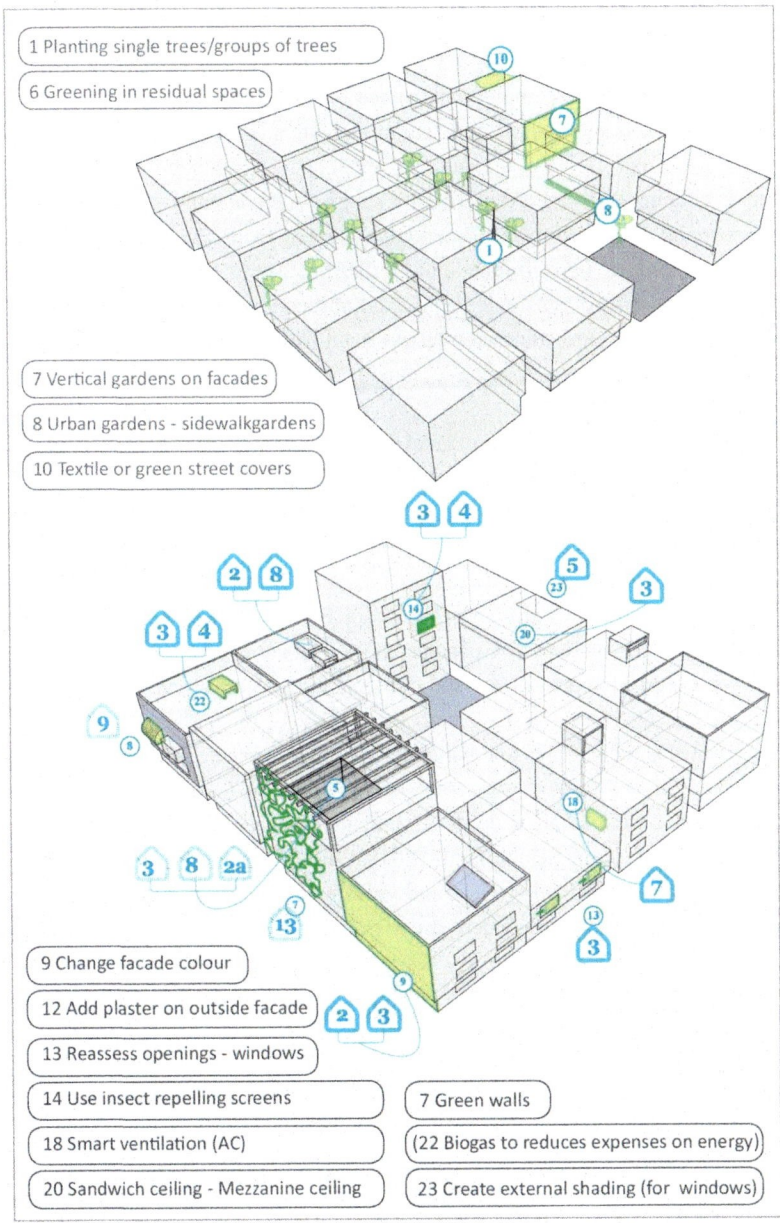

Source: Author, 2013.

For example, to relieve households from heat, the majority of those interviewed mentioned wearing lighter coloured clothing and using fans (CDS 2013), which can be described as autonomous coping measures. Other households adjusted the size and locations of windows (CDS 2013), which could be described as low level 'autonomous adaptation' as coined by Malik et al. (2010). Yet, financial constraints were common challenges for most households, and this prevented investments in physical and spatial adjustments to deal with heat (CDS 2013). Subsequent to this, the author developed a catalogue of adaptation measures (Figure 4) that could potentially support the community' spatial, physical and social organisation. The catalogue lists ten 'soft' (behavioural and organisational) and 32 'hard' (urban and physical) measures (Laue 2013). Most of these measures correspond to recommendations compiled in the IPCC's AR5 section of the WGII, including architectural and urban options for passive cooling, creating thermal mass, shading, green and white roofs, and green infrastructures, (IPCC 2014, pp.566-575).

From the above-mentioned catalogue, the PDP project consultants (Plan+Risk Consult) selected 15 measures to consider in a further feasibility study, with each measure being assessed for its co-beneficial qualities (Lückenkötter *et al.* 2016)[17] and the potential prevention of an overall maladaptation (IPCC 2014). This corresponds to the IPCC's WGII, within its AR5 recommendations on creating co-benefits in urban adaptation, particularly when selecting options that foster incremental change and sustainable transformation (IPCC 2014). With regards to prioritising and implementing co-beneficial measures, the PDP project in Ezzbet El-Nasr illustrates that process. Since then, the PDP project has grown and continues to conduct its activities on-site and other communities.[18]

As of 2017, nine small-scale development measures (pilot-measures) have been selected for implementation. In 2018, four architectural measures were realised in partnership with NGOs and private local businesses (PDP 2017). Three physical measures included street shading, wall greening and rooftop farming; others included capacity development and awareness-raising programmes on both the community and local administrative levels (PDP 2017).

---

17 Measures can be affiliated to four adaptation options or policies. These include 'no-regret options', 'low-regret-options', 'win-win options' and 'flexible management options', as coined by UKCIP (2007, p. 15).

18 This includes Masaken Geziret El-Dahab.

Climate Change Adaptation in Informal Communities | 203

Figure 4: Suggested measures listed in the catalogue for Ezzbet El-Nasr.

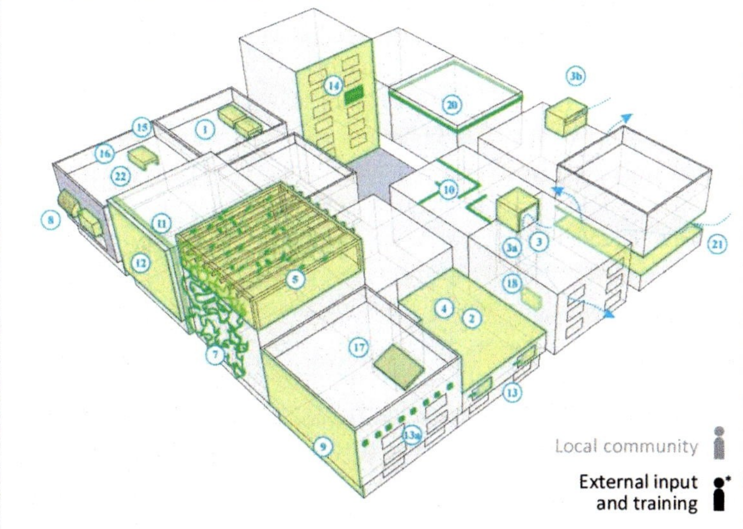

1 Build green roofs/roof top gardens	
2 Light coloured roofs	
3 Reuse shafts for ventilation and lighting	
3a Wind catcher towers	
3b Reuse the staircases	
4 Buffer/insulate the roof	
5 Add light weight structures on the roof	
7 Green walls	
8 Create external shading (for windows)	
9 Change facade colour	
10 Change of building design	
11 Build thicker walls	
12 Add plaster on outside facade	
13 Reassess openings - windows	
13a Reassess openings Wind tunnel flaps	
14 Use insect repelling screens	
15 Water storage space/tanks	
16 Power generators (conventional model)	
17 Solar and wind generators	
18 Smart ventilation (AC)	
20 Sandwich ceiling - Mezzanine ceiling	
21 Empty floor	
(22 Biogas to reduces expenses on energy)	
23 Open staircase, courtyard like space	

Legend: Local community; External input and training.

Source: Author, 2013.

Community-based solutions – The role of participation

As described above, in the initial phase of the PDP project extensive studies and interviews were conducted inside the community. It was thought that this programme could build on the previous experience of other community initiatives[19] that were already active in Ezzbet El-Nasr yet were not explicitly linked to climate-change adaptation. Hence, the community already knew about the external actors' involvement. In this case, intermediate and external local actors or champions helped to build a bridge between the community, the external partners and the assistance.

To initiate and, more importantly, maintain successful community-based soft and hard measures, the process, scope and success of the PDP seemed to be highly dependent on involving the local community in all of its segments. This included building trust and involving individuals who could potentially act as champions or drivers to mobilise various groups to join in on the inclusive participatory processes.

From within – The aspect of community

As was suggested above, when speaking of interventions on the local level, community involvement plays a crucial role. The success of these types of initiatives inherently requires active contributions from community members, particularly when identifying actors (internally or with input from outside), discussing issues, ideas and processes, and making decisions on needed measures.

The term 'participation' carries with it various interpretations and types (Arnstein 1969; Piffero 2009), yet commonalities include the indisputable aim (from within or without a community) to create knowledge, engage and empower community members, and ensure their commitment (Piffero in GTZ 2009) to influencing processes that are designed for their benefit (Piffero 1995). Referring to Arnstein's 'ladder of participation' concept (1969), community participation is preferably beyond technocratic measures and administrative dominance. Arnstein (1969) also argues for involving the local community in a genuine process of improvement, thereby creating a sense of ownership, in a process that emphasises the ladder's upper rungs (avoiding the lower rungs, such as manipulation) and creating a gradual process from developing 'partnerships' to 'delegated powers' and 'citizen control'. Hence, linking Arnstein's reflections on the process of community involvement to identifying co-beneficial adaptation measures and capacities in Ezzbet El-Nasr, it is evident that the early and close involve-

---

19 For instance, NGOs like 'Plan International' and local initiatives.

ment of various representatives in the process seems essential. Figure 5 illustrates a theoretical reflection on community-driven involvement within a spectrum that ranges from a household scale to a district scale, based on the author's observations in Ezzbet El-Nasr.

Figure 5: Levels and degrees of community involvement in Ezzbet El-Nasr.

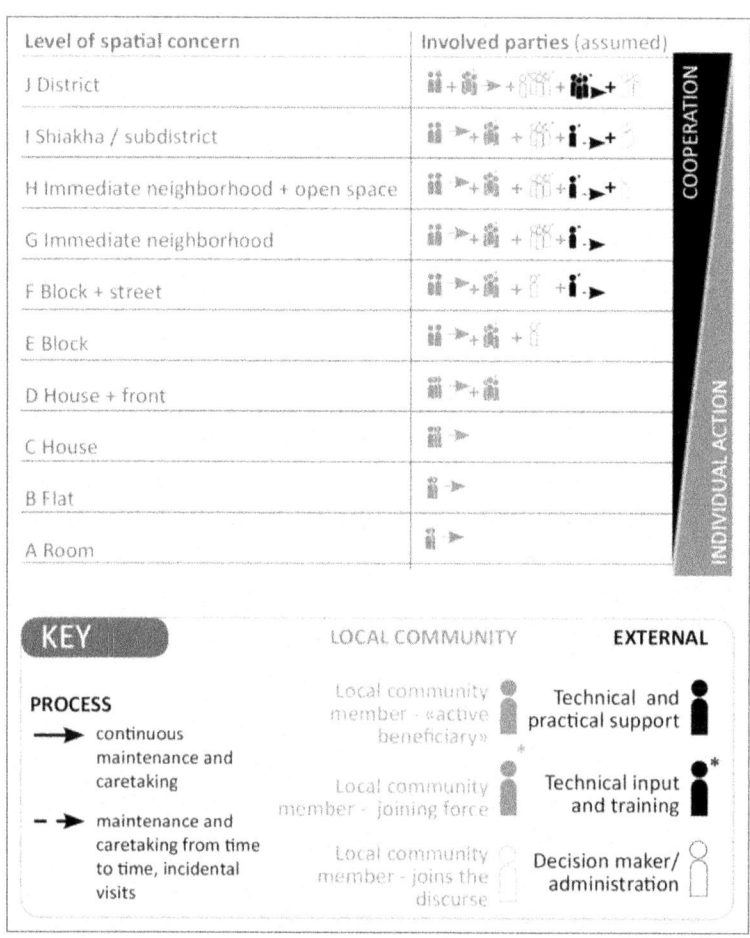

Source: Author, 2013.

*Figure 6: Scenarios for internal and external involvement of the community.
level. The example of Ezzbet El-Nasr.*

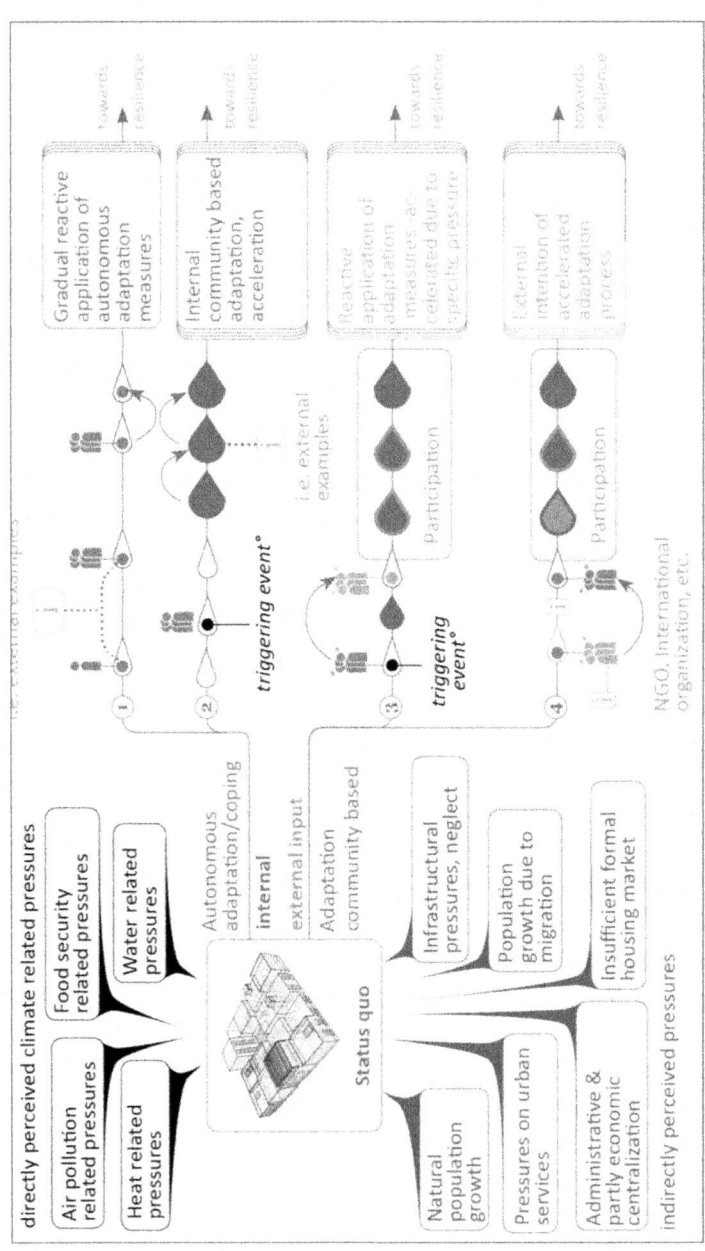

Source: Auhtor, 2019, adjusted from Author, 2013.

Community-based efforts to deal with climate change should pay special attention to involving vulnerable or marginalised community members, as this is heavily linked to health-related vulnerabilities. Hence, Verner (2013) and the UNFCCC (2018) suggest considering gender-specific and value-based approaches. In the surveys and interviews conducted in Ezzbet El-Nasr (2013), female 'agents' in particular were identified for becoming active participants in the community's social networks (Laue 2013); that is, to other female community members of different ages. Furthermore, children and youth were identified to play a crucial role in disseminating practices and awareness into families and households.

This is relevant as each adaptation measure and strategy might require a range of actors, depending on how and with whom and in which scope the actor is introduced. For example, planting a tree or making interventions at the building level can be both an individual or collective effort, varying according to whom benefits and in what context (see Figure 5 – levels D-J). However, other measures, including shared open spaces or soft measures, such as organising patrols, require a more complex set of actors. In some regards, this requires input and mobilisation from non-community members (i.e., NGOs, academia, value-based social movements).

In Between – Benefitting from local societal engagement and movements

In addition to increased research interest, there has been a continuous interaction and mobilisation between community members' housing realities, in informal urban areas and on community actors, that have resulted in interventions or social movements. Vincenti (2016, p.135) examined the role of new social forces in so-called 'value-based social movements' (VSMs) as playing an active role in the sustainable transition of post-revolutionary Egypt. Accordingly, these VSMs can and do result in collective action in social, political and spatial fields and represent the people's "readiness to individually and collectively construct lived alternatives in order to improve their respective communities" (Vincenti 2016, p. 136); hence, improved livelihoods and housing. In the context of the GCR, actors that have fostered such movements, so far, have been advocates like the 'Shadow Ministry of Housing' (n.d.), community architects and proponents of urban initiatives platforms, such as Urbanics since 2010 (Urbanics 2018), Tadamun (Froehlich 2017), and 'Takween Integrated Community Development'. Cooperation and collaboration among non-governmental actors have continued, to the date of this publication, and is documented on platforms such as the Cairo Urban Initiatives Platform (Cluster 2018a).

Moreover, academia also began offering channels for empowering, mobilising and encouraging local citizens in informal settlements to become involved in small- and medium-scale interventions that aim to improve livelihoods and living conditions in and around their immediate residential units. One example is the 'Ezbet Project', which was initiated by an academic staff member at the University of Stuttgart[20] and mobilises local students and community members.

From without – The role of external support

With a view to the above-mentioned reflections, interventions linked to housing on the community level seem to require significant overlaps not only with the real concerns of the residents within the respective community but also with the concerns of the city as a whole and, if needed, with impulses from outside.

Local knowledge about weather conditions and vulnerabilities that are thoroughly and jointly reflected by all involved actors is as essential as any statistical, meteorological and simulated data on a local urban community. Climate-change adaptation, on the city or community level, aims to ensure the prevention of any further damage and then to achieve resilience through growing knowledge. Hence, along with ensuring an awareness of climatic and non-climatic stressors, the recognition of interconnections may help identify and mobilise adequate responses. This could take place on different tiers; i.e., top-down adaptations through developing policies, regulations and investments for the benefit of the GCR in its entirety. This, however, as the WGII of IPCC'S AR 5 noted, may exacerbate inequalities among communities (IPCC 2014) due to differing amounts of social and financial capital on the local level. Therefore, bottom-up adaptation (community-based) efforts need to complement this and may require coordination and communication with authorities at the city level. Consequently, the IPCC sees a role for international partners in providing support (IPCC 2014) and in extending inclusive planning efforts (UNFCCC 2018) to (urban) communities with low capacities.

Referring back to the PDP programme in the GCR, as of the component's start in 2012, this has been undergoing current-practice testing for adaptation in informal settlements, adjusting to communities' actual conditions. As Figure 6 illustrates, there are several scenarios and corresponding degrees of external stakeholder involvement in the process of identifying and strengthening adaptive capacities at the community level. In all scenarios, social capital is being created,

---

20 Dr. Manal El Shahat, senior researcher at the University of Stuttgart, initiated the 'Ezbet Project' as a design competition in 2011, which evolved a project comprising interdisciplinary teamwork and projects.

yet with differing degrees of community involvement; hence, indicating different degrees of sustainable adaptation. The PDP project of GIZ and its local partners corresponds to the scenario at the bottom (illustrating a large share of mobilisation from external actors), which represents a donor-driven model that aims to support the local community to 'bounce forward' (IPCC 2014, p.549) within a limited time frame, whereas the scenarios that take place at the upper levels describe a stronger initiation that comes from the community side. Moreover, international philanthropic networks, foundations, and academia can play a role in facilitating and providing cross-references at both grassroots and community levels, focussing on vulnerable and marginalised segments of (urban) society (IPCC 2014).

Transferability OR Mutual exchange

Based on the above descriptions, one part of the initial question remains open: whether applying adaptive measures at the community level is transferable to other contexts that come with differing local and climatic specifics. A World Bank report entitled 'Clean Energy and Development: Towards an Investment Framework' (2006) states that, despite the global agreement that 'all countries are vulnerable to climate change' (World Bank 2006, p.9), the actual vulnerability levels and adaptive capacities may differ significantly among nations. Historically, low- and middle-income countries have remained unaccountable for climate impacts (Stern 2006, p.28), yet they incur the largest burdens from anthropogenic CO_2 emissions. Being among the most vulnerable (IPCC 2007, 2014; Satterthwaite *et al.* 2007; Stern 2006; World Bank 2006) these countries "can even less afford not to adapt" (Stern 2006, p. 443). This calls for cooperation among local and international stakeholders, while also acknowledging local circumstances.[21] Consequently, before and after the Paris Agreement, in 2015, the spectrum of official and non-governmental stakeholders, in particular, has been increasing knowledge transfer and experience across tiers, scales, and actors (IPCC 2014). For instance, the 2018 UNFCCC report on adaptation in human settlements mentions 'city-to-city partnerships on adaptation' as one aspect of peer learning to increase knowledge and the pace of applying adequate adaptive measures (UNFCCC 2018).

On the local level, with increasing knowledge and lessons learned in practice, strategies that include community-based efforts (i.e., the PDP project in the

---

21 Lessons learnt from previous community-based projects within arid urban contexts may be important references for strategic concepts.

GCR) feed into the transfer of knowledge. For instance, initially implemented in the context of rural communities, community-based adaptation principles were transferred to urban communities. This new knowledge can now serve as a reference to foster regional and international dialogues. Moreover, knowledge exchange and discourse can support the application of non-climatic developmental interventions and strategic considerations to create co-benefits in the context of housing in low-income communities. For instance, exchange in knowledge on urban upgrading measures and retrofitting for improved local microclimates can feed into a catalogue of climate responses and adaptation measures. As the IPCC recommends, civil-society partnerships on an eye-to-eye level, such as 'Shack/Slum Dwellers International' can contribute to sustainable community-based exchanges and monitoring (IPCC 2014, p.584).

Whereas, in the future Greater Cairo can share its experiences and lessons learned in the field of climate adaptation on the local level, it may well find constructive input from other cities within the region and worldwide that have struggled with similar issues of scale, socio-economic realities, or the interconnection of non-climatic and climatic factors. There is, however, still limited practice-oriented reference to climate-change adaptation to extreme heat in urban areas and in comparable socio-economic settings worldwide. Nevertheless, several African cities such as Johannesburg, eThekwini, and Cape Town (ICLEI 2019) have begun applying community-based approaches in their urban settings. For instance, in Soweto (Phalatse 2008, 2011), an intensive dialogue with and within local communities identified constraints and capacities and, hence, built the requisite community trust (Phalatse 2008) that allowed initiatives to become embedded in community-based processes for adaptation. Such promising stories (along with experiences that failed) will help adjust and develop community-based processes for adaptation in the case of Cairo and elsewhere. This mutual (constructive) exchange between cities and actors on lessons learned will be of essence when further developing approaches to foster the resilience of human settlements and communities.

CONCLUSION

This chapter looked into how the connection between climate-change adaptation and community involvement was reinforced through increasing knowledge and information exchange, particularly those linked to housing in informal urban areas. It illustrated how the Greater Cairo Region deals with the impacts and stresses of extreme heat and erratic weather events whose combination reduces the capacities of low-income households and communities to adapt, consequently resulting in the increased vulnerability of the region's population (Plan+Risk Consult 2013). A vast urban metropolitan region like the GCR requires holistic, long-term, comprehensive strategies that include adaptation on all levels for the sake of providing a 'collective good' (Pelling 2011, p.48) that does not exclude the most vulnerable segments of society. Currently, urban heat stress in the GCR and, in particular, in its informal areas seems to be subject to limited projects such as the PDP, a few bottom-up initiatives (Miit 'Uqba), and some research projects (GERF 2014). Nevertheless, knowledge is accumulating and interventions that tackle the environmental and heat-related aspects of climate change on an urban and built scale are beginning to be incorporated into mainstream development and community interventions. One example is the case of Ezzbet El-Nasr in the GCR, which is subject to development cooperation.

In respect to Ezzbet El-Nasr, one conclusion is that recognition of the connection between climate, the built environment, and housing is growing as the result of exemplary value-based community engagement (i.e., VMEs), and pilot projects are being introduced that are related to development cooperation and to diversifying the local and international academic discourse. Moreover, increased exposure to and growing knowledge on this topic can significantly contribute to developing a discourse on climate change across sectors and academic disciplines and the consequent complex aspects of adaptive housing. Information exchange and cooperation among the different actors across tiers are relevant to identifying and implementing co-beneficial measures and in fostering resilience.

Another conclusion is that measures on the community level can be physical or spatial but they need to be linked to communities' dynamics and diverse compositions, with personal and collective values playing a crucial role. Hence, adaptation in this context will require a particular balance between individual and collective awareness and community interaction and support, while (potentially) facing continuous neglect in the provision of services these communities need and also in formal governance. Here, the community and its people need to be in continuous communication and negotiation. The link to actual change (i.e., perceived or real improvements in livelihoods), however, will need to be subject to further monitoring and research. Moreover, the potential involvement of external actors (and champions) who act as catalysts needs to be sensitively built on lessons learned from previous experiences. Finally, looking at the question of transfer, a mutual (constructive) exchange between cities and actors on lessons learned will be of essence.

REFERENCES

Abouelmagd, S. (n.d.) 'The rehabilitation of inner-city slums in Cairo-a Livelihood perspective. The case Study of Ezbet-Haridy', Cairo-Egypt.

Agrawala, S., Moehner, A., El Raey, M., Conway, D., Van Aalst, M., Hagenstad, M. and Smith, J. (2004) 'Development and climate change in Egypt: focus on coastal resources and the Nile', *Organisation for Economic Co-operation and Development*.

Al-Gohari, S. (2010) 'Egyptian Approach to Informal settlements (ISDF)' [PowerPoint presentation], *Global Risk Forum, Davos*, available: https://de.sl ideshare.net/GRFDavos/egypt-for-idrc-2-june-2010-finalpptx [accessed 3 Nov 2018].

AlSayyad, N. (1993) 'Informal housing in a comparative perspective: On squatting, culture, and development in a Latin American and a Middle Eastern context', *Review of Urban & Regional Development Studies*, 5(1), 3–18

Arnstein, S.R. (1969) *A Ladder of Citizen Participation* [online], available at: http://lithgow-schmidt.dk/sherry-arnstein/ladder-of-citizen-participation.html #d0e75 [accessed 3 Nov 2018]

Ayers, J. and Forsyth, T. (2009) 'Community-Based Adaptation to Climate Change: Strengthening Resilience Through Development', *Environment: sci ence and policy for sustainable development* 51(4), 22–31

Bayat, A. and Denis, E. (2000) 'Who is afraid of ashwaiyyat? Urban change and politics in Egypt', *Environment and Urbanization*, 12(2), 185–199.

Bazrkar, M.H., Zamani, N., Eslamian, S., Eslamian, A., Dehghan, Z. (2015) Urbanization and Climate Change. In Leal Filho W., eds., Handbook of Climate Change Adaptation, Berlin, Heidelberg: Springer.

Beattie, G. and McGuire, L. (2019) *The Psychology of Climate Change Vol. 1*, London: The New American Library.

Bilgili, Ö. and Marchand, K. (2016) *Domain 3: Protection and Migration*, Thematic Input Paper – Agadir Regional Thematic Exchange Meeting, Bern, Switzerland: Swiss Agency for Development and Cooperation.

Center for Development Services (CDS) (2013) *Participatory Needs Assessment in Informal Areas – Cairo Governorate*, draft report on behalf of GIZ PDP, unpublished as of 11th May 2013.

Cities Alliance (2018) *Slum Upgrading Up Close – Experiences of Six Cities*, Washington.

CLUSTER (2018a) Cairo Urban Initiatives Platform, [online] available at: https://www.cuipcairo.org/en [accessed 3 Nov 2018].

CLUSTER (2018b) Urban Interventions in Saqiyat Mikki, Social media Platform [online] available at: https://www.facebook.com/clustercairo/ [accessed 3 Nov 2018].

Climate Changes for the Greater Area of Cairo (CSC) (2013) *Potential Impacts and Possibilities for Adaptation Options*, report on behalf of GIZ PDP as of June 2013.

Davis, M. (2006) *Planet of slums*, Verso, New York.

Dodman, D. (2009) 'Urban density and climate change'. *Analytical review of the interaction between urban growth trends and environmental changes*, (1).

Dreyfus, M. (2015) Adaptation to Climate Change in Cities, in Leal Filho W., eds., Handbook of Climate Change Adaptation, Berlin, Heidelberg: Springer.

Egyptian Environmental Affairs Agency (EEAA,: United Nations Framework Convention on Climate Change (UNFCCC) (2010a). *Egypt Second National Communication*, Cairo

Egyptian Environmental Affrairs Agency (EEAA, (MSEA: Ministry of State for Environmental Affrairs) (2010b) *Egypt National Environmental Economic and Development Study (NEEDS) for Climate Change*, Cairo: UNFCCC

Egyptian Environmental Affrairs Agency (EEAA) (2016) *Egypt Third National Communication*, Cairo

El-Batran, M. and Arandel, C. (1998) 'A Shelter of Their Own: Informal Settlement Expansion in Greater Cairo and Government Responses', *Environment and Urbanization* 10(1), 217–232

Ezbet Project (2018) [online], available at: https://www.ezbetproject.com/ [accessed 3 Nov 2018].

Fathy, H. (2010) *Architecture for the poor: an experiment in rural Egypt*, University of Chicago press.

Froehlich, P. and Al-Saidi, M. (2017) 'Community-based adaptation to climate change in Egypt status quo and future policies', *Climate Change Research at Universities,* Cham: Springer, 235–250.

Hassan, G.F. (2012) 'Regeneration as an Approach For The Development of Informal Settlements in Cairo Metropolitan', *Alexandria Engineering Journal,* 51(3), 229–239

Huq, S., Kovats, S., Reid, H. and Satterthwaite, D. (2007) 'Reducing risks to cities from disasters and climate change', *Environment and Urbanization,* Volume 19, 3–15.

Hunt, A. and Watkiss, P. (2011) 'Climate change impacts and adaptation in cities: a review of the literature', *Climatic change,* 104(1), 13–49.

International Council for Local Environmental Initiatives (ICLEI)2019) ICLEI Africa Interactive Decision Support Tool and Resilient Africa website, [online] available at: http://www.resilientafrica.org/page.php?ID=1 [accessed 25 Jan 2019].

Information and Decision Support Center (IDSC) /: United Nations Development Programme (UNDP) (2011). *Egypt's National Strategy for Adaptation to Climate Change and Disaster Risk Reduction*, Cairo. Egypt

Intergovernmental Panel on Climate Change (IPCC) (2007) 'Climate Change 2007: The Physical Science Basis. Contribution of Working Group I to the Fourth Assessment Report of the Intergovernmental Panel on Climate Change', in Solomon, Qin, D., Manning, M., Chen, Z., Marquis, M., Averyt, K., Tignor, M. and Miller, H.L., eds., Cambridge, United Kingdom and New York, NY, USA: Cambridge University Press, 996.

Intergovernmental Panel on Climate Change (IPCC) (2014) *Climate Change 2007: Impacts, Adaptation and Vulnerability. Contribution of Working Group II to the Fifth Assessment Report of the Intergovernmental Panel on Climate Change,* in Parry, M., Parry, M. L., Canziani, O., Palutikof, J., Van der Linden, P. and Hanson, C., eds., Vol. 4, Cambridge: Cambridge University Press.

Kadi, G. E. (1994) 'Le Caire, la ville spontanée sous contrôle' *[Cairo, the Spontaneous City Under Control] Monde arabe Maghreb Machrek*, 30–41.

Keeble, B. R. (1988) 'The Brundtland report: 'Our common future'. *Medicine and War*, 4(1), 17–25.

Khalifa, M. A. (2011) 'Redefining slums in Egypt: Unplanned versus unsafe areas', *Habitat International*, 35(1), 40–49.

Kipper, R. and Fischer, M. (2009) 'Cairo's Informal Areas Between Urban Challenges and Hidden Potentials Facts', *Voices. Visions, GTZ Egypt, Cairo: Published in the framework of the Egyptian-German Participatory Development Programme in Urban Areas (PDP)*.

Laue, F. (2013) *Coping with Climate Change – Reflections for Community Based Strategies in Cairo's Informal Settlements*, (MSc.), University of Stuttgart/Ain Shams University Cairo.

Lückenkötter et al. (2016) *Report on "Architectural" Adaptation Measures Suitable for Implementation in Informal Urban Areas: Climate Change and Adaptation in Informal Urban Areas of the Greater Cairo Region* –, GIZ PDP, Dortmund.

Madbouly, M. (2009) 'Revisiting urban planning in the Middle East North Africa region', *Regional study prepared for UN-Habitat Global Report on Human Settlements*.

Malik, A., Quin, X. and Smith, S.C. (2010) 'Autonomous Adaptation to Climate Change: A Literature Review', *IIEP Working Paper*, 2010–24, Washington, DC: Elliott School of International Affairs, George Washington University.

Maller, C. J. and Strengers, Y. (2011) 'Housing, heat stress and health in a changing climate: promoting the adaptive capacity of vulnerable households, a suggested way forward', *Health promotion international*, 26(4), 492–498.

McCarthy, J. J., Canziani, O. F., Leary, N. A., Dokken, D. J. and White, K. S., eds. (2001) *Climate change 2001– impacts, adaptation, and vulnerability: contribution of Working Group II to the third assessment report of the Intergovernmental Panel on Climate Change*, Volume 2, Cambridge University Press.

Moser, C. and Satterthwaite, D. (2008) 'Towards Pro-Poor Adaptation to Climate Change in the Urban Centres of Low- and Middle- Income Countries: Global Urban Research Centre', Working Paper #1, University of Manchester.

Organization for Economic Co-operation and Development (OECD) (2010) Cities and Climate Change, OECD Publishing, [online] available: http://dx.doi.org/10.1787/9789264091375-en [accessed 03 Oct 2018]

Pelling, M. (2007) *Urbanization and Disaster Risk, Panel Contribution to the Population-Environment Research Network*, Cyberseminar on Population and National Hazards, Palisades, New York: Population-Environment Research Network.

Participatory Development Programme (PDP) (2011) Maximising Use Value – Action Guide for Informal Areas, GIZ, Cairo.

Participatory Development Programme (PDP) (2017) Pilot Projects Factsheet, *unpublished*, GIZ. Cairo.

PDP (2018) Climate Change Adaptation and Urban Resilience, [online], available at: website http://www.egypt-urban.net/climate-change-adaptation-and-urban-resilience/ [accessed 03 Oct 2018].

Pelling, M. (2007) *Urbanization and Disaster Risk, Panel Contribution to the Population-Environment Research Network*, Cyberseminar on Population and National Hazards. Palisades, New York: Population-Environment Research Network.

Phalatse, L. (2011) Vulnerability assessment and adaptation planning for the city of Johannesburg, in Resilient Cities Congress, Bonn, Germany.

Piffero, E. (2009) *What happened to participation? Urban development and authoritarian upgrading in Cairo's informal neighbourhoods*, Volume 1, Odoya srl.

Plan + Risk Consult (2013) 'Conceptual and Analytical Framework: Community-Based Adaptation and Resilience to Climate Change in Selected Urban Areas of Greater Cairo', internal draft, Dortmund/Cairo

Raleigh, C., Jordan, L. and Salehyan, I. (2008, March) 'Assessing the impact of climate change on migration and conflict', in *paper commissioned by the World Bank Group for the Social Dimensions of Climate Change workshop, Washington, DC*, 5–6.

Rigaud, K. K., de Sherbinin, A., Jones, B., Bergmann, J., Clement, V., Ober, K. and Midgley, A. (2018) *Groundswell: preparing for internal climate migration*, World Bank.

Satterthwaite, D. et al. (2007) *Adapting to Climate Change in Urban Areas: the Possibilities and Constraints in Low- and Middle-Income Nations.*, Volume 1, IIED.

Séjourné, M. (2006) *Les Politiques Récentes de „Traitement" des Quartiers Illégaux au Caire*, (PhD), France: Université de Tours.

Shadow Ministry of Housing (n.d.) blog. [online] available: http://blog.shadowministryofhousing.org/p/english.html [accessed 25 Oct 2018].

Shehayeb, D. K. (2009) Advantages of living in informal areas. *Kipper R. et Fischer M. Cairo informal areas, between hidden challenge and hidden potentials, le Caire, GTZ*, 19–24.

Sims, D., El Shorbagui, M. and Séjourné, M. (2003) The case of Cairo, *Egypt UN Habitat, Global Report on Human Settlements*.

Sims, D. (2012) *Understanding Cairo: The logic of a city out of control*. Oxford University Press

Singerman, D., Amar, P. E. and Amar, P., eds., (2006) *Cairo cosmopolitan: politics, culture, and urban space in the new globalized Middle East*, Cairo: American University in Cairo Press.

Singerman, D. (2009) 'Cairo contested: Governance, urban space, and global modernity', Cairo: The American University in Cairo Press.

Steinberg, F. (1990) 'Cairo: informal land development and the challenge for the future', *The Transformation of Land Supply Systems in Third World Cities*, Avebury, Aldershot, 111–132.

Stern, N. (2006) 'The Economics of Climate Change: the Stern Review', Cambridge University Press

Tadamun (2013) 'Paving the Streets of Mīt ʿUqba, Tadamun' [online] available at: http://www.tadamun.co/?post_type=initiative&p=497&lang=en, [accessed 01 Nov 2018].

UK Climate Impacts Programme (UKCIP) (2007) *Identifying Adaptation Options* [online] available at: https://ukcip.ouce.ox.ac.uk/wp-content/PDFs/ID_Adapt_options.pdf [accessed 03 Nov 2018].

Urban Management masters Programme (UMP) Techinical University Berlin (2010) *Improving Informal Areas in Greater Cairo: The Cases of Ezzbet El Nasr & Dayer El Nahia*, Berlin: TU-Berlin.

United Nations Framework Convention on Climate Change (UNFCCC), V. (2015) Adoption of the Paris agreement. *United Nations Office at Geneva*, [online], available at: https://unfccc.int/sites/default/files/english_paris_agreement.pdf [accessed 03 Oct 2018].

United Nations Framework Convention on Climate Change (UNFCCC), (2018) Adaptation in human settlements: key findings and way forward Report by the secretariat.

United Nations Fund for Population Activities (UNFPA) (2007) 'In the Slums of Cairo, Home Is a Roof Over Your Head' [online] available: /news/slums-cairo-home-roof-over-your-head [accessed 01 Nov 2018].

United Nations Development Programme (UNDP) (2004) 'The Egypt Human Development Report 2004 – Choosing Decentralization for Good Governance', Egypt.

United Nations Development Programme (UNDP) (2013) *Potential Impacts of Climate Change on the Egyptian Economy*, Cairo.

UN-Habitat, U. N. (2003) 'The challenge of slums', *Global Report on Human Settlements*.

UN-Habitat. (2015) 'Slum almanac 2015–2016: Tracking improvement in the lives of slum dwellers'.

UN-HABITAT (2011) *Cairo – a City in Transition, Cities & Citizens – Bridging the Urban Divide*, Cairo.

Urbanics (2018) [online] available at: website http://www.urbanics.org/projects-activities/ [accessed 01 Nov 2018].

Verner D., ed. (2012) *Adaptation to a Changing Climate in the Arab Countries: A Case for Adaptation Governance and Leadership in Building Climate Resilience*, Washington DC: The World Bank.

Verner, D. (2013) *Adaptation to a Changing Climate in the Arab Countries: A Case for Adaptation Governance and Leadership in Building Climate Resilience*, Washington DC: The World Bank.

Vincenti, D. (2016) 'Sustainability transitions in Arab-Islamic countries: Egypt as a case study', *Agriculture and agricultural science procedia*, 8, 135–140.

Wamsler, C. (2008) 'Climate Change Impacts on Cities: Ignore, Mitigate or Adapt', *Trialog*, 97, 4–10.

Weart, S. (2013a) *Impacts of Climate Change* [online], available at: http://www.aip.org/history/climate/pdf/impacts.pdf [accessed 22 Oct 2018].

Weart, S.R. (2013b) *The Discovery of Global Warming* [online], available at: http://www.aip.org/history/climate/index.htm [accessed 3 May 2013].

WBGU–German Advisory Council on Global Change (2016), *Humanity on the move: 'Unlocking the transformative power of cities*, Berlin: WBGU.

Wodon, Q., Burger, N., Grant, A. and Liverani, A. (2014) 'Climate change, migration, and adaptation in the MENA Region'.

World Bank (2006) *Clean Energy and Development: Towards an Investment Framework.*

Zanaty Group (2013) *Draft report on Baseline Study: Outlining Three Indicators for the Participatory Development Programme in Urban Areas (as of 11th May 2013),* GIZ PDP, Cairo.

Interviews

Bayoumi, M. (2013) *International organizations and adaptation options in Egypt* [interview by F. Laue] UNDP, Cairo, 3 June 2013.

Chapter 9: From the Hyper-ghetto to State-subsidised Urban Sprawl

Old and New vulnerabilities in Buffalo City, South Africa[1]

Gerhard Kienast

URBAN POVERTY AND VULNERABILITY IN THE SOUTH AFRICAN CONTEXT

Even without climate change, the life of shack dwellers is full of risk due to densification, the poor condition of their housing and vulnerabilities to such hazards as heavy rains or fires. Since the advent of democracy in 1994, the South African government has undertaken great efforts to improve the lives of poor households by means of a massive programme of state-subsidised housing production, the extension of water, sanitation and electricity networks into formerly disadvantaged areas, and the provision of free basic services to households that fall under certain income thresholds. However, official housing policy soon came under criticism due to new settlements being situated in inadequate locations. Despite policy reforms that aimed at sustainable integrated settlements, an initiative set in motion in 2004, for many projects, past mistakes seem to have been repeated. Faced with shrinking budgets, an increasing number of households living in informal structures and growing unrest and demands for lives of dignity, the South African government declared the upgrading of informal settlements a national priority in 2010. So far, however, political expediency, en-

---

[1] Research for this paper was made possible by funding received from the School of Architecture, Urban and Landscape Planning of the University of Kassel and the German Research Foundation (DFG).

trenched networks of patronage and vested interests in the public housing complex have prevented a reorientation towards more incremental strategies.

Climate change is affecting South Africa by exacerbating uneven weather patterns, where arid settlements are expected to experience more heatwaves, drought and fires, while coastal areas are likely to suffer from sea-level rise, flooding and landslides. At the settlement level, climate change is likely to aggravate problems caused by poor urban management; for example, poor stormwater drainage systems that cause soil erosion. Increased storm intensity due to climate change will increase the risk of flash flooding in informal settlements in flood-prone areas and on sand dunes (Government of the Republic of South Africa 2011).

Urban planning has played 'a limited role in consciously reducing vulnerability to disasters or everyday risk' in South Africa (Van Niekerk 2013, p. 2). In fact, according to a study carried out by the South African Council of Scientific and Industrial Research (CSIR), in some municipalities, 'planning for everyday disaster resilience [...was not even deemed] part of the planning process, but rather as part of what the "environmental people" do' (ibid, p. 4). The pressure to provide housing and basic services has fixated planners and government on the very near future but it has failed to transform the post-apartheid economy in a sustainable way. Bringing together data on population and economic growth with climatic projections, like the expected change in the frequency of extreme rainfall events, the CSIR has identified regions of socio-economic vulnerability (Van Huyssteen *et al*. 2013).

The CSIR has stressed the importance of identifying in a timely manner the communities and areas at risk of being exposed to hazards, in the hope that geoscience and the application of spatial analyses will help practitioners determine the possible implications of projected risks for settlements and support the respective decision-making (ibid.). More recently, the CSIR was tasked with revising the Guidelines for Human Settlement Planning and Design (CSIR 2000) in order to address the challenges that can be expected as a result of climate change. The council's review points to the need to move toward dense and water-sensitive urban designs, among other initiatives (Van Niekerk *et al*. 2015). In this context, this paper traces a local practice of emergency resettlement and redevelopment, in a densely populated and highly vulnerable informal settlement, that was triggered by everyday natural disasters. It shows how disaster risk, geotechnical assumptions and infrastructural constraints have justified a new project of massive relocation to peripheral areas that have an eerie resemblance and physical proximity to former apartheid townships. Based on interviews with politicians, municipal officials, consultants and shack dwellers, analyses of plans and budgets, aerial photographs, newspaper articles, and site visits, this chapter argues that the relocation that has taken place has created new vulnerabilities without doing away with those it was supposed to overcome.

Figure 1a: Metropolitan municipalities of South Africa.

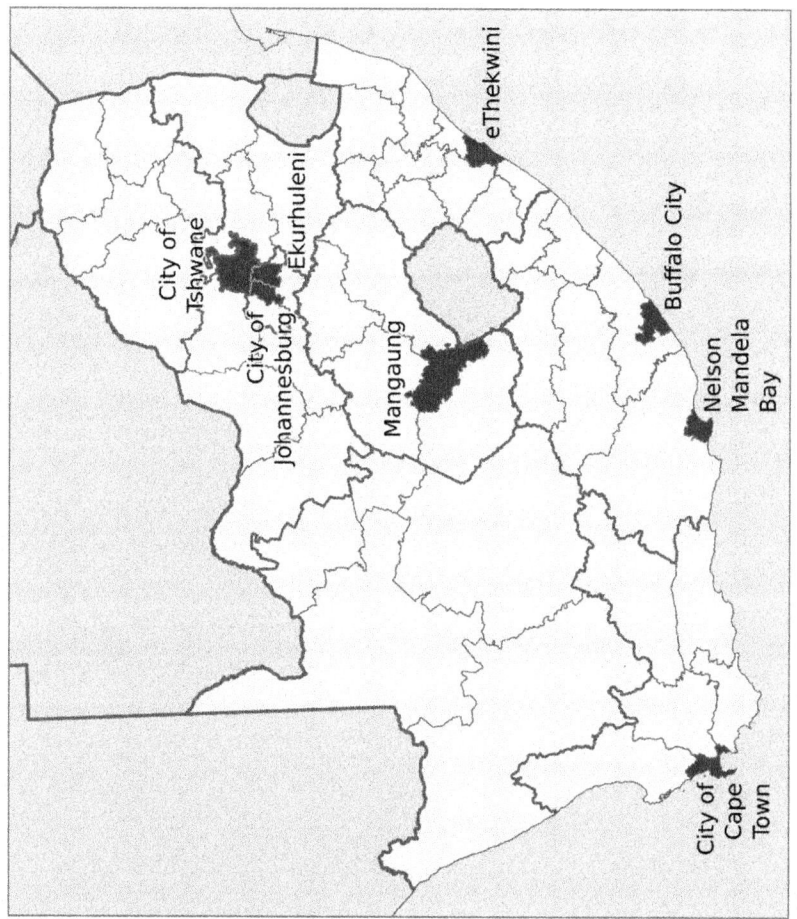

Source: Cartography: J.T. Wongnam based on Map of South Africa with district borders, 2016.svg by Wikimedia Commons.

222 | Gerhard Kienast

Figure 1b: Main places and built-up area in Buffalo City 2002.

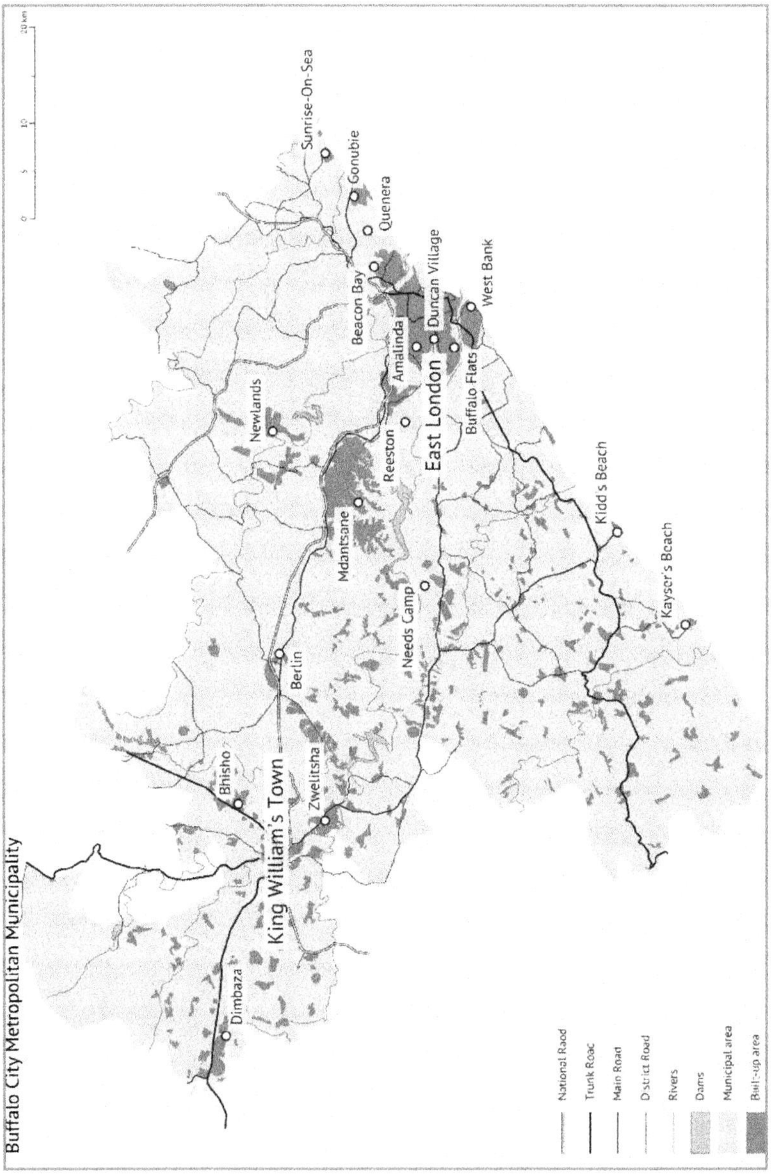

Source: Cartography: J.T. Wongnam based on BCM 2002 (Map B1 study area).

SOCIAL AND ENVIRONMENTAL VULNERABILITY IN THE LOCAL CONTEXT

Buffalo City: A low-growth, high-inequality environment

With 810,528 inhabitants, Buffalo City is South Africa's seventh most populous municipality (StatsSA mid-year population estimates for 2016, cited in ECDoH 2018). The municipality was only formed in 2000 when East London, King William's Town, Bhisho (the former capital of the homeland Ciskei), several black townships and their rural hinterlands were merged. In 2011, Buffalo City was elevated to the status of a metropolitan municipality. As a secondary city surrounded by former homeland areas, it must be considered one of the 'areas under the biggest population pressure' (Van Huysteen *et al.* 2013, p. 5). Although population growth in Buffalo City has been well below the national average (0.69% compared to 1.44%; Stats SA 2011), the incidence of households living in informal settlements is significantly higher than in other metropolitan municipalities (17% compared to the 12% average for all metro areas; StatsSA 2013 cited by Graham *et al* 2014, p. 12). The apparent contradiction between modest population growth and the high incidence of shacks may indicate that rural migrants use the city as a 'stepping stone' on their way to Johannesburg or Cape Town, where GDP per capita and chances of finding a permanent job are both much higher (Graham *et al.* 2014, p. 11). Notwithstanding the migration flows, Buffalo City is characterised by a discomforting continuity of precarious housing conditions and 'more and more' land invasions (interview with a municipal planner, March 2018).

According to Makiwane (2011; cited by Dlani *et al.* 2015, p. 178), climate change could imply that the municipality is faced with 'more frequent and severe flooding as a result of higher intensity storm events [...]. This will impact on human settlements, infrastructure, human health and place a greater burden on particularly impoverished communities.' The city's climate change strategy (BCMM 2014, p. 44) highlights the potential impact of increased precipitation on informal settlements located on flood plains; the strategy recommends city planners 'remove shacks in flood-prone areas [and] promote climate resilient settlements' (among others). Its authors also think it is 'likely' that droughts will intensify and it is 'almost certain' that there will be more extremely hot days with major consequences for vulnerable people and municipal infrastructure, possibly leading to an increased cost of water services (ibid., p. 126). Thus, they recommend "smart growth" planning a strategy that highlights high density, mixed-use, transit-oriented development [...] and directing city resources toward existing communities rather than diverting them to new development in outlying areas' (ibid., p. 81). The following case study shows that the municipality is still far from implementing these recommendations.

Duncan Village as a site of struggle and social deterioration

The highest concentration of informal structures can be found only five kilometres from the East London Central Business District (CBD), in Duncan Village, a township in the municipality of Buffalo City, Eastern Cape Province, South Africa (Figure 1). The area, originally known as the East Bank has been the main location of the country's black workforce since the 1880s and it has remained the primary scene of the local housing crisis since the industrial boom in the early twentieth century. The history of Duncan Village may be recounted as having been a sequence of failed attempts at urban renewal, starting with the construction of several hundred municipally managed rented homes in the early 1940s, under Governor-General Duncan, to whom the area owes its name. As the government could not do away with the village's wood and corrugated iron shacks, 'overcrowding and squalor' was blamed for a terrible tuberculosis epidemic (Ntsebeza 1993). In 1952, after police brutally dissolved an African National Congress (ANC) gathering, the area erupted in violent riots that were followed by a police massacre (Mager and Minkley 1993; Bank and Carton 2016).

For several decades, the East London council attempted to restructure the area in accordance with the Group Areas Act of 1950. Political activists and people without residence permits for the urban area were deported, black and coloured inhabitants were separated, and the old location was demolished. Duncan Village was supposed to become a settlement of standardised cottage housing where only married men with secure jobs were allowed to stay (Bank 2011, p. 70). In the 1960s and 1970s, the apartheid government built Mdantsane, a huge dormitory town 25 km outside of East London. The government's intention was to remove people from East London's urban areas and mitigate any future rural-to-urban migration. Although at least 8,000 families were displaced from the city (ibid., p. 194) and three quarters of the old East Bank locations were broken down, the state never completed these intended relocations. In 1985, the killing of an anti-apartheid leader sparked a new rebellion. Government forces committed another massacre but lost control over the township. The well-organised Duncan Village Residents' Association (DVRA) galvanised resistance and 'open[ed] up the township for immigration from surrounding rural areas' (ibid., p. 90). Effectively replacing state authority, the DVRA allowed shacks to be erected in backyards and open spaces, resulting in a population that had more than doubled by the time of the first democratic election in 1994.

In order to 'deliver concrete benefits to violence torn and crisis driven communities in major urban areas at an early stage' (SACN 2003, p. 38), the Government of National Unity embarked on six Special Integrated Presidential Projects (SIPP) and Duncan Village became one of them. Despite the local community's mistrust of the city administration, in an interview conducted in June 2015, the former project manager noted that a lot was achieved: '... we almost had to respond to crisis: Install new bulk infrastructure, build new roads, we even organised new schools, clinics, early childhood development centres, an old age home – still standing today!' Yet, as the project only built 1.000 housing units, it could not do away with the precarious conditions created by apartheid and mass migration. The persistence of high population densities and makeshift housing made Duncan Village highly vulnerable.

The biggest risk was people's dependency on paraffin (petroleum) for light and heating. According to Bank (2011, p. 102), between 1986 and 1992, alone, there were 208 fires in Duncan Village, destroying at least 1,151 huts. During the next six years, the number of destroyed huts doubled, probably due to a further increase in building density, and more than thirty people died. According to an evaluation done for the Human Sciences Research Council, the SIPP had intended to reduce the fire risk by connecting 5,000 illegally constructed buildings to the electrical grid, but electricity was too expensive for the inhabitants (Morrow and Engel 2003, p. 18). In contrast, the city council rejected the electrification of informal settlements even as a provisional measure and, thus, bears responsibility for the continued occurrence of tragedies (Bank 2011, p. 216). A particularly bad fire in June 2001 destroyed more than 400 shacks and killed a young girl. One year later, in August 2002, Duncan Village was hit by heavy flooding when two rivers that ran through the area overflowed. Thirteen people died, 3,000 were left homeless, and infrastructure and buildings worth R100 million (USD 16.6 million) were destroyed (FHISER 2004, cited by Kay 2005, p. 62). For the newly formed Buffalo City, Duncan Village represented a disaster area that needed massive intervention (Figure 2). According to one of the area's council representatives, there was 'intense pressure' to build housing in Duncan Village as quickly as possible (Kay 2005, p. 30).

Figure 2: Duncan Village study area as defined by the Local Spatial Development Framework.

Source: Kay, 2005, p. 17.

The growing impoverishment also added pressure. Due to the abolition of state subsidies to homelands industries after the 1994 elections and the resulting corporate closures, the whole region suffered from deindustrialisation. Thousands of unskilled and semi-skilled jobs were lost. While in the 1950s only a fifth of adults in Duncan Village were jobless, in the mid-1990s almost half of the adult population was unemployed (Bank 2011, p. 111). Despite the investments the SIPP made and the general recovery of the South African economy in the late 1990s, in 2001 only 17.5% of the residents were formally employed and only 11% earned more than R1,600 per month (then about USD 200) (BCM 2009, p. 27). With the term 'hyper-ghetto', taken from Wacquant (2008), Bank characterises Duncan Village as a racially stigmatised space trapped in a downward spiral within a post-industrial city (2011).

Duncan Village between redevelopment and relocation

In order to improve living conditions and reduce vulnerability in the area, in late 2003, the municipal planning department started to elaborate a local spatial development framework (LSDF). The plan aimed at a holistic renewal described as the Duncan Village Redevelopment Initiative (DVRI) in which the construction of state-subsidised housing was to gradually replace the area's shacks.[2] Due to the housing stock's high density, it was clear that the traditional typology of free-standing minimum-standard houses could only accommodate a very small proportion of the local population. Therefore, local urban planners, consultants and councillors agreed on the development of terraced row and semi-detached housing (Figure 3).

Figure 3: Duncan Village urban and housing design by The Matrix, commissioned for the Local Spatial Development Framework.

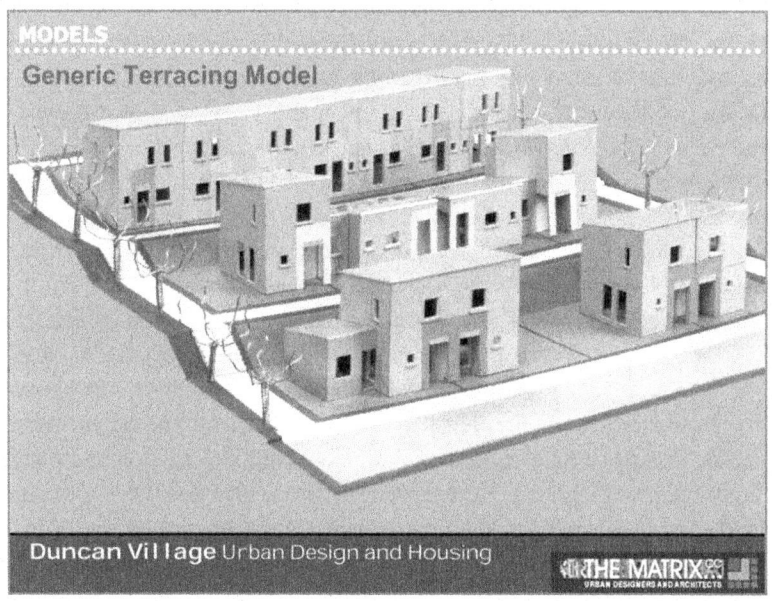

Source: BCMM 2013b, p.93.

---

2   It also included the pedestrian-friendly rebuilding of the main transport corridor, the creation of a multifunctional social infrastructure and the promotion of economic activities (Kay 2005, p. 66).

However, the people to be affected had little say in the planning process. Participation was always filtered through the elected ward councillors and thus was prone to political interference (Kay 2005, pp. 109–110; 113–116).[3] As newly elected leaders insisted on favouring native inhabitants over 'newcomers', the density target was reduced. In turn, both the number of families that should have been relocated and the need for suitable land increased (interview conducted 28 May 2015; BCM 2009, p.88; Ndhlovu 2015, p. 59).

According to the LSDF, over a period of twelve years at least 20,000 new homes were to be created. Only one-tenth of the new houses were supposed to be built in Duncan Village itself, yet even these were lacking in infrastructural prerequisites. The municipal engineering department insisted that new construction in Duncan Village and adjacent areas could only be permitted after the commissioning of a regional sewage treatment plant and the diversion of sewage to this plant. As long as these conditions were not met, only about 300 housing units were supposed to be built on this site. Almost 9,000 units were to be built on various sites within a ten-kilometre radius, but even these areas were subject to constraints. The only area where mass construction and resettlement could begin immediately was Reeston, the former buffer zone between East London and Mdantsane (see Figure 1). According to the planners, the area could accommodate more than 9,500 units. In other words, almost half of the population of Duncan Village was supposed to move to a no-man's land (BCM 2009, pp. 89–90, 164–168).

Reeston had been earmarked for low-income housing since the late 1980s (Reintges 1992). From a bird's eye view, the development of the area between the core city and its economically dependent satellite makes sense (Figure 1). However, if one were to have taken a closer look, one could have seen that Reeston was not very suitable for residential development. Deep valleys with irregular shapes and steep slopes prevented coherent development. The ridges where the housing was to be built upon, without the need for expensive foundations, were very narrow (Figure 4). Nevertheless, between 1996 and 1997, plans to develop Reeston were revived (interviews conducted 28 May and 10 June 2015). Even before work on the Duncan Village LSDF had begun, the Integrated Development Plan of 2003 to 2004 had earmarked more than R110 million (USD

---

3   Based on a 'qualitative attitudinal survey' and a series of consultative meetings (BCM 2009, p. 8–9; 31–33), municipal planners had concluded that 'many people are tired of the constant anxiety and suffering [...] and are becoming more willing to allow the government to provide a formal house located on a safer piece of land even if that means moving out of Duncan Village' (Foster 2004, cited by Kay 2005, p.63).

14 million) for housing construction in the area (BCM 2003, p. 32). Long before the Duncan Village LSDF had been officially adopted, Buffalo City Municipality (BCM) had begun relocating flood and fire victims to Reeston. Further, resettlement was seen as the only option for de-densification and a comprehensive redevelopment in Duncan Village.

Figure 4: Unfavourable topography for low-income housing development in Reeston (Buffalo City).

Source: Google Earth, Image © 2019 Maxar Technologies.
(aerial picture taken 17 May 2018; label 'New Life' added by the author).

Reeston as an example of state-subsidised urban sprawl

Since the early 2000's, Reeston has gradually been developed as another dormitory town that consists of far-flung single-family homes that were built to provide basic needs (Figure 5). However, building standards for the state-subsidised sector have improved over the years. At the beginning of the initiative, government-built houses consisted of corrugated iron roofs but not plaster walls with insulation; now, roofs are tiled and houses are insulated. However, the built environments that have been created still have an eerie resemblance to the apartheid-era township of Mdantsane, which has been described as a monotonous place 'marked by uniformity and separation, by loneliness and hardship, by starvation and unemployment and distance' (Minkley 1999, p. 217). Formal investment is limited to houses, internal roads, basic infrastructure (electricity, water, sanitation) and a few schools. All other functions that contribute to the village's social life and everyday commodities are provided from transport containers or shack-like structures, similar to the informal settlements Reeston was supposed to replace. (Using state-subsidised houses as shops is considered a misappropriation.) Fifteen years after construction began, it is obvious that the education infrastructure is insufficient as hundreds of school children rely on busses or long walks to attend schools in the town and the only secondary school that was established in Reeston has been extended again and again with corrugated iron structures.[4]

Figure 5: Unauthorised shop operating from a state-subsidised house in Reeston, Phase 3, Stage 3 ("New Life").

Source: Author, 2016.

---

4   On the basis of government-defined ratios, the authors of the DVLSDF had estimated that there would be a need for twelve elementary schools, five secondary schools, six health centers and two police stations, once the city extension area has reached its target population of 54,500 inhabitants (BCM 2009, p. 103). Due to the lack of coherent official reporting, it is difficult to establish the size of the current population. Based on a May 2015 estimate by a senior housing official, augmented by the recently built settlement known as "New Life" and assuming an average household size of 3.8 persons (a factor used by the municipality with regard to informal settlements), the area may now host more than 20,000 inhabitants. If the social facilities framework of the Duncan Village LSDF had been followed, then at least five primary schools, two secondary schools and two clinics should have been operational by now and a police station should soon be built.

The new housing development certainly does not match the criteria for a 'climate resilient settlement' formulated by the city's own climate change strategy (see above). Its density is too low, there is no mixed-use development and development was carried out without considering people's transport needs. While, so far, Buffalo City has been spared the crisis-level water shortages experienced, in September 2017, in Cape Town due to falling water levels in storage dams; Buffalo City also introduced water restrictions (Daily Dispatch, Sept 8, 2017). If droughts intensify in the future, then they are likely to be felt more severely in an area like Reeston, where almost the entire population depends on a free basic water quota and the low-density detached housing provides little shade.

While those parts of Reeston that are close to the watershed and the main transport artery[5] may be considered reasonably well-located, inhabitants at the bottom of the ridges are not better off than those who had to relocate to Mdantsane in the 1960s or 1970s. Although distributor roads connect the neighbourhoods to the main road, people are even more dependent on the core city than those living in the apartheid-era township, due to the difficult topography and the almost total lack of amenities and commercial activities. The situation is worse in an area officially described as 'Reeston Phase 3, Stage 3' but coined 'New Life' in the vernacular (see Figures 4 and 5). All interior roads were tarred but the main road linking the township to the rest of the city is gravel, which damages cars that are used as taxis, making some taxi drivers reluctant to travel to the area (Daily Dispatch, May 9th 2018). As people living far from the corridor must pay two taxis to take them to town, Reeston is a poverty trap for inhabitants who cannot afford to travel where they may find work.

Although former municipal planners defend their work, stating that they have made provisions for clinics, schools and commercial sites, no one claims to be proud of the outcome. Some blame other government departments for failing to 'follow housing development'. Others describe the project as a mistake 'because in Duncan Village, at least [... people] were close to working opportunities, your taxis, your transport and schools.' Yet, even planners who concede that Reeston is 'a bad example; or a good example of what not to do' seem to see no chance

---

5 Both Mdantsane and Reeston are located south of the watershed between the rivers Nahoon and Buffalo. Both areas are intersected by irregularly shaped valleys that have formed in the catchment area of the Buffalo River. Good access is only provided in the North, as the railway line between East London and King William's Town, the National Road No. 2 and the older R102 (the so-called Voortrekker Road) all follow the watershed.

to correct the error, stating that 'they have started on it, so we have to see it through now' (Interviews conducted 29 May and 10 June 2015).

Running to stand still: The persistence of informality in spite of housing allocation

The number of households from Duncan Village that have benefitted from this state-subsidised housing programme is unknown. Astoundingly, there are no official figures about relocation. According to a senior human settlement official, by mid-2015, around 4,500 households had moved to Reeston (Interview conducted 28 May 2015). Since then, 1,137 additional housing units were completed in 'New Life'. The construction of another 2,500 units was suspended when the procurement process was challenged (BCMM 2015a, p. 103).

Despite massive expenditures for infrastructure provision and housing in Reeston and other projects in the municipality, Buffalo City Metropolitan Municipality (BCMM) has not managed to reduce its precarious housing conditions. Based on the BCMM's annual reports, the average number of low-income housing units produced between 2007 and 2012 was calculated as 1,438. At this rate, it would take more than 50 years to fill the backlog and provide for future need (CS Consulting / Afesis-corplan 2014, p. 8). By 2015-2016, the municipality had only completed 936 'top structures' (BCMM 2017, p. 15). In Duncan Village, in particular, the municipality had hardly made any progress in reducing its precarious housing conditions. This was also acknowledged by the current portfolio councillor for human settlements who explained:

'... we planned for the redevelopment of Duncan Village [...] but the challenge is the influx. [...] there is land invasion, which is the crisis in the whole metro. [...] As human settlements we are doing our job as per the mandate, but we still have no control measures to stop people rebuilding shacks' (Interview recorded 16 November 2016).

Municipal officials from the planning and engineering departments blame political interference and the housing department's lack of sophistication for the municipality's inability to defend the spaces it created through relocation. One of the planners explained that, in order to fulfill his mission, the developer contracted by the municipal human settlements department would have to perform three tasks at the same time: while homes are being built at Reeston, residents of Duncan Village would have to be moved, block-by-block, into so-called temporary relocation areas and at these vacated places the company would then need to immediately begin preparations for new construction:

'You got to clear a block at the bottom of the hill because your sewerage pipe will work up as you go [in order to gradually connect houses to the sewer system]. [...] And you have to be building houses here at the same time that you are building elsewhere; because of these [issues], 1,000,500 would come back to Duncan Village, 500 would be built in Reeston, roughly, and then there is still the question of these guys [residents who have no right to a state-subsidised home]. So, you got to be building in two places at once. You've got to have your admin organised because you have to move people to a TRA [temporary relocation area]; make sure that no extra people arrive in that TRA; it's only the people from that block; and then you got to work out: 'From you guys, who wants to go to Reeston? Who wants to come back to Duncan Village?' and who's not going to qualify. And you got to have a place for all three. [...] You gotto have a production line. Eesh – it's not happening' (Interview conducted 29 May 2015).

The concept of block relocation was already well formulated during the planning process (Kay 2005, p. 152). However, political interference in the processes of beneficiary registration and housing allocation undermined implementation. According to a senior official from the engineering department:

'[T]he councillors have got in and they said: 'no, you cannot only help one area!' So, instead of taking 1,000 people, they would take 50 there, 50 there... the area was still too dense! [...] The whole plan fell through because it was not done in a systematic way' (Interview conducted 17 July 2018).

Even a former portfolio councillor who was responsible for housing allocation acknowledged that "people were identified, registered and then approved [without...] taking into consideration the block movement". Yet, according to her account, this practice has now been stopped, and the only reason the DVRI still has not been able to reduce the number of informal structures is that construction was stalled after litigation over procurement processes (Interview conducted 08 March 2018).

Be that as it may, in terms of disaster risk reduction, the project was not very successful. As is evident from the analysis of aerial pictures, 15 years after the floods of 2002 even some areas inside the 100-year flood lines are still being invaded. While re-naturalisation along the Amalinda River has managed to reduce the risk of another natural disaster, areas along the Umzonyana River, which were empty when the 2013 aerial picture was taken, have since been reoccupied (Figures 6a, b and c).

Figure 6a: Excerpt of 1-in-a-100-year floodlines included in the Duncan Village Local Spatial Development Framework showing the Gesini settlement on the west bank of the Umzonyana River before the floods of 2002.

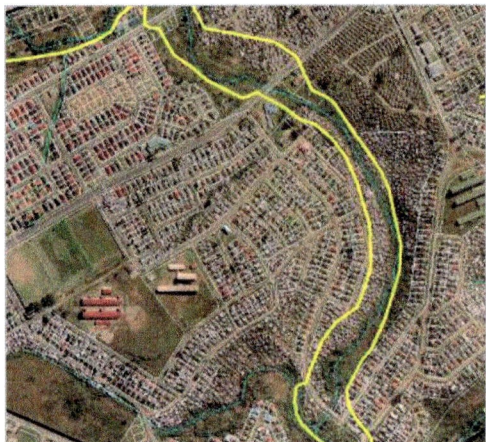

Source: BCM 2009, p. 35.

Figure 6b: Aerial picture taken in 2013.

Source: Buffalo City Metropolitan Municipality (unpublished).

Figure 6c: Aerial picture taken 31.10.2017.

Source: Google Earth, Image © 2019 Maxar Technologies.

Everyday risks: The reluctant delivery of basic sanitation and electricity services

Even after the launch of the DVRI, living conditions in Duncan Village's informal areas remained appalling. Many people who were living in shacks relied on public toilets from the apartheid era and the so-called bucket system. Even if the redevelopment plan had been followed to the letter, many inhabitants would have had to wait a decade before they could have got a fully serviced house. Still, there was no plan for interim measures. In May 2009, a study by the Eastern Cape NGO Coalition showed that, on average, 333 shack dwellers had to share one public toilet (Daily Dispatch, 19 May and 27 May 2009). Angry community protests against the lack of service delivery made it clear that, fifteen years after the first democratic elections, shack dwellers had lost patience waiting for fully serviced housing (Daily Dispatch 28 July 2009 and 18 March 2011). During the next three financial years, Buffalo City provided 26 'movable ablution blocks'[6] (BCMM 2011, p. 45; BCMM 2013a, p. 59). Yet, as the lack of maintenance and security persisted (Mbi 2015), it is no wonder that service-delivery protests became a common feature in the area (Mukwedeya 2016).

---

6 Although locally described as 'ablution blocks', the sanitary facilities do not provide showers or wash rooms but only public toilets and open-air sinks.

The other main source of vulnerability continues to be the lack of access to safe energy, which causes a permanent risk of shack fires. In keeping with South Africa's progressive Bill of Rights, the ANC government introduced a policy of free basic services for households whose income fell below certain thresholds. Part of this policy consisted of a monthly allowance of 50 free kWh of electricity. Since free basic services could only be delivered to households that were connected to the respective (electricity, water and sanitation) networks, shack dwellers missed out on most of what should have been provided by law. Yet, they developed an impressive ability to illegally tap into these networks.

In the 2009/10 financial year, the Buffalo City administration reported a dramatic increase of illegal electrical connections, called izinyoka (snakes) in the Xhosa language. In reaction to this development, the council decided to pilot the electrification of informal dwellings in Duncan Village (BCMM 2011, p. 41). Since the municipality depended on co-funding from the national government, the electrification of shacks only began in earnest in 2013/14. Since then, the municipality has connected more than 5,600 households in informal settlements, including more than 1,600 in Duncan Village (Figure 7). However, the official electrification process also clashed with 'illegal electrical connections, which cause[d] delays on site as they [had] to be removed before work [could] proceed; theft of copper [...and] vandalism to equipment' (e-mail communication with BCMM Electrical and Energy Services Department, 15 August 2018). Therefore, the BCMM electrical department drew up a restrictive list of minimum criteria for electrification[7] that cast uncertainty about the future of the programme.

---

7 Easements, flood-prone areas and private land are considered off limits. In order to avoid wasteful expenditures, the department expects assurances that 'the community supports the proposal and is willing to co-operate with the opening up of access roads where necessary [...], keep these access roads clear; supply and organize local labour where required; and help prevent tampering with or on-selling of electricity supplies'. It also requires a 'formal layout' from the municipal planning department. The general manager is clear that 'many informal areas do not and will never meet [...these] requirements' (e-mail correspondence, 17 August 2018). Although several parts of Duncan Village have been connected to the grid, he has no optimism that this will continue: '... in some areas it is so dense, [...] you have got to walk through one shack to get to the neighbour behind you. [...] So, we cannot get electricity in there' (interview conducted with BCMM Electrical and Energy Services Department, 17 July 2018).

Figure 7: Electrification of informal settlements in Duncan Village.

Source: author, 2015.

Figure 8: Illegal electricity connections on the floor of a dwelling in Amalinda.

Forest (Buffalo City).

Source: author, 2018.

Meanwhile, every year in Buffalo City, between 2012 and 2015, there have been more than 180 so-called 'informal fires' that literally happened 'every other day'. In most cases, the cause of the fire was not reported. Where a cause was indicated, candles appear to have been the major cause, followed by arson. An analysis of the fuel type used in the affected households seemed to indicate that electricity-related problems (exploding electrical cords; illegal connections; burnt-out switches, etc.) surpassed paraffin as the major cause of fires[8] In 2013/14 alone, 16 people lost their lives due to 'informal fires'. In 2014/15, this number dropped to 6 (BCMM 2015b, pp. 23–31).

According to a council report cited in the local newspaper, between July 2016 and February 2017, alone, the metro lost R95.8 million (approximately USD 7 million) in revenue from electrical generation due to illegal connections. At the same time, it was reported that 63 people had been killed by illegal electricity connections in the municipality's informal settlements over the three-year period from 2014 to 2017.

'The settlement hardest hit by electrocution deaths is Duncan Village which has recorded 20 between 2014 and 2017, followed by Mdantsane which has recorded 10 deaths. The ages of the victims range from two years to 48 and most of those who die are male' (Daily Dispatch, 19 June 2017).

These reports show that even after the initiation of the municipal electrification programme, people who are living in shacks still risk their lives (and those of their neighbours) to get free access to electricity. Given the programme's slow pace and restrictions, some may never benefit from it and feel conflicted between waiting to obtain a safe, legal connection to the electrical grid or risking the dangers of using paraffin against those of izinyoka. In any case, they are subject to everyday risks that may appear much higher and certainly more immediate than those looming from climate change.

CONCLUSION

The paper has traced the history of Duncan Village, an iconic black working-class neighbourhood which successfully resisted the racist relocations of the apartheid era but has become increasingly impoverished. This condition has

---

8 This interpretation is tenuous since information about the fuel type was available in less than 15% of incidents.

hardly improved through the recent redevelopment efforts that have taken place since the new millennium. This shows that local planners faced with overcrowding and natural and everyday disasters saw no alternative but to conduct a new massive relocation programme to a peripheral area. Since the new settlements were only serviced with the most basic infrastructure, due to their lack of integration in the local economy and the prohibitive costs of transport, resettlement has created new vulnerabilities for these inhabitants. The perpetuation of urban sprawl through low-income housing is also problematic in terms of climate change because the dominant settlement typology is already resource-inefficient, so if Buffalo City has less water available in the future it will be even more difficult to service this population.

Meanwhile, attempts at de-densification in Duncan Village have failed, partly due to the low pace of new housing construction and partly due to a disingenuous resettlement process that has failed to carry through the block clearance the planners had promoted. Again and again, new informal housing filled spaces that were opened up by the relocation of shack owners. Municipal officials and local politicians provide different explanations for this phenomenon. No matter whether people allocated to housing in Reeston sub-let their new housing or rented out their former shack, no matter whether the space that was vacated became occupied by a rural migrant or a youngster who could no longer stand living in a shack with his parents or aunt, the trend in reoccupation points to the high demand for a place to live in the city and the fact the state-subsidised housing programme is nowhere close to filling this gap.

The DVRI was established on the premise that government would be able to replace the informal housing in Duncan Village and create infrastructural preconditions for its redevelopment over a twelve-year period. Fifteen years after the start of the planning process and nine years after the formal adoption of the plan, these assumptions need to be reassessed. Given the balance of the initiative so far, there is a strong argument for shifting the focus toward the provision of interim services and disaster management in informal settlements in Duncan Village and beyond. The projected risks of climate change point in the same direction: If municipalities are serious about reducing the risk of disaster, then they must start by accepting the status quo and focus on energy safety, water and sanitation, the clearance of flood-prone areas and the implementation of basic systems of storm-water management. Although the relationship between energy safety, shack fires and climate change may be indirect, given the number of lives lost due to fires and electrocution, climate-change adaptation in a poverty-ridden area like Buffalo City must be balanced with or include the reduction of such everyday risks.

REFERENCES

Bank, L. (2011) Home Spaces, Street Styles: Contesting Power and Identity in a South African City, London: Pluto Press.

Bank, L. J. and Carton, B. (2016) 'Forgetting apartheid. History, culture and the body of a nun', Africa 86 (03), 472–503.

Berg, N. P. and Öberg, M.-L. (2005) Urban living rooms in Duncan Village – a project focusing on public space. (M.A.), School of Technoculture, Humanities & Planning, Blekinge Institute of Technology.

Buffalo City Metropolitan Municipality (BCMM). (2011) Annual Report Financial Year 2009–2010.

Buffalo City Metropolitan Municipality (BCMM). (2013a) Annual Report Financial Year 2011–2012.

Buffalo City Metropolitan Municipality (BCMM). (2013b) Spatial Development Framework Review October 2013.

Buffalo City Metropolitan Municipality (BCMM). (2014) Climate Change Strategy.

Buffalo City Metropolitan Municipality (BCMM). (2015a) Annual Report 2014/2015.

Buffalo City Metropolitan Municipality (BCMM). (2015b) Disaster Management *Annual Report 2014/2015*.

Buffalo City Metropolitan Municipality (BCMM). (2017) Annual Report 2015/16. VERSION 115 – 20/07/2017, Buffalo City.

Buffalo City Municipality (BCM). (2003) Integrated Development Plan Review: 2003/2004. Report on Amendments to IDP 2002.

Buffalo City Municipality (BCM). (2009) Duncan Village Redevelopment Initiative. Local Spatial Development Framework. Final Report approved November 2009.

CS Consulting & Afesis-corplan (December 2014) Buffalo City Metropolitan Municipality Informal Settlement Upgrading Policy and Strategy. Produced for the National Department of Human Settlements, the National Upgrading Support Programme and Buffalo City Metropolitan Municipality.

CSIR Building and Construction Technology (2000) Guidelines for Human Settlement Planning and Design, Pretoria.

Dlani, A., Ijeoma, E. O. C. and Zhou, L. (2015) Implementing the Green City Policy in Municipal Spatial Planning: The Case of Buffalo City Metropolitan Municipality, Africa's Public Service Delivery and Performance Review 3 (2), 149–182.

Eastern Cape Department of Health (ECDoH) (2018) Annual Performance Plan 2018/19.

Graham, N., Leslie, M. and Palmer, I. (2014) Design and Implementation Evaluation of the Urban Settlements Development Grant (USDG) – Buffalo City Implementation Report (Department of Human Settlements).

Government of the Republic of South Africa (2011) The National Climate Change Response White Paper.

Kay, D. (2005) Shack settlement planning Duncan Village, South Africa, East London: University of Fort Hare.

Mager, A. and Minkley, G. (1993) 'Reaping the Whirlwind. The East London Riots of 1952', in Bonner, P., Delius, P, and Posel, D. eds., Apartheid's Genesis: 1935–1962, Johannesburg: Ravan Press, Wits University Press.

Mbi, A. (2015) Duncan village's communal toilets pose dangers to health, [online], available at: http://wwmp.org.za/elitsha/2015/06/01/duncan-villagescommunal-toilets-pose-dangers-to-health/ [accessed 20 May 2018].

Morrow, S. and Engel, K. (June 2003) 'Ten-year Review. Buffalo City' in Human Sciences Research Council (HSRC), eds.

Mukwedeya, T. G. (2016) Intraparty Politics and the Local State: Factionalism, Patronage and Power in Buffalo City Metropolitan Municipality, (PhD), University of the Witwatersrand, Johannesburg.

Ndhlovu, P. (2015) Understanding the local state, service delivery and protests in post-apartheid South Africa. The case of Duncan Village and Buffalo City Metropolitan Municipality, East London. (M.A), University of the Witwatersrand, Johannesburg.

Ntsebeza, L. (1993) Youth in urban African townships, 1945–1992. A case study of the East London townships. (M.A.), University of Natal, Durban.

Reintges, C. (1992) 'Urban (mis)management? A case study of the effects of orderly urbanization on Duncan Village', in. Smith, D.M. eds., The Apartheid city and beyond, Urbanization and social change in South Africa, 99–109, London: Routledge, Witwatersrand University Press.

South African Cities Network (SACN) (2003) South African Urban Renewal Overview, available at: http://pdf.usaid.gov/pdf_docs/Pnadh380.pdf, [accessed: 14 June 2018].

Statistics South Africa (Stats SA), Census 2011 Municipal factsheet, Pretoria.

van Huyssteen, E., Le Roux, A. and van Niekerk, W. (2013) 'Analysing risk and vulnerability of South African settlements: Attempts, explorations and reflections', Jàmbá: Journal of Disaster Risk Studies, 5 (2).

van Niekerk, W. (2013) 'Translating disaster resilience into spatial planning practice in South Africa: Challenges and champions', Jàmbá: Journal of Disaster Risk Studies, 5(1).

van Niekerk, W., Petzer, E., Ndaba, D. N., Pieterse, A., Rajab, A. and Kruger, T. (2015) 'Revising the South African Guidelines for Human Settlement Planning and Design (the Red Book)', in Gibberd, J. and Conradie, DCU., eds., Smart and Sustainable Built Environment (SASBE) Conference 2015, South Africa: University of Pretoria, 135–141.

Chapter 10: Learning From Co-Produced Landslide Risk Mitigation Strategies in Low-Income Settlements in Medellín (Colombia) and São Paulo (Brazil)[1]

Harry Smith, Soledad Garcia-Ferrari, Gabriela Medero, Helena Rivera, Françoise Coupé, Humberto Caballero, Wilmar Castro, Alex Abiko, Fernando A. M. Marinho, Karolyne Ferreira

CO-PRODUCTION AS AN APPROACH TO LANDSLIDE RISK MITIGATION

Low-income communities across the Global South provide themselves with housing and services (see, e.g. Casanova in Chapter 3 of this book). There has been increasing recognition of this, with urban policy and management initiatives focused on supporting and supplementing community-based efforts, ranging from financial mechanisms to co-production arrangements though these are still rare. Approaches to co-produced service provision in the urban South have been examined in a growing literature, as reviewed, e.g., in d'Alençon et al.

---

[1] This paper has been produced based on the collaborative work of the above authors, together with the communities of Pinares de Oriente, El Pacífico and Carpinelo 2 in Medellín, and supported by the Mesa de Vivienda y Servicios Públicos Domiciliarios de la Comuna 8, Mesa de Desplazados de la Comuna 8, Corporación Con-Vivamos and Corporación Montanoa; and with the community of Vila Nova Esperança in São Paulo, supported by TETO Brasil, and with the active involvement of staff from the Instituto Geológico and the Instituto de Pesquisas Tecnológicas of the State of São Paulo.

(2018). Service co-production is increasingly seen as a way of securing sustainable access to key services, such as energy, water supply, sanitation and waste management, relying on contributions from residents as well as from public or private agents (e.g. Allen 2012; Batley and Mcloughlin 2010; McGranahan 2013; Mitlin 2008; Moretto and Ranzatto 2016). The concept of co-production was initially developed in the late 1970s, where it focused on the delivery of services, as 'the process through which inputs used to produce a good or service are contributed by individuals who are not "in" the same organisations. Co-production implies that citizens can play an active role in producing public goods and services of consequence to them' (Ostrom 1996, p. 1073).

Although various interpretations of co-production have emerged since this initial conceptualisation and there is currently a good deal of ongoing experimentation with approaches to co-production, it could be argued that these have in common that 'Co-production stems from voluntary cooperation on the part of citizens (rather than compliance with laws or city ordinances) and involves actives behaviours' (Brudney and England 1983, p. 63). Watson (2014) identifies both commonalities and differences between co-production and approaches to participation that have developed in planning, such as collaborative or communicative planning. According to Watson (2014), commonalities include: a concern with how state and society can engage in order to improve the quality of life of populations; taking an incremental, evolutionary and social learning approach to social change and state action; and assuming a context of democracy and the ability of 'active citizens' to engage collectively and individually. The differences identified by Watson (2014) include: co-production tends to work outside established rules and procedures of governance in terms of engagement with the state; co-production focuses more on delivery processes and management than participatory planning; bottom-up co-production does not necessarily share the belief of collaborative and communicative planning in debate per se as being able to address issues of power relationships between the actors involved; some co-production approaches rely more on 'learning by doing' than on talk and debate; and some bottom-up co-production approaches have an intention to up-scale local practices through global networks, which is not a characteristic of state-led co-production or collaborative and communicative planning.

A particular manifestation of co-production in relation to service provision is 'institutionalized co-production', which according to Joshi and Moore (2004, p. 40) is 'the provision of public services (broadly defined, to include regulation) through regular, long-term relationships between state agencies and organised groups of citizens, where both make substantial resource contributions'. This is characterised by: (1) long-term arrangements developed on a regular basis; (2)

moving away from standardised contractual and/or semi-contractual agreements towards continual renegotiation; and (3) the sharing of control of resources, authority and power between citizen groups and the state. This goes beyond the technical organisation of service delivery, involving the political dimension of resource management i.e., the distribution of power around service delivery (McGranahan 2013).

However, the co-production of risk mitigation in low-income communities is much less common, well-known and understood. Key hazards that low-income communities in the Global South often face include landslides, flooding and fires, as well as the range of socio-economic, institutional and sometimes political threats that heighten their vulnerability. Such events are becoming increasingly frequent and impactful through a combination of ongoing urbanisation and the changing weather patterns that accompany climate change. Working in partnership, researchers at the Universidad Nacional de Colombia Sede Medellín, Heriot-Watt University and the University of Edinburgh, together with community leaders, identified the need to explore the scope for co-production as an approach to help vulnerable communities to address the risk of landslides that affects many settlements in the north-eastern sector of Medellín. This resulted in the first participatory action research project (November 2016-October 2017) called, 'Resilience or resistance? Negotiated mitigation of landslide risks in informal settlements in Medellín'[2]. Participatory Action Research (PAR) can be viewed as a way of 'bringing participation into action research' (Elvin and Levin, cited in Khanlou and Peter 2005, p. 2234). In this project, PAR was the method used to explore the feasibility of the process of co-production discussed earlier, since the outcomes of a PAR methodology should be focused on action and developing new knowledge with emancipatory results for the community (Khanlou and Peter 2005).

In this case, a good deal of what we envisaged as being co-produced was knowledge: of the landslide (and other) risks the community was exposed to, and of the possible ways of addressing these in a way that involved different stakeholders. The project was undertaken by a multidisciplinary team that covered sociology, planning and slum upgrading, geotechnics and environmental engineering, and architecture and construction. The aim of this project was to explore the scope for, and acceptability of, landslide-risk-reducing strategies for informal settlements from the community and state perspectives. The project also sought to understand the barriers to landslide-risk-reducing strategies and to identify

---

2   This was funded by the UK's Global Challenges Research Fund / NERC / AHRC / ESRC Building Resilience programme as project NE/P015557/1.

politically and practically viable approaches to landslide-risk-reducing strategies within a wider and more complex context of social and physical risk (see Smith et al. 2017). The concept of 'resilience' in the project title was interpreted following Vale's (2014) identification of 'pro-active preventive resilience', as opposed to 'reactive/restorative resilience', and as a politically engaged form of resilience with a focus on the issues of 'whose resilience' and 'whose city', as advocated by Vale (2014). In the second part of the title, 'resistance' refers both to the approach of community organisations in north-eastern Medellín in dealing with local government in relation to urban planning and landslide risk, in terms of opposing risk-related evictions and defending the right to remain on the land, as well as to 'resistance' as a form of 'resilience' – see Alvarez et al. (2019).

The exploration of community-based disaster-risk management (CBDRM) harks back to Maskrey (1989) and subsequent literature, with most of this focussing on what communities can achieve through spontaneous community disaster-risk management organisation (CDRMO) or in collaboration with universities and/or NGOs (see, e.g., Tanwattana 2018). A few initiatives have been documented and promoted in the literature involving communities working together with government organisations in monitoring landslide risk and implementing landslide-risk mitigation measures, such as MOSSAIC in the Caribbean (Anderson and Holcombe 2013), and Alerta Rio in Brazil. The latter collects relevant data in every neighbourhood of the city, with community involvement, and publishes its results online, with residents developing small emergency plans and mitigation strategies using updated data (Rahman 2012). These initiatives, however, have not tended to be conceptualised or analysed in terms of co-production.

In the area of Medellín, there has been increasing interest in finding ways of involving the community in risk monitoring, such as the project undertaken by the Universidad de Antioquia and the Corantioquia Foundation from 2011-13 to design and put in place an environmental monitoring social network for early warnings of flooding, flash floods and landslides in strategic locations across the 80 municipalities where Corantioquia operates.[3] Key actors were communities and municipalities, using social cartography as a basis for the design of the monitoring network and hand-made easy-to-use instruments to measure rainfall, etc.,

---

3   Corantioquia is a state-financed organisation that operates within the Colombian Department of Antioquia with the institutional objective of managing the implementation of policies, plans, programmes and projects related to the environment and renewable natural resources. Additionally, Corantioquia oversees that all statutory activities are undertaken according to the guidelines issued by the Ministry of the Environment.

supplemented by electronic instruments for verification. The project trained community members and installed pluviometers (devices used to measure rainwater) and water-level recorders, and was followed up by a further project in 2015 that took place in three municipalities. However, these experiences do not appear to have been evaluated.

In terms of mitigation, Empresas Públicas de Medellín (EPM – the municipal utilities company) has established a programme of 'community brigades' to detect water leaks in the water supply system, which are rife particularly in informal settlements. These 'brigades' are formed temporarily to undertake 3 to 4 days of work every year, managed by EPM, and identify leaks and replace informal water supply systems with non-conventional temporary systems installed jointly by community members and volunteers from EPM (EPM 2015). These 'non-conventional temporary systems' are those that are neither structural nor permanent and can provide physical, social or environmental aid, such as undertaking basic upgrades to internal plumbing fixtures within individual houses; helping to manage an overgrown tree within the immediate vicinity of a neighbourhood; and establishing community links within different neighbourhoods (EPM 2015). This is not primarily a landslide-risk reduction initiative, nor a permanent form of co-production, but it reflects the increasing (though still scarce) attempts to address the complex issues of risk mitigation and service provision in vulnerable urban areas a context within which the 'Resilience or resistance?' project experimented further with encouraging results.

PILOTING THE CO-PRODUCTION OF LANDSLIDE RISK MONITORING AND MITIGATION IN MEDELLÍN, COLOMBIA: THE EXPERIENCE OF PINARES DE ORIENTE

The first project piloted the co-production approach during 2017 in a neighbourhood in Comuna 8, Medellín, where the international Colombia/UK research team worked with volunteer community researchers to: understand the perceptions of risk (among community, public sector and third sector); pilot community-based monitoring of landslide risk using mobile phone technology; test low-cost community-built emergency landslide-risk mitigation works; and identify mechanisms for joint decision-making between community and public sector agencies to mitigate risk.

The activities developed to reach these objectives were centred in a neighbourhood located in the upper part of the central-eastern area of Medellín, in

Comuna 8, called Pinares de Oriente (see Figure 1). It is located between 1,738 and 1,824 metres above sea level, covers 1.52 hectares, and is inhabited by 180 families – approximately 800 inhabitants – 80% of whom are victims of the internal social and armed conflict that Colombia has gone through. Colombia has been 'hostage to an intermittent internal war' causing a rural exodus to cities and placing particular pressure on the country's largest cities, such as Medellín (Garcia Ferrari et al. 2018). This conflict has been endured as 'three key waves'. There is little reliable data quantifying the number of deaths and internally displaced people in the first wave, La Guerra de Mil Dias, (1899–1903); the second wave (1946–1957) led to an estimated death count of 200,000 to 300,00 and the forced migration of 2 million people, which was equivalent to a quarter of the national population. In the third wave (1984–1999), the continued political violence led to 1.7 million people being forcefully displaced from their homes (Garcia Ferrari 2018, p. 4). Low-income settlements that are informally built and outside of the municipal land-use plan, are to a large extent inhabited by the internally displaced people (IDP) that had arrived in Medellín during the last wave. According to the municipal land-use plan, part of the Pinares neighbourhood is on urban expansion land that has been identified for integrated upgrading and part is outside the urban perimeter; i.e., on rural land. 'La Loquita 1' ravine crosses the settlement, but it only carries water during periods of heavy rain. The local authority has identified in the neighbourhood an area of no risk in the lower part, an area of mitigatable risk, and a non-recoverable area of high risk, which is also the area outside of the urban perimeter, where approximately 70 families are located.

Figure 1: Location of Pinares de Oriente, El Pacífico and Carpinelo 2 in the city of Medellín, Colombia.

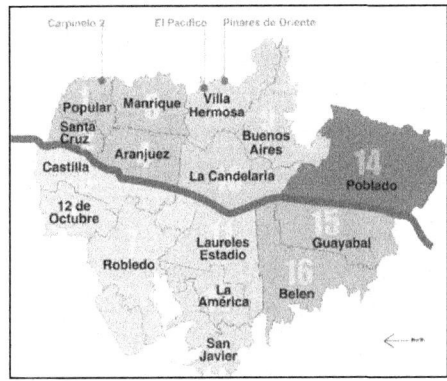

Source: Adapted by the authors from a map by Alcadía de Medellín.

Perceptions of risk

Exploration of the perceptions of risk included two focus group meetings with residents and community leaders; sixteen semi-structured interviews with community leaders and residents of Pinares; and six semi-structured interviews with key players from the public sector, in meetings with the people directly responsible for institutional relations with the community on the issues directly related to the process. In addition, workshops and working processes involved third sector organisations. Perceptions of risk among informal settlement residents were explored at different times, from when they arrived in the settlement to during the project implementation. Most interviewed residents have known some risk during their lives, including floods, landslides and fires. The perception of whether they currently live in a risk area is more varied, from ignorance or lack of concern for the conditions of the site due to other concerns that are more urgent and immediate such as subsistence, to knowledge of the risk and willingness to face the consequences. This is influenced by how they see the role of the municipality in relation to risk, which they link to the possibility of eviction. Public sector interviews revealed that state organisations agree on the importance of intervening on the edge of the city and on the need to control new land occupation and to have a positive view of emergency mitigation interventions while integrated neighbourhood upgrading also takes place where conditions permit.

Monitoring of landslide risk

The research team collaborated with a group of residents who were interested in the process and who participated as volunteer community researchers as they were motivated by the knowledge that their participation would bring improvement to their neighbourhood and subsequently to their individual home. The idea was to establish several WhatsApp groups, each of these groups being responsible for taking photographs at several predetermined monitoring points. The photographs were received in Edinburgh and analysed by looking at the following points: chronological comparisons of the images; comparisons and correlations of the images with the average monthly rainfall level; evaluations of mass movements; identification of the most critical points from the point of view of the hazard. These WhatsApp groups became general platforms for monitoring, and volunteer community researchers uploaded various media: photographs, audio clips and videos (Figure 2).

The monitoring work started with the technical team taking preliminary reconnaissance walks with community residents (community researchers) so as to identify hazards, risk conditions and potential monitoring points. Interviews with residents had identified concerns about moisture, water springs and floods. Using the information provided by the community and the technical team's appraisal, fourteen initial points where the community monitoring work would take place were defined in a joint participatory mapping workshop. Once the points were known, the technical monitoring group in Edinburgh prepared a detailed guide to facilitate monitoring by the community, which indicated the point to be monitored, the frequency of observations, and the safety conditions that needed to be taken into account during these activities.

Figure 2: Screenshots of one WhatsApp Group ('Grupo 4'), showing the images taken by volunteer community researchers of various monitoring points within Pinares de Orente.

Source: Images uploaded by volunteers from the Pinares de Oriente community and screenshots by Helena Rivera, 2017.

The manual or guide was used as the basis for a workshop/training session with community volunteers who were interested in participating in the monitoring. Topics covered included clarifying the meaning of the term 'monitoring' and its importance in a community risk management process, as well as the great importance of taking photos periodically and systematically. The images thus produced could then be technically analysed by the Edinburgh-based group. The initial selection of monitoring points was extended by participant residents during a subsequent field walk, in which each of the volunteers was given instructions on the specific way in which the photographs should be taken, indicating the importance of the physical feature to be observed.

The monitoring was carried out between the months of May and October 2017, covering a dry period and a rainy one. At the end of this monitoring, the experience was evaluated in two community workshops, and the community researchers, supported by the academic team, shared their experience in the project and its results with the local authority organisations and NGOs.

Through their participation in the monitoring process, community researchers demonstrated that residents in low-income neighbourhoods, with appropriate technical support, are able to be involved in a landslide hazard monitoring system and to collaborate with academic researchers in data collection for analysis. Community researchers took part in the experience in order to improve the community and because they understood the importance of the process. Lessons were learned during this pilot experience about the limitations faced by this type of community participation and on the possible ways in which these community research processes could be optimised. These included the following:

- difficulties regarding the regularity of photograph taking and sending, linked to other priorities and events in the volunteers' daily lives;
- decrease in the number of participants, with only two out of the six initial monitoring groups sending photos throughout the process, due to technical difficulties with the mobile phone, changes of the residence of some participants, and family circumstances; and
- the detail of the photograph: some sent small videos which, although important in communicating the seriousness of flooding in the settlement during heavy rain, did not contribute to the specialists' technical analysis of the images.
- feeling fully engaged: relying exclusively on the technical analysis of the photographs being done by experts in geolog and geotechnics led to the community researchers feeling less engaged in the pilot experience because they never saw or understood how their photographs were being analysed and used.
- the factors that were identified, together with the community researchers, as possibly leading to more continuous participation, were: local administration of the WhatsApp networks, instead of abroad; closer accompaniment of community researchers through the more frequent presence of a member of the ac-

ademic research team, or possibly students of the university that accompany the process; concentration of effort in a smaller number of monitoring points within the community; and activities in which the methods and results of the analysis of the images collected by the community researchers are shared, so as to reinforce these volunteers' understanding of the process. These informed the strategy adopted in the second project, which is described in the next main section of this paper.

Mitigation of landslide risk

This action research component was based on two main elements: technical analysis of the conditions of the land and buildings, identifying factors that could contribute to landslide hazards, and linking this analysis to the identification of monitoring points; and the establishment of action strategies that are the result of community collaboration and intervention. Therefore, the priorities identified during the project were the result of multidisciplinary workshops, taking into account the knowledge of the expert members of the project's technical team (geologists, engineers, architects, sociologists, etc.), and the community. During these workshops, the community shared their concerns, particularly during the rainy periods, their specific knowledge of the area, identifying key points, and their willingness to take part in the participatory monitoring and risk mitigation processes.

For the technical analysis, an initial roof survey was carried out with the support of university students and two local NGOs: Con-Vivamos and Corporación Montanoa. This was supplemented by perceptual surveys that enabled the establishment of a hierarchy of spaces and networks that, in turn, enabled the prioritising of the points of intervention as well as the more detailed definitions of the character of the works to be executed in each place. This analysis required a considerable investment of time by the technical staff of the research team, given the precariousness of the graphic and cartographic information available.

Analysis of open spaces, buildings and drainage identified four levels of water management linked respectively to four levels in the drainage network, which provided a basis for the prioritisation of low-cost community-built emergency mitigation works. These levels are: (1) at the municipal level, a drainage network situated under the main access roads, which are under the responsibility of the Municipality; (2) at the community/street level, drainage along lanes and stairways, which are the responsibility of the neighbourhood association; (3) at the lane and alley level, drainage in semi-private areas between houses, which are the responsibility of groups of residents living around these houses; and (4) at the residential level, individual houses, which are the responsibility of their owners. The project gave priority to the tertiary network, with some interventions in the secondary network when deteriorating or deficient areas were identified. A number of interventions were also carried out in individual dwellings, generally in the case of houses that affect others, always seeking to benefit the neighbourhood.

Figure 3: Mitigation works in a semi-private area between houses (tertiary network), in Pinares de Oriente.

Source: Wilmar Castro, 2017.

The works were arranged to be carried out by groups of neighbours through 'receptions' (convites) or community events during the weekends, supplemented with partially paid work during the week (Figure 3). The construction was led by the consultant architect for the project, and guided and coordinated by a local builder. The community self-build works were carried out during the months of September and October 2017. The initial intention had been that some of the sites where works were carried out were to be included in the monitoring process, but this was not possible as these works were carried out in the final stage of the project. At the end of this period, the mitigation experience was evaluated in a community workshop, and the residents who took part in the convites shared the results from their evaluation with local government organisations and NGOs in subsequent workshops, supported by the academic team. The project demonstrated the potential of mitigating risk, throughout an informal settlement, with a very low budget, community self-build and technical advice.

Seeking community-state agreements over landslide risk mitigation

Ultimately, the pilot project sought, through a collaborative process, to identify ways and mechanisms for developing a sustainable process for the co-creation of a risk mitigation strategy and its implementation through agreements between the communities in the informal settlements and the relevant state agencies at different scales, based on the lessons learned from the activities carried out in relation to perception, monitoring and mitigation. In Spanish, this agreement-seeking process is referred to as concertación.

Agreement (concertación) was achieved at two levels: At the district (comuna) level, within the wider community, addressing the deep differences between the Local Administration Board (Junta Administradora Local) and the Working Groups on Housing and Internally Displaced People (Mesas de Vivienda y de Desplazados): a meeting between these organisations and a joint call for an open council meeting (Cabildo Abierto – a legally-binding type of meeting). This is important for two reasons: (1) because the local administration board, which is the lowest level of local government in Colombia, with administrative responsibility at the district (comuna) level in urban areas, and is elected by residents, has the capacity to convene meetings with the municipality at the city level: and (2) the Working Groups on Housing and Internally Displaced People can mobilise the community due to their constant work in the neighbourhoods these are community-based organisations that coordinate community action across districts and across the city, and are increasingly vocal in relation to the need to address risk mitigation in addition to other issues that have traditionally been on their agendas, such as recognition of informal settlements, land regularisation and titling and neighbourhood upgrading.

At the level of the community of Pinares, after the Cabildo, a working group was established with participation of the community of Pinares and four departments of the municipality (Planning (DAP), Disaster-Risk Management (DAGRD), Housing (ISVIMED) and the Urban Development Company (EDU)), which are to look at the possible ways forward for the settlement's at-risk area, once the risk survey plans have been approved. In addition, it was agreed that the larger interventions required to mitigate risks (channelling of La Loquita, box-culvert and screens to protect from rock falls) would be analysed to see if these could be addressed using municipal resources.

The community-local government working group around Pinares was established during a series of steps designed to provide opportunities to establish co-working practices between the local government and the community, which had the following sequence:

- A community evaluation workshop, with the participation of the community-based researchers (residents of Pinares de Oriente) and leaders, which included a role play exercise to help the community prepare for the multi-stakeholder workshop at neighbourhood level.
- A multi-stakeholder workshop at neighbourhood level, with the participation of representatives of the community and those responsible from the main relevant public organisations, which took place in the settlement and included an opportunity for the community volunteers to show the local government officials the results from the monitoring and mitigation pilots on-site.
- A workshop with NGOs and other organisations that work with the community, and whose participation the research team considered important towards the roll-out of the experience in the follow-on project.

Evaluation of the pilot monitoring and mitigation projects, and multi-stakeholder workshop discussions showed that the following factors can facilitate the process of reaching agreement among the different stakeholders involved in landslide-risk mitigation (in this case mainly community and local government): (1) engagement with the different stakeholders from an early stage, though not necessarily together in the beginning; (2) knowledge of the capacities and responsibilities of each stakeholder; (3) consideration of timescales (in this case, a focus on the short term – 'the meantime' – was key in achieving agreement between community and local government); and (4) consideration of the resources that can be brought to bear, including community resources.

THE ROLL-OUT OF CO-PRODUCTION OF LANDSLIDE RISK MONITORING AND MITIGATION IN MEDELLÍN AND SÃO PAULO

The above pilot experience was rolled out, during 2018, in two further communities in Medellín, and another one in São Paulo, in order to explore and identify the issues that may arise in transferring the pilot experience to different socio-economic and political contexts within the same city (but in neighbourhoods and districts with different histories) and in a city in a different Latin American country. This was achieved through a project called 'Co-production of landslide risk management strategies through development of community-based infrastructure in Latin American cities', which ended in May 2019.[4]

The experience of replicating co-production of landslide risk monitoring and mitigation in El Pacífico and Carpinelo 2 in Medellín

In Medellín, the follow-on project was implemented in one settlement within the same district (Comuna) as the pilot project and in another in a different district (Figure 1). El Pacífico is located at the high end of Comuna 8 (not far from Pinares), on land that is partly classed as at high risk because of its being within the officially required setback from 'La Rafita' ravine, partly outside the official urban perimeter, and partly within a forest reserve. According to a community census undertaken in 2016, there are 184 households, with the majority age group being that between 18-29 years old and with 79% of the population having been displaced by the armed conflict. Originating around 1995, this densely built-up and consolidated settlement has a strong history of community organisation, with a Junta de Acción Comunal and a track record in engaging with the municipality (Figure 4).

---

4   Funded by the UK's Global Challenges Research Fund / The British Academy Cities & Infrastructure programme – project number CI170338.

Figure 4: El Pacífico (left) and Carpinelo 2 (right), in Medellín.

Source: Images taken by the Medellín research team, using a drone, 2018.

Carpinelo 2 is a more recent and much less consolidated settlement. It is located in Comuna 1 at the north-eastern tip of Medellín, high up above the city on a steep slope overlooking the next municipality to the north. On the upper edge of a wider neighbourhood called Carpinelo, which started to form in the 1970s and was recognised in 1993, Carpinelo 2 started to form in the late 1990s and early 2000s and became a neighbourhood in its own right in 2012. Carpinelo as a whole has approximately 2,600 households, and Carpinelo 2 is a less densely inhabited part of this, with a considerable amount of open space and lower access to public services, with untreated water, e.g., being tapped into it from a pipe higher up the hill and distributed to houses via pipes installed and charged for by people linked to the armed groups that control the territory. There have been recent instances of evictions and house demolitions in the neighbourhood due to imminent landslides, but residents continue to engage in cutting into the hillside and moving earth to build homes (Figure 4).

Perceptions of risk

In both communities, the research team went through a lengthy negotiation process with locally-based NGOs that have been supporting the two communities (respectively, Convivamos and Corporación Montanoa), establishing rules of engagement with the community in setting up the processes and looking towards the future sharing of the results and the appropriate acknowledgement of those involved in the co-production of knowledge. The process of interviewing community residents and leaders faced some interruptions due to national events, such as the presidential elections, but was eventually completed with 13 interviews in El Pacífico and 15 in Carpinelo 2. Perceptions of risk in each settlement vary somewhat, with residents in El Pacífico being more concerned about rock falls, as well as reporting some flooding and problems with poor building quality, while in Carpinelo 2 there was more explicit concern with landslides and with water including the link between water and landslide risk.

Monitoring of risk

Building on the lessons learned from the pilot project in Pinares, the participatory mapping and training of the volunteers who were to undertake community-based monitoring took longer, with more sessions taking place with the community members, while at the same time limiting the number of monitoring points (4 in El Pacífico and 6 in Carpinelo). In addition, the technical problems and perception of distance between data collection and data analysis that were found in the pilot project were addressed by establishing a system of small weekly top-ups of volunteers' mobile phone allowances in exchange for weekly photographs, with the latter being sent to a WhatsApp group that was managed by a community leader in Medellín (who is part of the research team), rather than to the UK-based researchers.

Figure 5: Community volunteers in Medellín analysing the landslide-risk monitoring data they had collected.

Source: Carlos Montoya, 2018.

This resulted in more consistent participation of community volunteers and therefore in more systematic data collection. In addition, instead of relying exclusively on technical analysis of the photographs by experts in geological and geotechnics a process that had not led to the community researchers feeling fully engaged in the pilot experience in the follow-on project, community workshops were held at regular intervals so as to allow joint analysis of the sets of photographic data by community volunteers together with the research team (Figure 5). This not only helped towards developing the community's knowledge of their own territory but also, and even more importantly, towards their capacity to engage other stakeholders with systematically collected data of their own, thus strengthening the community's involvement in the co-production of landslide risk management.

Risk mitigation

In terms of mitigation, a major difference with the pilot project was the lack of funding available to implement small self-built works. In the follow-on projects, the emphasis was on the co-production of a strategy for each of the settlements, which provided the respective community organisations with a document that recorded possible interventions and mapped the stakeholders that would need to be involved in their implementation, for the Junta de Acción Comunal to take forward. It was considered that the hierarchy of spaces and networks developed in the pilot project remained valid for the two further communities in Medellín, while the importance of the principle of linking walking routes with water drainage became more evident. A particular challenge was faced in El Pacífico, where the high ratio of land occupation by construction and the little amount of space for circulation (of both people and water) raised the possibility of proposing a certain level of building removal, which in itself would risk creating conflict within the settlement.

Agreement-seeking (concertación)

In relation to agreement-seeking, the follow-on project benefitted from both what was shown to be possible by the pilot project and a general move towards an improving community/state relationship in the city (whereas the community/academia relationship has already been positive for a much longer time). The state has tended to feel under pressure from community mobilisations, but more sophisticated forms of engagement between the two have been lowering the tensions. An example of this is the in municiaplity having awarded a prize for citizen participation to the 'Hillside Neighbourhoods School' (Escuela de Barrios de Ladera), an initiative that brings together academia and community organisations in NE Medellín, with the support of Convivamos, and which has incorporated the experience of the projects that are presented in this paper. In addition, almost as a repeat of the research team's experience of presenting the pilot work at a public Cabildo in 2017 for Comuna 8, in 2018 the Medellín research team leader was invited to facilitate a further Cabildo that addresses neighbourhood improvement and risk management across the whole of north-eastern Medellín. Comuna 8 civil society has become a spearhead in the demand for appropriate risk management, resulting in the municipality prioritising the commissioning of micro-zoned risk assessments for this city district, ahead of all the others. This is seen as a first step toward a risk management plan for the whole of north-eastern Medellín.

Transferring the experience of landslide risk management co-production to São Paulo

The transfer of the pilot experience and lessons learned in the case of Medellín to the context of São Paulo was facilitated by two visits of the Brazilian research team to Medellín, where they took part in the final forum that was held there to disseminate the results of the pilot experience and where they also visited and took part in workshops in the participating communities; participation in theme-focused webinars involving the three research teams in Brazil, Colombia and the UK; and weekly project management skype meetings. Replicating and contextualising the experience in São Paulo was not an easy task, with initial reflections mainly highlighting the differences in socio-political and security contexts and in the way that contact between the research teams and potentially participating communities was established.

In early 2018, the São Paulo research team had started working with an informal settlement in the south-east of the city, Morada do Sol, which consists of areas at risk of landslides. Contact was initiated with the community through a relationship that the University of São Paulo has with state-level civil defence in the district of Butanta, where the settlement is located. Representatives from Civil Defence recommended working in this settlement because of its level of community organisation, and the research team visited the area and held a community workshop. However, visits soon had to be suspended because of clashes between police and druglords, which turned the settlement into a no-go area for outsiders. The Brazil-based research team then turned to a contact within the NGO CEDECA (Centro de Defesa da Criança e do Adolescente – Centre for the Defence of the Child and the Adolescent), an organisation that is working in a low-income settlement in Sapopemba, on the eastern edge of the city. The settlement is divided into two parts, a cluster of dwellings at the top of a hill that is partly constituted by rubbish the inhabitants tip down the hill, and another cluster in the valley. Landslide risk here involves not only soil movements but also rubbish sliding as well as catching fire. Initial meetings with the CDEC and a community leader were promising, but it eventually became clear that powerful individuals who were building relatively high buildings for rent in the settlement did not welcome external interference, and the research team had to discontinue the engagement.

Figure 6: Location of communities where the transfer of experience was attempted in São Paulo (left) and an aerial view of Vila Nova Esperança (right).

Source: Prepared by the authors using Google Maps.

Eventually, through the NGO Teto, the Brazil-based research team established contact with the main community leader of Vila Nova Esperança, a 450-household settlement in the south-west of the city, which has landslide-risk issues, including areas classified at high and very high risk. The 60-year old neighbourhood, which is surrounded by a protected forest, is involved in a process of land regularisation which in principle is not applicable to high and very high-risk areas unless mitigation works are carried out hence the community leader's interest in involving the community in the project. Having finally agreed to a collaboration with the community by August 2018, the Brazilian team was able to adapt the Medellín experience to Vila Nova Esperança. It undertook interviews with the community, started a community-based monitoring system based on four agreed monitoring points, and assessed the requirements for community-based mitigation.

The experience of transferring the approach internationally from Colombia to a Brazilian context allowed the team to draw out preliminary lessons regarding the limitations faced by this type of community involvement and on the possible ways in which these community research processes can be optimised. These lessons included the following:

- different participatory surround: understanding the socio-political and security contexts is fundamental and will have an impact on the way a project is co-produced. The socio-political and security contexts will vary widely even amongst continental neighbours, so addressing this at an early stage is fundamental;
- including a community member within the academic research team: the way that contact between the research teams and potentially participating communities is established has an impact on the level of trust that the academic team has within the community. This 'trust' is fundamental for co-production;
- linked to the above point, different socio-economic processes within the neighbourhoods can enable or hinder community willingness to engage with external actors, and the involvement of a community member in the research team from the outset can help understand these processes;
- landslide diversity: the type of potential landslide and its secondary effects will, like all so-called 'natural' hazards, vary widely between geological regions and settlement characteristics. In this case, the project had to momentarily contend with rubbish sliding and the secondary effect of catching fire, both of which require an entirely different set of mitigation strategies.

CONCLUSIONS

The research shows that different levels and ways of understanding landslide risk can be found within different communities, linked to the history of each particular settlement, which in turn affects how such communities engage with external agencies (e.g., local government) in relation to this endeavour. In addition, risk governance and management involve different approaches in different cities and are linked to the general approach to informal settlements in each city and to state capacity. The tendency has been to focus on post-disaster attention and recovery rather than prevention and mitigation, with the latter manifesting mostly in interventions which run counter to establishing relationships of co-production (e.g., preventative evictions).

The projects described in this chapter have explored alternative ways of engaging vulnerable communities and the local government in each city in co-producing landslide risk management strategies. Lessons learned along the way suggest the need to engage the community as much as possible not only in data collection and in implementation of emergency mitigation works but also in the analysis of the data they collect, in developing their own knowledge and understanding of their territories, and in the development of settlement-level strategies they can use in lobbying local government for resources and in prioritising actions together with local government agencies. The experience of trying to roll out the pilot project to other communities in Medellín and to transfer it to a different context in the city of São Paulo highlights the influence the socio-political and security context can have on such replication as well as the importance of considering the routes to engaging vulnerable communities in this kind of work.

As climate change and the continued informal growth of cities on hazardous terrains increase their inhabitants' exposure to potential disasters, developing ways of co-producing landslide-risk mitigation that optimises the use of community and state capacities to provide safe homes is becoming increasingly urgent. The two projects that are described and analysed in this chapter have shown both the potential and the challenges not only of developing such co-produced landslide-risk-management approaches but also of the co-production of knowledge to underpin the development of such approaches through collaboration between academia and the community primarily, as well as with NGOs and the relevant legal government organisations. On reflection, a key element underpinning success in the co-production of research appears to be the existence of shared objectives between academia and community, as it can be achieved especially in the Colombian cases, and the open acknowledgement of these as well as of the differences in the agendas of the key actors. This also applies to the involvement of other actors, with an example being the protracted and detailed negotiations that took place between the academic researchers and the NGOs supporting the two communities that the experience was rolled out to in the second project in Colombia. This ranged from dealing with issues around what the project deliverables would be, to the recognition of joint authorship. Thus, our experience in these projects tells us that co-produced research requires transparency in the agendas, confluence in the objectives, and a willingness to negotiate and resolve differences that may emerge during the research process, which is inevitable given the open-endedness of participatory action research.

REFERENCES

Alfaro d'Alençon, P., Smith, H., Álvarez de Andrés, E., Cabrera, C., Fokdal, J., Lombard, M., Mazzolini, A., Michelutti, E., Moretto, L. and Spire, A. (2018) Interrogating informality: Conceptualisations, practices and policies in the light of the New Urban Agenda, *Habitat International,* 75, 59–66.

Alvarez de Andrés, E., Cabrera, C. and Smith, H. (2019) Resistance as resilience: A comparative analysis of state-community conflicts around self-built housing in Spain, Senegal and Argentina, *Habitat International,* 86, 116–125.

Allen, A. (2012) Water provision for and by the peri-urban poor: Public-community partnerships or citizens co-production? In I. Vojnovic (Ed.), *Sustainability: A Global Urban Context* (pp. 209–340). East Lansig, MI: Michigan University Press.

Anderson, M. G. and Holcombe, E. A. (2013) *Community-Based Landslide Risk Reduction: Managing Disasters in Small Steps.* Washington D.C., USA: World Bank.

Batley, R. and Mcloughlin, C. (2010) Engagement with Non-State Service Providers in Fragile States: Reconciling State-Building and Service Delivery. *Development Policy Review,* 28(2), 131–154.

Empresas Publicas de Medillin (EPM). (2015) Brigadas de Mitigación del Riesgo, available at: http://2015.sostenibilidadgrupoepm.com.co/gestion-social-y-ambiental/nuestra-gestion/temas-materiales/calidad-y-seguridad-de-losprodu ctos-y-servicios/brigadas-de-mitigacion-del-riesgo/

S. Garcia Ferrari, H. Smith, Coupe, F. and H. Rivera. (2018) City profile: Medellin. *Cities,* 74, 354–364.

Joshi A. and Moore, M. (2004) Institutionalised Co-production: Unorthodox Public Service Delivery in Challenging Environments. *The Journal of Development Studies,* 40(4), 31–49

Khanlou, N. and Peter, E. (2005) Participatory action research: considerations for ethical review. *Soc Sci Med,* 60(10), 2333–2340.

Maskrey, A. (2011) Revisiting community-based disaster risk management. *Environmental Hazards,* 10(1), 42–45

McGranahan, G. (2013) *Community-driven sanitation improvement in deprived urban neighbourhoods. Meeting the challenges of local collective action, co-production, affordability and a trans-sectoral approach.* Research Report, SHARE.

Mitlin, D. (2008) With and beyond the state – co-production as a route to political influence, power and transformation for grassroots organizations. *Environment and Urbanization,* 20(2), 339–360.

Moretto, L. and Ranzato, M. (2016) A socio-natural standpoint to understand coproduction of water, energy and waste services. *Urban Research & Practice,* 10(1), 1–21.

Parodi, O., Waitz, C., Bachinger, M., Kuhn, R., Meyer-Soylu, S., Alcántara, S. and Rhodius, R. (2018) Insights into and Recommendations from Three Real-World Laboratories, *Gaia,* 27, 52–59.

Rahman, T. (2012) Landslide Risk Reduction of the Informal Foothill Settlements of Chittagong City Through Strategic Design measure. MA Dissertation, BRAC University, Dhaka, Bangladesh.

Smith, H., Garcia-Ferrari, S., Medero, G.M. and Rivera, H. (2018) The role of 'connection' in participatory management of landslide risk in low-income settlements in Medellín, Colombia, 18th N–AERUS Conference 2017 on *Why urban in a hyper-connected Global South?* Politécnico di Milano, September 14–16 2017.

Tanwattana, P. (2018) Systematizing Community-Based Disaster Risk Management (CBDRM): Case of urban flood-prone community in Thailand upstream area. *International Journal of Disaster Risk Reduction,* 28, 798–892.

Vale, L. J. (2014) The politics of resilient cities: whose resilience and whose city? *Building Research & Information,* 42(2), 191–201.

Watson, V. (2014) Co-production and collaboration in planning – The difference. *Planning Theory & Practice,* 15:1, 62–76.

Bio Notes

Abiko, Alex, is a civil engineer, professor at the Escola Politécnica (School of Engineering) of the University of São Paulo, co-ordinator of the "Engineering and Urban Planning" Teaching and Research Group at the Civil Engineering Department of the Escola Politécnica, and of Poli-Integra, which is the Extension Courses Programme of the same School. He has developed research, been involved in consulting, supervised students at the masters and doctorate levels, and published in books and journals, particularly on urban sustainability, urban planning and governance, housing management, social housing and favela upgrading. He currently coordinates the Commission for Special Studies on Sustainable Development in Cities and Communities of ABNT, the Brazilian Association of Technical Standards.

Annisa, Shaharin, is an academic researcher and lecturer at the Department of International Urbanism at the University of Stuttgart. Born in Bangladesh but raised in Oman, she completed her bachelor's degree at the German University (GUtech) in Oman, studying urban planning and architectural design (UPAD). Later, she joined the UPAD department as a teaching and research assistant, for two years, on topics of housing and public space. Furthermore, she was involved in the design, construction and monitoring phase of Gutech's Eco-friendly house. She finished her master's degree at the University of Stuttgart in the program Integrated Urbanism and Sustainable design (IUSD) researching on understanding the spatial effects of migration and the livelihoods of Bangladeshi migrants in Oman. She was part of the EZBET project based in Cairo from 2017, where she worked on the understanding the development of informal settlements and was involved in understanding participatory needs assessment. She is the co-founder of MCTspaceLab, an initiative based in Oman, working with community empowerment. Her interests lie in topics of migration, housing, human rights, and she places a great interest in bottom-up approaches.

Bayro-Kaiser, Fabio, is a research associate and PhD candidate at the RWTH Aachen University, Faculty of Architecture, Chair and Institute of Urban Design. Born in La Paz, Bolivia, in 1984, he graduated as an architect at UCB in Tarija-Bolivia, in 2015 and completed a master's in building biology at the University of Lleida, Spain, in 2016. From 2010 until 2016, he worked at the office for architecture and planning 'mKaiser' in Tarija-Bolivia, where he focused on housing, neighbourhoods and urban development and the cultural landscape.

Boanada-Fuchs, Anthony, is a trained architect and urban planner with a Ph.D. in International Development Studies (IHEID). After completing a postdoc and undertaking visiting positions at the University of São Paulo (USP-CEM), University of Lausanne (UNIL-IDG), University of Basel (Europainstitute), and the ETH Zürich (CASE), he started working at the University in St.Gallen, where he is currently a project manager at the St. Gallen Institute of Management in Latin America (GIMLA). His research and teaching efforts are situated at the intersection of scientific research and practice and thematically focus on affordable housing programs, the role of real-estate developers in urban development, the systematization of knowledge in urban policy-making, and government responses towards informality.

Caballero, Humberto, is a geological engineer who is responsible for undergraduate and post-graduate programmes in geological engineering and environmental engineering, and in environment and development at the National University of Colombia (Medellín). Caballero has a strong track record in the application of expertise in earth sciences to the field of risk management in mountain areas, especially in urban areas with a history of serious events with loss of life and property. He is highly skilled in engaging in risk-management training / education of low-income communities, and has long-standing links with the public sector through research and consultancy; e.g., in work undertaken on the institutional coordination of geotechnical, geological, hydraulic and erosion control, for the metropolitan area of the Aburrá Valley. His inter-disciplinary work includes collaboration with Prof. Françoise Coupé on risk management.

Casanova, Marielly, is a licensed architect from Venezuela, holds a master degree in architecture and urban design from Columbia University in NY, and, in 2017, she defended her PhD thesis, "Social Strategies Building the City: a Reconceptualisation of Social Housing in Latin America", at the University of Duisburg-Essen. Casanova's work focuses on the intersection between urban planning and social inequality. Her main expertise and interests lie in participatory planning, and the co-production and co-implementation of projects of diverse nature. She analyses the potential of neighbourhoods in different contexts for the conception of urban strategies and projects that can be implemented in collaboration with local stakeholders. Casanova also teaches non-conventional research methodologies for the assessment of urban issues and her teaching experience extends to Columbia University, the ETH Zürich, and the University of Duisburg-Essen. In addition, Casanova has worked as a project manager, in urban and community development projects, for different public and private organisations.

Coupé, Françoise, was an associate professor in the Faculty of Social Sciences and Economics at the National University of Colombia (Medellín) between 1972 and 2003. Since her retirement in 2004, Françoise has been a professor emeritus at the university. Between 2001 and 2003, Prof. Coupé was Director of the Environment in the Government Department of Antioquia and has consequently led various committees that are of crucial significance to the project her chapter in this book is about, such as President of the Management Boards of CORNARE, CORANTIOQUIA and CORPOURABA; co-ordinator of various inter-institutional committees and lead co-ordinator of numerous education, investigation and social projects. Since 2013, Prof. Coupé has been a member of the general Advisory Board for the Planning Department in Medellín, with particular focus on the city's development plan.

Ferreira, Karolyne, graduated in geography with a master's in urban and civil engineering from the University of São Paulo. Ferreira is an expert in urban resilience and risk management and has worked on and been an instructor in socioenvironmental impact studies. Her research topics have focused on urban resilience, urban planning, governance, risk management and natural disasters. She has publications related to landslide risk management, urban resilience and civil defence

Fokdal, Josefine, is senior researcher and lecturer at the department of International Urbanism at the University of Stuttgart. After completing her diploma in architecture and international urbanism from TU Berlin (DE), and a Masters from Ball State University (USA), Josefine obtained her PhD in 2014 from TU Berlin on the topic: Embodiment of the Urban-Relational Space in the Mega City of Guangzhou. Her field of expertise and publications includes a variety of topics related to processes of transformation and urbanisation with an emphasis on spatial theory, housing, governance, participation, informality, co-production and rapid urbanization with a geographical focus on Asia.

Garcia-Ferrari, Soledad, is a senior lecturer at the Edinburgh School of Architecture and Landscape Architecture, University of Edinburgh. Professionally qualified in architecture and urbanism in Uruguay, her research focuses on current processes of urban development and regeneration in Latin America and Europe. She was awarded her PhD in urban studies in 2007 at the School of the Built Environment, Heriot-Watt University. Soledad has extensive expertise in research in recent planning strategies in Medellín and led the Medellín Urban Innovation project that was funded by the British Council. She is currently leading research in Mexico, which focuses on developing collaborative approaches to climate-change-related risk. She has taught in the faculty of architecture in Montevideo, the University of Seville, and was invited as a speaker at the School of Architecture, CEU in Madrid. She is currently at the University of Edinburgh, where she is Dean of Latin American Studies and Director of the Edinburgh University Centre for Contemporary Latin American Studies.

Hossain, Md. Zakir, is a professor of urban & rural planning and course coordinator in the Master's of Urban and Rural Planning Programme at Khulna University, Bangladesh. for He holds an MSc from the University of Antwerp and D.Phil from the Heriot Watt University. Before coming to academia, Zakir worked as a development practitioner concerned with urban health and governance in Bangladesh. He specialises in the grounded theory approach to the study of climate change, poverty and resilience. Besides teaching at Khulna University, he is also implementing research projects which particularly address the coexistence between vulnerability and resilience, poverty, migration and the asset-based approach to development. He is also embarking on a new project concerning resilience building, with particular attention on the vulnerability of children in different climatic disaster zones of Bangladesh. His work has appeared in a number of peer-reviewed scholarly journals, including the Journal of Climate Strategies and Management, Environment, Development and Sustainability, and Sustainable Built Environment.

Kienast, Gerhard, is an urban and regional planner; alumni of TU Berlin, Instituto Politécnico Nacional, Mexico City, and the Centre for Rural Development (Humboldt-Universität); has worked as an advisor for organisational development for the German Development Service (DED) in Mozambique and South Africa; carried out research into the design of urban development grants in the European context and the functional and social integration of new large housing projects in Germany; is a former lecturer and currently a researcher and PhD candidate at the Department for Urban Regeneration and Planning, University of Kassel, working on a DFG-funded research project on spatial development frameworks and locational decision-making in South Africa. His areas of interest include urban governance and participation, planning performance, and housing policy.

Laue, Franziska, is research associate and lecturer at the International Urbanism Institute, and course co-ordinator for the M.Sc. Double Degree IUSD at the University of Stuttgart. She studied architecture (TU Berlin) and has a M.Sc. IUSD Double Degree (Stuttgart, Cairo). She also worked for the GIZ's UDP in Aleppo, Syria from 2007-2011, and for Egypt's PDP in 2013. Since 2003, she is also involved in local and international conferences, exhibitions and publications on local identity, local challenges of climate change, and informal urban development in the MENA region, particularly in Damascus (2012), refugee camp improvement strategies (DAZ, UNRWA 2012, 2014), and on urban heritage conservation and archiving on Aleppo (2010 -ongoing). She is involved in the strategic discourse on post-conflict recovery in the MENA region since (2011-ongoing). Currently, she researches on strategies for community-based climate-change adaptation in the MENA region. Since 2018, she has represented the institute at Stuttgart's multi-stakeholder working group on localising the Sustainable Development Goals "Mein Stuttgart mEine Welt".

Ley, Astrid, is chair of International Urbanism and course director of the international master program MSc Integrated Urbanism and Sustainable Design (IUSD) at University of Stuttgart. She also works as an urban development consultant and trainer to bilateral and international development agencies (oikos human settlement research group). She holds a degree in architecture and urban design from RWTH Aachen and a PhD from TU Berlin. Prior to her position in Stuttgart she was urban development research analyst at the German Advisory Council on Global Change (WBGU) and post-doc in a research project on "Housing for the Urban Poor: From Local Action to Global Networks" as well as lecturer at Habitat Unit, TU Berlin and University of Witwatersrand, Johannesburg. Her expertise and publication record include topics related to urbanization in the Global South, housing processes, the role of local governance, participation, co-production and civil society.

Marinho, Fernando A. M., is an associate professor at the University of São Paulo and teaches courses in civil engineering, mining engineering and geology. His research is related to geotechnical aspects of soils, in particular in the unsaturated condition. Marinho undertakes research in several states in Brazil and abroad. He is a consultant for government agencies and works within the geotechnical industry.

Medero, Gabriela, is a professor in geotechnical and geo-environmental engineering at The Institute for Infrastructure and Environment, School of Energy, Geoscience, Infrastructure and Society (EGIS), Heriot-Watt University, Edinburgh, UK. She is a civil engineer and her research interests focus on the thermo-hydro-mechanical behaviour of soils from micro-level to large-scale mechanisms such as landslides. She has been researching tropical soils, unsaturated soils and associated failure mechanisms for over 20 years, with international collaborations in Latin America, Europe and Asia.

Mera, Wilmar Castro, is a consultant and researcher in risk management, specifically in territorial vulnerability and environmental education. He has also explored the field of the social perception of risk and its relationship with institutional trust in mega-projects in the city. He is an environmental administrator, specialist in environmental education with a master in environment and development from the National University of Colombia (Medellín). Together with Professor Françoise Coupé and Elizabeth Arboleda at the National University of Colombia (Medellín), he has participated in different research projects with a focus on themes around habitat, risk, community development, territorial vulnerability, the co-production of knowledge, and resilience. Wilmar has participated in the preparation of the 'Municipal Disaster-Risk Management Plan of Medellín and Rionegro', the formulation of public policy for dweller protection and in the evaluation of the likelihood, vulnerability and risk of torrential floods in the Department of Antioquia, Colombia.

Mukaddim, Syed, holds a master's degree in urban and rural planning from Khulna University, Khulna, Bangladesh. He obtained his bachelor's degree in social science (Anthropology) from the Independent University, Bangladesh. He has been teaching at the primary and secondary levels. His research interests include anthropogenic changes in different aspects of human lives. Recently, he has developed an interest in the area of climate change and its associated affairs; to name a few, identity and migration in relation to climate change, housing and land owing mechanisms of such forcefully displaced people, and so on. Beside his academic endeavours, Syed likes to read books and code computer programs – mostly plug-ins for financial market trading systems. He is also active in financial markets as a futures trader.

Rahman, Md Ashiq Ur, is a Professor of Urban and Rural Planning Discipline of Khulna University, Bangladesh. He is highly motivated in working in the field of pro-poor housing initiatives in Bangladesh and other developing countries. He gained his MSc in Urban Development Planning programme of Development Planning Unit of University College London and was awarded with PhD in Urban Studies from Heriot Watt University, Edinburgh, United Kingdom. His field of research interest and career motivation lies in pro-poor urban development initiatives. He believes that individuals have their own capabilities and combining those capabilities towards democratic development is essential. In the recent past, he worked as Research Fellow of the Alexander von Humboldt Foundation at the Department of International Urbanism of Institute of Urban Planning and Design, University of Stuttgart, Germany.

Rivera, Helena, is a visiting lecturer in Landscape Architecture and Urbanism at the University of Greenwich. She was awarded her PhD in Regional Planning in 2015 at the Bartlett School of Planning, UCL, where her research focused on applying transferable lessons from British New Towns into contemporary housing policy. Rivera is a professionally qualified architect, chartered by the ARB and RIBA, and is founder and director of A Small Studio Ltd. Helena undertakes work in both a professional and academic capacity related to architecture and urbanism out of her studio in London. Helena has worked as a research associate with Prof. Harry Smith and Dr. Soledad Garcia-Ferrari on several projects in the Global South. She has recently been a visiting guest at the UK All-Party Parliamentary Group on New Towns, 2018-2019.

Santoso, Jo, studied urban planning, architecture, sociology, eonomic planning in Darmstadt, Berlin and Hannover, Doktor-Ingenieur in Urban History 1981. He was also a member of the teaching staff at Hochschule der Kunste Berlin before returning to to Jakarta, Indonesia, in 1983. Between 1984 and 1996 he worked as planner in several Newtown Projects in Indonesia; i.e., as chief planner of the Bumi Serpong Damai New City, Lippo Village and Bukit Semarang Baru/Semarang. He has also worked as a consultant for different development agencies, like the World Bank, the Asian Development Bank and for the Germen Technological Cooperation (GTZ) in different Ministries in Indonesia. In 2003, he returned to the academic world and set up the Master's Program for Urban and Real-Estate Development at Tarumanagara University in Jakarta and was the head of the program until 2018. He is presently head of Tarumanagara Urban Laboratory and works as an individual expert for diverse ministries and local governments in the fields of housing, urban planning and the development of tourist destinations. He has also been guest professor at a number of universities; i.e., TU Karlsruhe; TU Darmstadt, Department of Social Science; the University of Frankfurt; and Willems Business College Sydney; and has given public lectures at European, Asian and American Universities. Among his publications, the most well-known is The Fifth Layer of Jakarta (English) and Kota Tanpa Warga (City Without Citizens (Indonesian).

Sikder, Sujit Kumar, is a research associate at the Leibniz Institute of Ecological Urban and Regional Development (IOER) in Germany within scientific Area 'Monitoring of Settlement and Open Space Development'. His academic experiences and research interests are focused on the topics of urban data science and innovations in geoinformation for better spatial decision-making. He is committed to contributing to the transdiciplinary research domain for improved quality of urban living. Dr. Sikder was awarded a PhD in engineering (Dr. Ing.) from the Institute of Geodesy and Geoinformation at the University of Bonn, a master's of science (M.Sc) from the Technical University of Munich (TUM), and a bachelor's of urban and rural planning (BURP) from Khulna University, Bangladesh.

Smith, Harry, is a professor at The Urban Institute, School of Energy, Geoscience, Infrastructure and Society (EGIS), Heriot-Watt University, Edinburgh, UK. An architect and planner, his research interests focus on how people produce and manage their built environment, ranging from institutional and governance issues in planning and housing to physical design. Harry has undertaken much of his work with an international focus, collaborating with partners in Latin America, Europe and Africa, examining planning and housing issues, community empowerment, participatory processes and user involvement in the production of the built environment, and partnership approaches to the design and long-term maintenance of open space, mainly from a qualitative perspective. He has published widely in the planning and development literature, particularly in relation to governance of human settlements in the Global South.

Yang, Shiyu, is a Ph.D. candidate at the Institute of Urban Planning and Design, University of Stuttgart. She studied architecture in Tsinghua University, Beijing, and obtained a bachelor's degree of architecture in 2014 and a master's degree of architecture in 2016. Shiyu started her doctoral research in October 2016 and the working title of her dissertation is "Space production of migrants in urban villages in China – the case of Beijing". Her research interests include informality, migration, and housing, as well as Lefebvre's theory of space production. Shiyu has several experiences of presenting her research at international conferences, including: the 2018 AESOP Annual Congress "Making Space for Hope" in Sweden; the 19th N-AERUS Conference "Housing and Human Settlements in a World of Change" in Germany; and the 11th IFoU Congress "Reframing Urban Resilience Implementation" in Spain. Since April 2017, she has also been teaching in seminars within the Master's Program of Integrated Urbanism and Sustainable Design at the University of Stuttgart.

Social Sciences

kollektiv orangotango+ (ed.)
This Is Not an Atlas
A Global Collection of Counter-Cartographies

2018, 352 p., hardcover, col. ill.
34,99 € (DE), 978-3-8376-4519-4
E-Book: available as free open access publication
E-Book: ISBN 978-3-8394-4519-8

Mozilla Foundation
Internet Health Report 2019

2019, 118 p., pb., ill.
19,99 € (DE), 978-3-8376-4946-8
E-Book: available as free open access publication
E-Book: ISBN 978-3-8394-4946-2

James Martin
Psychopolitics of Speech
Uncivil Discourse and the Excess of Desire

2019, 186 p., hardcover
79,99 € (DE), 978-3-8376-3919-3
E-Book: 79,99 € (DE), ISBN 978-3-8394-3919-7

**All print, e-book and open access versions of the titles in our list
are available in our online shop www.transcript-verlag.de/en!**

Social Sciences

Michael Bray
Powers of the Mind
Mental and Manual Labor
in the Contemporary Political Crisis

2019, 208 p., hardcover
99,99 € (DE), 978-3-8376-4147-9
E-Book: 99,99 € (DE), ISBN 978-3-8394-4147-3

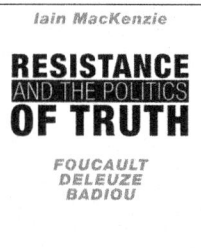

Iain MacKenzie
Resistance and the Politics of Truth
Foucault, Deleuze, Badiou

2018, 148 p., pb.
29,99 € (DE), 978-3-8376-3907-0
E-Book: 26,99 € (DE), ISBN 978-3-8394-3907-4
EPUB: 26,99 € (DE), ISBN 978-3-7328-3907-0

Alexander Schellinger, Philipp Steinberg (eds.)
The Future of the Eurozone
How to Keep Europe Together:
A Progressive Perspective from Germany

2017, 202 p., pb.
29,99 € (DE), 978-3-8376-4081-6
E-Book: 26,99 € (DE), ISBN 978-3-8394-4081-0
EPUB: 26,99 € (DE), ISBN 978-3-7328-4081-6

**All print, e-book and open access versions of the titles in our list
are available in our online shop www.transcript-verlag.de/en!**